# THE NAZI SÉANCE

Books by Arthur J. Magida

*Opening the Doors of Wonder*
*The Rabbi and the Hit Man*
*How to Be a Perfect Stranger*
*Prophet of Rage*
*The Environment Committees*

# THE NAZI SÉANCE

*The Strange Story of the Jewish
Psychic in Hitler's Circle*

ARTHUR J. MAGIDA

palgrave
macmillan

THE NAZI SÉANCE
Copyright © Arthur J. Magida, 2011.

First published in 2011 by
PALGRAVE MACMILLAN®
in the United States—a division of St. Martin's Press LLC,
175 Fifth Avenue, New York, NY 10010.

Where this book is distributed in the UK, Europe and the rest of the world,
this is by Palgrave Macmillan, a division of Macmillan Publishers Limited,
registered in England, company number 785998, of Houndmills,
Basingstoke, Hampshire RG21 6XS.

Palgrave Macmillan is the global academic imprint of the above companies and
has companies and representatives throughout the world.

Palgrave® and Macmillan® are registered trademarks in the United States,
the United Kingdom, Europe and other countries.

ISBN 978–0–230–62053–7

Library of Congress Cataloging-in-Publication Data

Magida, Arthur J.
    The Nazi séance : the strange story of the Jewish psychic in
  Hitler's circle / Arthur J. Magida.
        p. cm.
    Includes bibliographical references (p. ) and index.
    ISBN 978–0–230–62053–7 (alk. paper)
      1. Hanussen, Erik Jan, 1889-1933. 2. Clairvoyants—Austria—Biography.
  3. Clairvoyants—Germany—Biography. 4. National socialism and
  occultism. I. Title.

BF1283.H235M34 2011
943.605'22092—dc23
[B]                                                        2011023664

A catalogue record of the book is available from the British Library.

Design by Newgen Imaging Systems Ltd., Chennai, India.

First edition: December 2011

10 9 8 7 6 5 4 3 2 1

Printed in the United States of America.

"It does not follow that what is mysterious must necessarily be miraculous."

—*Johann Wolfgang von Goethe*

"Two things fill the mind with ever-increasing wonder and awe . . . the starry heavens above me and the moral law within me."

—*Immanuel Kant*

# Contents

★　★　★

*Eight pages of photographs appear between pages 154 and 155*

# "He Cannot Doubt the Genuineness of His Mission"

Germans take advantage of warm weather; they know it won't last long. So with the sun high in the sky and the temperature settling into a comfortable zone, a private yacht sailed south from Berlin on the Spree River, passed a large castle on an island opposite the town of Kopenick, where it turned east onto the Dahm River and continued its slow, leisurely cruise toward Lake Scharmützelsee, another forty miles away. Scharmützelsee—seven miles long—was the largest of a series of thirty lakes in the area; most were linked to each other with canals and waterways like a string of aquatic pearls. And there, not far from the spas and the cabins and the manor houses dotting the shore, the *Ursel IV* moored. The small group on the forty-foot boat didn't care about the people who lived there—they were in their own little universe. The *Ursel* had everything its passengers could desire—luxurious staterooms, teak paneling, chandeliers, handmade furniture, chilled wine, delicious food. They could have anchored in the lake for several days and not run out of supplies. Or fun. Some of the guests on the *Ursel* went skinny-dipping, which had become fairly common in Germany of the day: Nude sunbathers lined the riverbanks and lakeshores all over the country. By the early 1930s, Germany had become a nation of sun worshippers. If the Weimar Republic couldn't save itself from the runaway inflation of the 1920s and the jobless-ness of the Depression, perhaps the rest of the universe—the sunny side—would. But as the late afternoon turned to dusk, some of the women on the *Ursel* began dancing nude on the deck. Local residents were scandalized: They were country people who liked their quiet and their propriety. Yet they had a hard time putting down their binoculars while watching from the shore, especially as one of the men on the *Ursel* motioned to a beautiful blonde to stretch out on a deck chair. She closed her eyes as the man swept his hands just above her face, then lay still as he whispered and gestured over her. To the people on the shore, he appeared to be casting a spell over her. She began moving slowly, then faster and faster until she was writhing, as if in the embrace of a lover. Yet no lover was in sight, and the man in his white flannels standing above her had not touched her. No one had.[1]

The people who lived along the lake didn't know that the man in white flannels was Erik Jan Hanussen, the most famous mentalist in Germany and an accomplished hypnotist who performed at some of Berlin's most majestic theaters. Since a Czech court had acquitted him of charges of fraud eighteen months earlier, Hanussen's fame was greater than ever. His fame had brought him many prizes: the yacht; a few limousines; a large, sprawling apartment in Berlin next door to the Bendlerblock, a complex of gray buildings that was the nerve center of the German military—or what passed for a military under the spite-ful Versailles Treaty; and women, always women, for Hanussen loved women and they loved him. Back in Berlin, he had a different lady on his arm almost every night, and he loved parading them through cafés and nightclubs after his performances.

Hanussen had come a long way from his origins as a poor Jew in Vienna—his real name was Hermann Steinschneider. Now he had this terrific boat, a plaything beyond the dreams of most Jewish boys who had survived Austria's ghettoes, and he had interesting friends (mostly from show business, politics, or the arts) who snapped up invitations to join him on the *Ursel*. Hanussen was a good host and an effective entertainer, even offstage. He enjoyed telling his guests that their fun and games on the boat were really a form of worship of Saraswati, the Hindu goddess of music, art, and creativity. Hanussen knew that wrapping himself in the mysterious East made him more exotic. In fact, he understood that this was one reason his friends—and his fans—found him so alluring.

That day on the *Ursel*, Hanussen was paying close attention to one particular guest, a tall, blond man with clear, almost translucent, blue eyes—Count Wolf-Heinrich von Helldorf. Helldorf came from German nobility. He also was the head of the storm troopers in Berlin—the Nazis' private army: brownshirted shock troops who took the law into their own hands, dispensing terror and pogroms in the name of their fuehrer and messiah, Adolf Hitler. Unlike other storm troopers, Helldorf didn't have the face of a killer, a thug's mug. Rather, he bore a certain rectitude, or at least the appearance of rectitude—the benefit of his descent from generations of blue bloods. His cultivated mien was useful to the Nazis: it assured financiers, industrialists, and nobles, whose support Hitler needed to gain power, that the Nazis could be trusted; that, indeed, they were as sensible as they were ambitious.

It was improbable that Hanussen would own a boat like the *Ursel*. It was more improbable that Helldorf would be his friend. But the two men needed each other. Berlin was a dangerous city, with rampant crime and frequent, sometimes fatal, street brawls between Nazis and Communists. Helldorf made sure Hanussen was safe. In exchange, Hanussen bailed out Helldorf: The count was always in debt, and his private life was a wreck. He was separated from his wife and was on bad terms with his mother after welching on his promise to pay her rent. Sometimes he even was behind on his own rent. On one occasion he "forgot" to pay for a new Mercedes. And he was always late paying his personal tailor and the trainer he hired for his racehorse. There were other debts as well, all from a gambling habit Helldorf couldn't shake. Luckily, he could always count on a handout from Hanussen. All he had to do was sign an IOU, which Hanussen would add to the growing pile of chits he kept in a safe in his apartment.[2]

The word in certain circles in Berlin was that Hanussen provided Helldorf with more than money: He procured drugs and women, although on the *Ursel* that day, according to stories that would soon be circulating in Berlin, Helldorf and Hanussen had other pleasures in mind. After watching Hanussen hypnotize that lovely woman into the throes of orgasm, Helldorf reportedly whispered something to Hanussen, who smiled and called over a beautiful fourteen-year old boy, Kabir. His parents—friends of Hanussen's—had thought their son would enjoy a cruise with the famous psychic. "Kabir," said Hanussen, "the count says you have to be punished because you touched the ladies where you shouldn't have." The men grabbed Kabir. "Tie him up," Hanussen ordered. "The count himself will inflict the punishment." Helldorf hit Kabir with his riding crop. The more Kabir cried, the harder Helldorf hit him, beating the boy until he fainted.[3]

That was just one of the stories about how Hanussen conducted his life and about the people he associated with. The rumors about the psychic were often extravagant and invariably fed by resentments and fears arising from his friendships with some of the top Nazis. This common response to Hanussen's maneuverings was not new. By the early 1930s, he was well enmeshed in a lifelong pattern of cementing alliances that were dubious, spurious, and unapologetically self-serving. In time, he would become so close to the Nazis that he pledged to "be the first, if necessary, to devote everything I own and am...to the altar of Germany. I have encountered the readiness for sacrifice among all those who stood behind the banner of the [Nazis'] National Concept; I know that Adolf Hitler sacrificed his all for this idea;...I have observed selflessness, integrity and true patriotism among the millions who back Hitler...and so I have...no choice but to demonstrate my respect and gratitude, unhesitatingly, to serve the truth."[4]

Such confessions would come later. And, of course, they would seem impossible, given the Nazis' anti-Semitism—and the fact that Hanussen was Jewish. But for now, Hanussen was content to sit quietly late at night on the deck of his boat and discuss human nature with his friend Count Helldorf. While they agreed that some men were born to be masters, Hanussen declared that ordinary people "need the threat of punishment. It does them good. Without fear, they wouldn't know what to do." Helldorf pursued this idea: "The *Herrenmenschen* [the master race] have to reign. The *Untermenschen* [the subhumans] have to obey. With the storm troopers, we will strike hard and merciless against them. Above all things, we will not go easy on the Jews."

Turning confidently toward Hanussen, Helldorf said, "As a member of the Danish gentry"—for Helldorf knew Hanussen only by his phony Danish name—"you appreciate the attitude of our Nordic race, don't you?" "Of course,'" said Hanussen. "Of course."

Helldorf was pleased. With these foreigners, you never knew whether you had a comrade or a moralist on your hands. Then, suddenly, concerned about his host, he asked Hanussen, "Are you tired?"

"Yes, I am," Hanussen said. "I always get tired when hypnotizing people. It wears me out."

"Staying with you has been very nice," Helldorf said as they walked toward their staterooms. "I hope we will remain friends."[5]

★  ★  ★

And remain friends they did, with both men laboring under their own illusions: Helldorf believing Hanussen was Danish and Hanussen indulging in deceptions of his own making. Another disparity separated them: with his regal bearing and courtly manners, Helldorf was emblematic of the old Germany; Hanussen's piercing eyes, bushy eyebrows, slightly oversized ears, average height, and relentless drive implied that he harkened from a world distant from aristocrats and wealth—the world that had coddled and produced a man like Helldorf. Reaching the stratosphere where Hanussen now resided was one of the illusions in which he specialized since, like all illusionists, he was constantly negotiating between the world he created and the world that exists. Most illusionists can separate the two. Not Hanussen. He persistently mistook his illusions for reality, although it must be said that he worked so hard at creating them that by the end of his shows, he was drenched in sweat. It was not easy being "Europe's Greatest Oracle Since Nostradamus," but Hanussen's persistence was central to pursuing his dreams and seducing his audiences. Almost everything the man did illustrates how much he enjoyed his underlying drama and his certainty that he could manipulate not only his most devoted admirers but also some of the more incendiary personalities of his time. Hanussen's pleasure was doubtless enhanced by the fact that only he was aware that the persona he so adroitly invented relied on a fragile and dubious safety net: his shameless, tireless audacity.[6]

Looking at the arc of Hanussen's career—from small-time carnie in Austria and Czechoslovakia to the most controversial mentalist in Europe—one surprising trait stands out: a sporadic honesty, a tic at odds with the scams in which he specialized. "I am nothing but a traveling salesman," Hanussen told a reporter in Vienna in the 1920s, "but I choose my clients myself. Those who are most likely to buy my product are the ones I choose. I observe them very carefully. Their most important characteristics for my 'experiments' to be successful are imagination and a desire that everything I perform work out.... They don't even care if it is true.... After my first 'experiment' [in a show] has been successful, they all share a faith in my power and know that it is useless to oppose me in any way."

And who was in Hanussen's audience? "Idiots," he said. "Imbeciles." "Crazy hysterics addicted to wonder." "Unhappy and unfortunate people"—all desperate for wisdom, even from him. "Most of all," Hanussen said, "they are children. Their sadness comes from the fact that they don't have a teacher, a father, a boss, a friend who impresses them enough that they can trust them. Why do these people come to me? Because I am stronger than they are, more audacious, more energetic. Because I have the stronger will. Because they are children and I am a man."[7]

"I wouldn't dream," said Hanussen, "of being the one to talk the poor devils who come to me out of their illusions.... Let these dear people believe in their miracles.... With courage, will power, energy and impertinence, you can twist 2,000 people seated in front of you around your finger."[8]

These revelations came during an interview Hanussen had with a reporter in Vienna almost a decade before his career reached its zenith. Still naive and not quite polished, his arrogance was apparent in his casual condescension toward his admirers. In subsequent years, Hanussen would smooth this over with a veneer of charm and sophistication.

Some people, particularly ladies, would find him irresistible. And yet he spoke a certain truth during that interview in 1922: many people who seek clairvoyants *do* wish that life were simpler, easier, less cumbersome, containing fewer questions and more answers. But Hanussen was foolish in his contempt for the people who came to see him. They were his meal ticket. Without them he might as well have been a *real* traveling salesman, going from city to city and theater to theater selling not miracles and wonders but widgets and doohickeys: a merchant of junk, not of slick conjuring and lively patter. By revealing himself to the reporter in Vienna, Hanussen put his foolishness on full display. Eventually he learned that charm, polish, and discretion were his best defense against skeptics and critics. These traits helped him cement his friendship with Nazis. His money didn't hurt either.

★   ★   ★

Hanussen's knack for puffing himself up got him in endless trouble. He especially liked taking what was not his—other men's women, other performer's acts, other people's trust. Some of these troubles were resolved in courtrooms—so many, in fact, that perhaps no other performer in the twentieth century was involved in so much litigation.

The worst of Hanussen's misadventures would be his Faustian pact with Hitler and the men close to him. Hanussen became so confident that he was in their good graces that one of his final acts went several steps too far in testing their patience. This was not a wise move: the Nazis had little patience to begin with. In this culminating assertion of his powers, Hanussen inserted himself in the machinations of the new Reich—a foolish venture for a man so unschooled in politics, so certain that he could carry the day through personality, persuasion, charisma, and confidence. By employing the occult—or, at least, his version of the occult—so selfishly, Hanussen entered a dark realm from which there was no retreat and no escape. Leading up to this errant and singular moment in early 1933 were other reckless impulses: not only did Hanussen bribe the top storm troopers, treat them to orgies on his yacht, and loan them his limousines, he also provided them with a warehouse full of boots at a time when their supplies were so scarce they sometimes were photographed barefoot. And beginning in the summer of 1932, Hanussen's weekly journal in Berlin—part newspaper, part gossip sheet, part astrological almanac—kept up a steady drumbeat for the Nazis, with headlines blaring "The Stars Tell Us Hitler's Greatest Days Are Coming Up" and "Cosmic Laws Determine the Decision for Hitler." Soon after that, Hanussen began conferring with Hitler himself in the fuehrer's favorite hotel in Berlin, the Kaiserhof, assuring him that the cosmos—and the masses—were on his side.[9]

Politically, Hanussen was truly an innocent. Indeed, his only interest in politics was gauging whose power and influence he could yoke to his advantage. Hanussen's ideology was not political. His creed was founded solely on self-preservation, a hunger for fame, a lusting for wealth, and a willful ignorance of the moral ambiguity that dwelled in his soul. If Hanussen had been more aware of his interior world, he might have acted differently. And if he had been more aware of the world around him, he would have known that the storm troopers, those thugs whom Helldorf was commanding in Berlin, had been waging terror on the city—and especially on Jews and Communists—for several years.

★ ★ ★

In February 1927, the Nazis received their first major write-up in the press in Berlin when they held a meeting in the neighborhood of

Wedding, a Communist stronghold. As Joseph Goebbels, the Nazis' propaganda chief, was about to speak, Communists moved closer to the podium to protest. They were attacked by storm troopers armed with chains, brass knuckles, sticks, and iron rods. Eighty-five Communists were badly wounded; three storm troopers were hospitalized. The next month, Goebbels ordered four hundred storm troopers to beat up any Jews they encountered in cafés or walking on the streets. They sent hundreds to the hospital. Four years later, in 1931, Count Helldorf personally sent fifteen hundred storm troopers to assault Jews leaving synagogues on Rosh Hashanah, the Jewish New Year.[10]

The storm troopers—officially, the Sturmabteilung, or SA for short—had been formed in 1921 to keep order at Nazi meetings. That didn't satisfy them for long, not with their virile self-image. Their name hadn't been chosen idly: *Sturm* means "tempest" or "attack"—exactly the sort of aggressive steamrollering these men fantasized about. Soon they were breaking up meetings of other political parties—tactics that pleased Hitler, who gloated that the Nazis had "recently been described as a savage, brutal horde, unafraid of using any means. I am very happy to hear this since I expect that this will make my aims and my party feared and known." In the early 1920s, after he personally led the SA against a meeting where a Bavarian federalist was speaking, Hitler was sentenced to three months in jail. He served one month and left prison a martyr for the movement he was building. "It's all right," he told the police. "We got what we wanted." He could also say that he had now fulfilled the promise he had made a few months before: "The National Socialist movement will in the future ruthlessly prevent—if necessary, by force—all meetings or lectures that are likely to distract the minds of our fellow countrymen."[11]

The Nazis' vision of violence and discipline appealed to the veterans of World War I who formed the first cadres of storm troopers. They appreciated the Nazis' total obedience to a leader, their complete merging of the party with the Fatherland, their near-absolute negation of the individual who existed only to serve the community. As the economy got worse in the Weimar Republic and desperation set in, they were joined by unemployed men who had no place else to turn. Then they were joined by thugs and criminals. The Nazi ideology didn't necessarily appeal to them—somewhere between half to 70 percent of storm troopers never joined the party. In fact, the Nazis' standard tropes—the Jews or the Versailles Treaty or more land for Germans—rarely cropped up in short essays that a number of SA members wrote in these years about why they became storm troopers. Rather, according to many of the essays, unemployment was why they joined. After all, by late 1933, more than one million Germans had been jobless and destitute for several years. The Nazis knew these men were willing to do anything for food and shelter. The SA ran soup kitchens and operated hostels for the poor and the homeless—converted barns, abandoned warehouses, empty storage rooms: anyplace with some square footage where a few men could bed down for the night. Spartan accommodations. Free accommodations. Joining the SA meant you had a full stomach and a roof over your head. As more people became unemployed, more joined the SA until it had 60,000 men in 1930; 170,000 in 1931; and more than 4 million by 1934.[12]

Being a storm trooper was also a chance to play soldier in a country brought to its knees by the Treaty of Versailles—that vile document that ended the Great War but humiliated the Fatherland. The storm troopers' marches, wrote one German, were "a substitute for Kaiser parades"—vast, endless rivers of men, with Adolf Hitler standing in for his highness and pride, terror, and fear employed to restore the nation to its glory. "In all confidence," Hitler wrote, "we can go to the limits of inhumanity if we bring happiness back to the German people."[13]

It would be overly speculative to say that Hanussen was oblivious to this violence. No one in Berlin could have been that blind. But it barely fazed him. Accustomed to enchanting others, he seems to have counted on his easy charm to beguile everyone he came in contact with, even the Nazis. What he didn't understand was that the Nazis were immune to charm. Their heavy-handedness—their aesthetics were more like a sledgehammer than a scalpel—gave them little tolerance for the subtlety in which Hanussen specialized. Asked by a friend in the early 1930s about Hitler, Hanussen replied, "Adolf looks more like an unemployed hair dresser than a Caesar." By that date, anyone with more sense would have kept his mouth shut. But for Hanussen, life was an illusion, a play, a charade. Not long before his death, he finally saw the sham he had been living. As he wrote a friend, "I always thought that business about the Jews was just an election trick of theirs. It wasn't." Hanussen was not just a master of deception; he was a master of *self*-deception. Somehow, he wanted to convince the Nazis that not *all* Jews were capitalists, Communists, or scum. His failure to do this can charitably be attributed to Hanussen's naïvêté. More surely, it refutes Hanussen's claims of being a clairvoyant: Even the least psychically endowed European could intuit Hitler's hate for Jews.[14]

Like Hanussen, Hitler was a sorcerer. The most whirling of dervishes, he screamed and yelled at rallies, his eyes glazed while he pounded away with incantations from a demonic realm, certain that he knew the future and that only he could lead the German people into it: glorious, noble, and triumphant. Between the world wars, Germany was ripe for this sort of magical thinking, and no one was more magical than Hitler, though an ambitious, ridiculously naive Jew who proffered his own magic to the masses would attempt to sway both the masses and the fuehrer, believing that if Hitler was the new God, then the magical Jew would be Hitler's favored prophet.

At first, Hanussen was a traditional mentalist—someone who acknowledges he is only simulating psychic powers, openly *pretending* he can read minds, divine the future, or assay someone's character, all in the service of entertaining—and befuddling—his audience. But by the late 1920s, Hanussen was presenting himself as a genuine psychic, assuring his fans that he communed with the mysterious forces that shape our destiny, returning with truths and revelations that illuminate our dull and meager lives, lives stunted by the narrow and limited dimensions that we cannot see beyond. As one German wrote in the 1930s, "A clairvoyant, face-to-face with his public, goes into a trance. That is his moment of real greatness. . . . He believes what he says; carried away by a mystic force, he cannot doubt the genuineness of his mission." This early supporter of national socialism was talking about Hitler. He could have been writing about Hanussen.[15] Ultimately, what Hanussen dispensed was wonder, without which life can be hollow and drab: Free will remains, but it's weighed down by the repetition of dull and deadening responsibilities. Wonder takes us beyond the quotidian. It tells us that the ordinary is just too much of a drag to put up with. In his own way, Hanussen understood this shrewd insight that verges almost on genuine wisdom.

Start to finish, and even while treating his friend Count Helldorf to long cruises on his yacht, Hanussen's was a life of magical thinking. Yet he was not alone. Millions of people in Europe and America were also oblivious to the conflagration that lay ahead. Unlike Hanussen, they did not claim to be prognosticators or seers, to having superpowers or operating out of time and space. Ordinary people with ordinary vision, they were not ready to forgo their hope in the essential goodness of human beings. In time they would; they would have no choice. Hanussen was different. He straddled the juncture between tribal loyalties and personal adventurism, between the Nazis' fascination with the occult and the rationalism of traditional Jewish thought; between the 1920s demimonde in Berlin and the looming Nazi nightmare. In certain ways, Hanussen was typical of the European Jews who operated along the margins of society. They did this by necessity, not choice: There were limits to how far they could enter into mainstream society. But what could be more marginal than reading minds and performing magic, than teetering along the thin ledge between reason and logic? The Jew was already the Other. Hanussen would take Otherness in a new direction, emphasizing less his difference from Christians than his ability to expand their universe, to channel visions and prophecies to a people craving a future where they would stand tall, towering over the pygmies who had humiliated and emasculated them, assuring them that Germany would rise from the ashes and that only one man—obscure and undistinguished for most of his life—was capable of leading them to this hallowed and exalted land.

PART ONE

# The Wonderful Land of Make-Believe

If we lose a sense of the mysterious, life is no more than a snuffed out candle.

—*Albert Einstein*

# CHAPTER 1

# One of the Finest Liars in Europe

In 1930, at the age of 41, Hanussen published his autobiography, *Meine Lebenslinie (My Lifeline)*, the only account of his early years. *Meine Lebenslinie* reads like a Horatio Alger novel grafted onto amateur metaphysics and stale legends from show business. As our only source for Hanussen's life before he became famous, it should be approached with a jaundiced eye. If you can consider it an album of Hanussen's whims and imagination, it's a fun read. Otherwise, it's simply the jottings of an already puffed-up showman puffing himself up some more.

Throughout *Meine Lebenslinie*, Hanussen tells us that he was a genius at manipulating people, even as a baby. "I made my parents marry," Hanussen proudly declares, looking back on his parents' elopement in 1889. His mother, 20-year-old Julie Kohn, was pregnant by Siegfried Steinschneider, who was 11 years her senior. Outraged, Julie's father, a wealthy furrier, tracked the couple down and had them arrested, Hanussen says without explanation, for vagrancy. Hanussen narrowly missed being born in a prison cell in Vienna: his mother was released 15 minutes before his birth.[1]

Next in Hanussen's infantile manipulations was "bringing my parents back together." His father escaped from prison, climbed over the garden wall surrounding his in-laws' house, and searched their villa for his wife and child. When young Hermann began crying wildly, Siegfried used the wailing to locate Julie and the baby. Her family was so busy quieting Hermann that they didn't realize their son-in-law was in the house. Using the baby's crying as a distraction, Hermann's father grabbed "my mother's hand and disappeared with her." A few hours later, Siegfried returned, "took me by my diaper and kidnapped me. Smart little boy that I was, I didn't make any noise."

This baby was wise beyond his years. He united his parents, then helped his father save his mother from her cold, mean family. From conception on, he was a savant—even in soiled diapers.

Hanussen's parents traveled constantly: His father was an actor, his mother, a singer. Roaming through Austria and Italy with low-budget troupes, they never made much money but always took baby Hermann with them. When he was three, his parents worked at a theater in Hermannstadt, a city in central Romania. The Steinschneiders lived in the rear of a house that faced "Corpse Alley," a narrow lane leading to a cemetery. Every day, funeral corteges passed by, filling the air with dirges, grief, and gloom. One night young Hermann woke up with a start and ran "as if led by an invisible hand" to the nearby apartment of his favorite playmate, Erna. Leading her to the cemetery, he told her to crouch behind a tombstone. Seconds later, Hanussen wrote in *Meine Lebenslinie*, "there was a terrible explosion" in Erna's parents' apartment. Luckily, no one was hurt. This, Hanussen said, "was my first experience of clairvoyance."

Hermann's second experience with clairvoyance came soon after that. Every day he rode out to the countryside with a man named Martin, who hauled dung from the town's stables in his wagon to the fields of the local farmers. One day a storm approached while Martin was heaving dung onto a field. Grabbing the reins, Hermann yelled, "Go!" Seconds later, lightning struck the tree the wagon had been standing under.

Looking back at these incidents with Erna and Martin, Hanussen said in *Meine Lebenslinie* that "the gift of clairvoyance is recognized early in someone's life." Maybe so, but more revealing is that, from an early age, Hanussen did not trust females. Not long after he saved Erna, she "let me down. A glazier moved into our building with his two sons. From that moment, she never looked at me again. Women are evil!" To Hanussen—as a boy and as a man—women were fickle and unreliable. It was better to leave them before they left you. In Hanussen's account, little Erna was the first of many females who would give him a lifetime of headaches.

After a few months in Hermannstadt, Hanussen's family returned to Vienna, always one step away from poverty and crammed into an apartment so tiny that Hanussen called it a "cabinet." They were not the only Jews in Vienna who were poor, but it may have seemed that way. The Rothschilds lived there, most of the city's doctors and lawyers were Jewish, and Jewish professionals were so well integrated into Viennese society—top to bottom—that even women in the royal family consulted a Jewish obstetrician. To a considerable degree, a frantic compulsion to assimilate accounted for the success of these Jews. The city had the highest conversion rate of any Jewish community in the world. It also had some of the worst self-hatred: Vienna's second-richest Jew—the banker and railroad builder Baron Maurice de Hirsch—vowed "to prevent Jews from pushing ahead too much," and an influential critic, Karl Kraus, himself a Jew, urged Jews to abandon their beliefs, their rituals, their mannerisms—*anything* that made them distinct and separate.[2]

The Steinschneiders rarely had time to think about how they fit into the broader world. Their life was a constant struggle, partly because Siegfried had no trade from which he could earn a reliable living. About all he could peddle was his gift of gab. That was how he had wooed Julie and how he was now trying to survive as a salesman. But the Steinschneiders never forgot they were Jewish, and they didn't let little Hermann forget either. Yet there is no indication that the local community remembered them, that any shuls or Jewish welfare organizations reached out to them. Or, indeed, that Siegfried or Julie sought their help. If anything, they were alone and drifting into an oblivion that was made worse when Julie died in 1899. She was 30 and had been sick for months. Hermann was nine.

To attempt to escape their poverty and their grief, Siegfried and his son moved to Boskovice, a small Czech town about 160 miles away. They were happy to be out of Vienna. And there, it seems, young Hanussen learned how to excel at the kind of pranks that would be the basis for his more sophisticated tricks in later decades.

After reading about the Roman emperor Nero, Hermann got the idea of doing to Boskovice what Nero had done to Rome: burn it down. Early one morning, he and some friends stole some paint and brushes, smeared "Rome Is Here" on most of the houses in town, and set fire to an old mill. As the villagers gathered to watch the fire, Grasel, a notorious thief, ran out of the mill. The police had been searching for him for months. The daughter of a local tailor also ran out of the mill: Grasel had a gift for seducing women. Hermann was immensely pleased with himself. "Boskovice of all cities," he wrote in *Meine Lebenslinie*, "had the honor of catching Grasel. I was the hero of the day and, normally, I would have qualified for the reward."

But the circumstances are not normal when you're an arsonist. Hermann received five ducats—not the hundred-ducat reward the government had offered for Grasel's capture. The boy also received a beating from one of his teachers—25 strokes with a cane. As an adult, Hanussen tried to be stoical about this. "God knows," he wrote, "there are always two sides in life. On one side, there was the friendly community with the ducats; on the other, the strict teacher with the cane." As the mill went up in smoke, so did Hermann's faith in fairness. Grasel had terrorized towns and villages. Hermann had caught him. Those hundred ducats were his, he figured, even if he had started a fire that threatened the town. Instead, he was caned. If any lesson stayed with him, it was that justice has its limits. Meeting the law halfway, at best, was preferable to observing it strictly. After his mother died and his father could barely provide for them, after receiving only five ducats of the promised hundred, and after his teacher caned him, Hermann concluded that the only person he could rely on was himself.

Or so it would seem—*if* Hanussen was telling the truth. There *had* been a bandit named Grasel. Unfortunately, he was hanged in 1818—eight decades before Hanussen said the man ran out of a burning mill in Boskovice. The real Grasel came from a family of thieves: His grandfather, his parents, and at least one cousin all had been jailed for stealing. Grasel first went to prison when he was nine years old. When the police caught up with him a few decades later, they charged him with 205 crimes, including a few murders. Sixty thousand people watched his hanging. Few of them heard his last words: "So many people." Hanussen also had a vocation that attracted people, though he never attracted a crowd as large as the one that watched Grasel's hanging. Fueling Hanussen's career was a deep and unshakable conviction that he could outsmart everyone—little Erna in Hermannstadt, the rubes in Boskovice, and, eventually, the audiences that filled the theaters where he performed and the Nazis who were conspiring to seize Germany. Like Grasel, Hanussen was not humble. Unlike Grasel, he would not hang. His enemies would find another way to deal with him.

Hermann and his father returned to Vienna three or four years later. Around this time, Hanussen had a bar mitzvah, although he does not use that term in his autobiography. Rather, he says, he had a confirmation. Confirmations for Jewish girls had begun in the mid-nineteenth century in Vienna, but they still were rare by the time Hanussen was of bar mitzvah age, which would have been about 1903. And anyway, boys were not eligible for them. Yet in those years some Viennese Jews referred to bar mitzvahs as confirmations, perhaps to draw less attention to their religion. Hanussen may have used the term in his autobiography for that exact reason. Nowhere in *Meine Lebenslinie* does he state that he was Jewish. That would have been bad for business.

Hanussen does state in *Meine Lebenslinie* that his father soon remarried—and that Hermann despised his new stepmother. Desperate to get away, Hermann thought he found his escape with a singer who performed in the garden of the Red Pretzel, a tavern just below the Steinschneiders' apartment. She performed every night, and Hermann had a great view of her show. She was pretty. She was talented. And she was 45 years old. That didn't stop 14-year-old Hermann. The lovers decided to run away, but they needed money. Ever resourceful, one afternoon Hermann lowered most of his family's possessions—vases, pictures, bookcases, clothes—by rope into the tavern's courtyard, where his lover was waiting. Then he shimmied down the rope. Hermann was almost to the ground when his father came home.

Even more than Hanussen's story about Grasel, this foiled elopement carries the whiff of fiction: A 14-year-old's fling with a 45-year-old is buffoonery, the furniture lowered to the garden is nonsensical, and the father's brilliantly timed return home is farcical. The whole scene is pure slapstick—a nod to what had not yet been viewed on the screen in 1903, which is when this incident allegedly occurred. Not viewed because, in 1903, no one was making films like this. But it is similar to films that Hanussen would have seen by the time he wrote *Meine Lebenslinie*—two-reelers with Charlie Chaplin, Buster Keaton, or the Keystone Kops, extended skits that played fast and loose with logic and common sense, all of which the adult Hermann Steinschneider enjoyed twisting to his own benefit. For his elopement story, Hanussen lifted a trope from silent films and inserted it into his own life. It lends his teen years a certain glamour. Unfortunately, it was as real as the tricks that he later performed: riffs on a reality that he conjured up. Whatever Hanussen's inadequacies, he more than compensated for them by concocting a convincing land of make-believe.

If Hermann couldn't be with the lovely singer from the Red Pretzel, then he would follow her in another way: He would become an entertainer. So not long after his father stopped him from running away with a woman three times his age, Hermann asked the manager of a vaudeville show passing through Vienna for a job.

"Have you worked anywhere else?" the manager inquired.

"Of course," Hermann lied. "I've been performing for five years."

"Then you must have started very early."

"I'm a natural," Hermann blustered. "It runs in my blood."

The manager told Hermann he could try out that night. He ran home, pawned all his clothes, and bought a tuxedo with tails. At a hairdresser's, he traded the watch he had received for his bar mitzvah for a wig and a phony beard that he was sure would make him look funny that night. Fueled by coffee and strudel, he sat at a café jotting down jokes for his routine.

The show began at a tavern at five o'clock. Wearing his new tuxedo, wig, and beard, Hermann grew anxious as the night wore on, wondering if he would ever be called onstage. Around midnight, he asked the manager when he would have his turn.

"Oh, you still want to perform?" the manager said. "All right, go on stage and do your stuff."

Hermann climbed the few steps to the stage, looked around nervously, and blurted out a few jokes. They fell flat. He tried some more. No one laughed. Finally, a long hook came out from the side of the stage, ending Hermann Steinschneider's debut in show business. The only joke of the entire incident occurred the next day when his father couldn't figure out why his son was wearing a tuxedo to school.[3]

Again: an improbable story in Hanussen's autobiography.

And again: Hanussen manufactures his own world—one part fantasy, one part moxie, one part making his father look like a jerk. Throughout *Meine Lebenslinie*, Hanussen accorded his father no respect. Calling him "My Old Man," Hanussen mocked and belittled him as having no trade and no skills, no place in the world and no place in his son's heart. There was a total lack of affection between the two, according to Hanussen's account of these years. Weak, frail, and gutless, Siegfried served only one function for young Hanussen: he provided a model of what Hermann would never be. And as he had with his father, Hanussen would repeatedly relish bringing down to size anyone who was stronger, older, or wiser than himself.

Hermann's debut as a comedian at that tavern was a flop, but after having his moment in the spotlight, he couldn't turn away from it. A few months later, he ran away from home, hoping to get by on writing songs and funny monologues, briefly joining a circus, then a theater company in Neustadt, a town about five hundred miles from Vienna. He hated the director. "There have been many times in my life when things didn't go well for me," Hanussen wrote in *Meine Lebenslinie*, "but it's never been worse than with director Bill." He also hated Bill's son, Ferdinand. One night, Hermann and Ferdinand began arguing while performing in a skit as army officers. Pulling out the sabers that were part of their costumes, they stabbed each other in front of the audience. Hermann was immediately fired.

For days, Hermann wandered around town. A prostitute, realizing that here was someone in even worse condition than she, gave him her last few coins. Desperate to buy a meal, Hermann drifted from tavern to tavern, telling jokes and hoping for handouts. He got schnapps, beer, and wine, but no one gave him a cent, and his pride stopped him from outright begging. "You must keep in mind," he assured the readers of his autobiography, "that I was no vagabond, but an intelligent guy from a good family."

He slept wherever he could—once in a kennel next to an over-sized dog. He worked in the fields for a day or two and wasn't asked to return—he was no good at manual labor. He worked for another theater company. No one came to its shows. The actors weren't paid. They slept in the fields. They were all as hungry as Hermann. Finally, a circus took him in, almost as a charity case.

"Look, boy," Mr. Pilcher, the director, told him, "you're young and you need something to eat. Hungry bones only end up being living dirt. Real actors may look down on us as imposters, but we work hard so we can eat. And we always do."[4]

Hermann learned enough about the circus to fill many roles and to earn his keep. Sometimes he would negotiate with local officials for rental space for the circus. Or he would be "Harry, the famous bareback rider." Or "Marini," a gymnast. Or "Mr. Gari, the famous tightrope walker." Or "the unbelievably funny clown, Mr. Clapp-Trapp." And once, as "the famous actor, Hermann von Brandenburg," he played

Judas in a passion play. Of all the jobs Hermann Steinschneider had with the Circus Oriental, this was the most delicious: a Jew playing the Jew who betrayed the Jew who was the Son of God.[5]

At the time, many small troupes like this were bouncing around Europe. Most had no more than a comedian or two, a strongman, a few horses, a monkey, a clown, a juggler. Some had a tent; most didn't. And many, like the one young Hermann joined, were run by Gypsies, who, Hanussen later said, were his "best friends ever." The best of his best friends were an odd couple: a giant and a pony. Heinrich the Giant was so tall Hermann barely reached his shoulders. They hung out all day, went to taverns at night, and slept in the stable, where Hermann doted on a pony named King, lovingly grooming him and bringing him fresh food he swiped from the fields while returning from his nightly carousing. A grateful King let Hermann rest his head against his soft, warm belly at night, barely moving so as not to wake his devoted friend.[6]

This was the most idyllic time of Hanussen's life. He was relaxed. He wasn't always trying to prove himself. And for the first time in his life, he was receiving unwavering and unconditional love. Heinrich the Giant protected him "like his own blood." And of his pony, Hanussen wrote, "King, my sweet King," there had never been "comrades who understood each other as well as we." After miles of wandering and years of loneliness, Hanussen found a home—in a stable.[7]

★   ★   ★

This peaceful interlude ended, as these things often do, because of a woman. In a small village, Heinrich fell in love with Anna, the daughter of a brewery owner. The strongman was always sighing "like an elephant" over her, and Hermann, barely into his teens and with no appreciation for the powerful and unpredictable ways of the heart, couldn't stand it. His strongman was now a weak man, and a girl—of all things—had done this to him. One day Heinrich, who was illiterate, asked Hermann to write a love letter for him. Determined to end "this unbearable situation," Hermann sent Anna a note ending the romance.[8]

Heinrich was furious, and Hermann was devastated. "The whole incident was a true disappointment to me," he lamented. "Our whole friendship was ruined by a skirt."[9]

One night, after the wagons were loaded, Hermann hid in the bushes, watching the circus rumble out of town "until my eyes hurt and a cloud of dust covered the entire caravan." When the dust settled, Hanussen stood up, took a deep breath, and decided he was ready "to rejoin civilization." Unfortunately, civilization wasn't ready for someone whose skills were limited to getting into fights, sleeping in stables, and betraying Jesus in a passion play.[10]

Again, Hermann wandered aimlessly. He was down to his last few pennies when he saw an ad in a paper:

*Zookeeper Wanted*
*For Animal Training*
*(Lions, Tigers, Dogs, Polar Bears)*
*Candidates must have experience as tamers and be able to present*
*the ensemble in afternoon shows*[11]

At the circus—a huge enterprise with a hundred employees and a long caravan of wagons and even its own chapel—Hermann located the manager, who sized up the scrawny teenager.

"Have you done this kind of work before?" he asked.

"Of course."

"And you're familiar with training animals and presenting them in a show?"

"Of course."

"Good. Then go talk with Mr. Johnson. He'll show you the animals."[12]

Johnson may have been one of the more famous lion tamers of the day, but he was a complete coward around his wife, Mabel, who was small, skinny, cross-eyed, and, according to Hanussen, all seeing and all knowing. One eye looked to the right. One eye looked to the left. "She saw everything and she missed nothing," Hanussen wrote. "The poor guy had a hard life with her by his side," which may explain why Johnson was a lush.[13]

Hermann fed the lions—from outside the cage. On his fourth day with the circus, Johnson got drunk. Barely able to stand, he draped one of his beefy arms around Hermann and walked him over to the lion's cage. "I can't do the show," he said. "These beasts lunge at me when I'm drunk." But Hermann could do it. "You've seen everything you need to know," Johnson assured the young man. "You can wear my costume. When the lions smell a different costume, they attack whoever's wearing it."[14]

Johnson's only advice was to keep an eye on Sultan, one of the more feisty lions: "If you walk past him, he'll try to grab you with his paw. Crack the whip and lash him until he stands on his pedestal and quiets down."[15]

Hermann went to the dressing room, got into Johnson's costume, and ran his hands fondly over the epaulettes. "What can happen to me?" he thought. "I'm wearing Johnson's costume." He treated it like a talisman that could save him from whatever he was walking into.[16]

The other performers formed two lines for Hermann to walk through to the cage. He marched bravely toward the lions, entered the cage—and froze: there was no way Johnson's costume could protect him from these monsters. Then he realized that the lions already knew what to do. He just had to follow their lead. With every crack of his whip, they did what Johnson had taught them. Then Hermann got cocky and started shouting at them. They roared back and Sultan, the lion Johnson had warned Hermann about, refused to balance on a ball Hermann rolled in his direction. As the boy walked up to Sultan to scold him, the lion roared and swatted at him. Remembering what Johnson said, Hermann slapped Sultan across the face with the handle of the whip. Sultan winced, sighed, and, to quote Hanussen, "mumbled an apology." Indeed, Hanussen would humbly assert, "It was like this always is in life: the bolder one wins." Sultan returned to being docile and Hermann—a kid who had no idea what the hell he was doing—was temporary ruler of these dangerous beasts.[17]

Hermann had always thought of himself as a hero. Now he *was* one, and it felt good. But as he was about to take off Johnson's costume, he caught himself in the mirror: He was pale and white. He wasn't a hero. He was just a scared kid. Then he looked at the outfit he was wearing. It wasn't Johnson's costume; he was wearing the tightrope walker's tights. He "began shaking so much" he had to sit down, realizing he "was lucky not to have come across this mix-up five minutes earlier when I beat Sultan in the face."[18]

Hermann learned one principle from the debacle: "Imagination and fantasy are the only thing that count in life." Finally, he was being honest with the readers of *Meine Lebenslinie*. It's preposterous to think that he ever walked into a cage of lions. He may have worked as a lackey at a circus, perhaps grooming the domesticated animals or feeding (from outside their cage) some of the more exotic ones. But it strains credulity that any circus would let a teenager walk into a cage full of wild beasts if its lion tamer was too drunk to perform. And Hanussen could not have run his hands fondly over the epaulettes before walking into the cage because there weren't any, not if he was actually wearing tights.[19]

Like any creative act, Hanussen's yarns provide insights into their author. His literary drama came at the expense of fact. His writing was a device that, more than anything else, was intended to manufacture sympathy for himself but, when examined carefully, only bred suspicions about its author. Hanussen devoted his life to illusion, to conjuring up realities that were entertaining, mystifying, boggling. His autobiography is no exception. How he presented himself in print was consistent with how he presented himself onstage. But a life devoted to weaving illusions is not a reliable life, and one danger was that Hanussen risked fooling himself. If a life is constructed on a lie—and on a lie that is eminently successful—why pay any attention to the truth?

By now, we've followed Hanussen through the years when he had little fame and even less money. We've heard that he brought his parents together as an infant in Vienna; that he saved little Erna's life as a tot in Hermannstadt; that he was a juvenile delinquent in Boskovice, setting fire to a barn and nabbing a famous robber; that as a teenager he courted a singer three times his age and walked into a cage full of lions. The list goes on. It will get longer, as you will soon see. All these stories come from Hanussen. There is no way to confirm them. During this phase of his life, no one was chronicling his adventures. A rascal and a scoundrel, he is *always* the hero of his stories: falling flat on his face, again and again, then redeeming himself, bringing the cheering crowd to its feet demanding more miracles from this undersize, underestimated maestro. He knew the world was not coming to him for truth. Illusionists and mentalists don't dabble in truth. As Chekhov said, "Any idiot can face a crisis; it's the day-to-day living that wears you out." The world was coming to him for hope—the hope that life is more than what it seems, that we can survive the grinding exhaustion of the day-to-day–ness of our lives. If we grant Hanussen this intention, his fictions are more than fabrications; they are parables of what might be.

So we enter into a compact with the Hanussens of the world. We allow them to make us smile, to brighten our day, to jolt us into wonderment. In turn, we are their willing and compliant audience—a small price to pay for pleasure and, on a good day, an even smaller price for the joy of being amazed. Yet it is essential to recognize that even illusionists have ethics. As the preeminent American magician Teller told me, "A magician puts a frame of truth around his lies that prevents them from doing harm." The illusionist is honest about his dishonesty, aware of how easy it is to persuade the gullible and tractable to be in awe of profound and esoteric secrets. Jewish law—for, indeed, Hanussen was Jewish—imposes a similar obligation: A magician must admit to having no special powers. Claiming otherwise muddies the holy and the mundane, the sacred and the fake. Later in life, Hanussen would forget about these obligatory confessions. That lapse would bring him great fame...and much trouble.[20]

# CHAPTER 2

# The Psychic Gravedigger

Hermann left the circus not long after his (alleged) triumph with the lions. He had to get out of there: Mabel, the lion tamer's wife, couldn't keep her hands off him. First, that 45-year-old singer back in Vienna wanted to run away with him; now the lion tamer's wife had a crush on him. Still in his teens, he was a magnet for older women—or so he claimed—a dubious assertion not only because of the hormonal complexities in these May-December romances but also because Hanussen's distinction between truth and fantasy was murky at best.[1]

Hermann bounced around in a few more circuses, eventually ending up in Vienna, where he wrote songs, jokes, plays—anything that would give him enough money for food and rent. And in May 1912 he married a woman named Herta Samter. Almost all we know about her is that she was a prompter in a small theater in Vienna and was three years older than Hanussen. Most likely, a rabbi officiated at the wedding. Also, Herta was probably pregnant.

Soon after their son was stillborn, Hermann left Herta. The marriage was too constricting. He needed to get away. So he sailed to Turkey with an opera company. Hermann had no right to call himself a singer, but people do strange things when they're desperate, like crash an audition, mouth the words as other singers are harmonizing, and sign the roster with the name of a singer who doesn't come forward for his audition when his name is called. In Istanbul, the director almost died of a stroke, the producer went bankrupt, and the company's stars paid their fare back to Vienna out of their own pockets while the rest of the cast was stranded in a strange and not very hospitable place with no money to get home. Hanussen, always quick with his tongue, convinced a theater owner to let them perform if they could pay the fee for the theater *after* their show.[2]

Using their last pennies, Hanussen and his friends printed elaborate posters announcing a performance by Vienna's "best operetta ensemble" of Franz Lehar's latest operetta. The posters listed 40 performers and promised that Lehar himself would conduct the show and that, for a grand finale, fireworks would spell out the initials of the sultan of Turkey.[3]

When the group sold enough tickets on the night of the show to pay for their trip home, Hermann handed the money to one of his singers, telling him to leave the theater and meet him later. Of course, there was no Lehar, no fireworks, no operetta, no set, and no costumes. Hermann had just stitched together songs that members of his ensemble knew into what amounted to more of a variety show than an opera.[4]

As the audience sat waiting for the fireworks after the last song, the singers tried to steal away backstage. The theater owner blocked them, yelling for his money *and* for the fireworks. When the audience heard him—this was a small theater—they, too, began shouting, demanding refunds. With a near-riot on his hands, Hermann tried to calm the crowd.

Facing the audience alone, Hanussen was frank about his predicament: "We performed the best we could for you.... My dear ladies and gentlemen, if you insist, we will give you your money back. But I beg you: please give us that money as a present. Do something good for people who came to your country. When we are back in Vienna, we will think of you. It is true: we didn't have a fireworks show in honor of your sultan. But you can praise him even more by helping some stranded entertainers find their way back home."[5]

It took a few moments for the crowd to absorb what Hanussen said. This wasn't the ordinary patter at the end of an operetta, the climax where the handsome leading man gets the beautiful leading lady. This was a man pleading to go home. One by one, they began clapping and stomping and showering Hermann with money. The theater owner even waived his rental fee. Hermann had averted a disaster, but the singers who were huddling backstage didn't know that. All they heard was a wild ruckus. Sure that Hermann was being torn apart by an angry mob, they ran to their hotel, leaving him to fend for himself.

By the time Hermann got back to his room, the rest of the cast had disappeared. They were thoughtful enough to have written a brief note to him: "Please don't be angry. It's better if one man suffers for everybody than everybody suffers for one man."[6]

Hermann didn't suffer: He had enough money for a ticket to Vienna. In fact, Hermann bought *two* tickets for second-class cabins— separate cabins. A few days later, he boarded a ship, the *Baron Beck,* accompanied by a pretty cabaret singer from Vienna who was also stranded in Istanbul. Hermann was so flush that he had bought her a ticket, too. Her name was Betty Schostak.

Their cabins were just down the hall from each other . But Hermann knew he could do better for himself, especially with first class full of elegant and wealthy people. So he told the captain he was Titta Ruffo, a famous baritone, and offered to perform on the ship. Honored to have such a noted celebrity onboard, the captain moved Hermann into first class. Nothing was too good for his famous passenger.

Using Ruffo's name was beyond ridiculous. The real Ruffo was called the "Voce del Leone"—the Voice of the Lion. He had an enormous voice and a powerful stage presence. His high notes thrilled audiences. In the opera world in the early twentieth century, only Enrico Caruso was more famous than Ruffo, although many critics said Ruffo was the finest baritone of his generation. Knowing that everyone would realize he was a fraud as soon as he sang a single note, Hermann scheduled his performance for the fifth day of the cruise. At that point, the ship would be near Corfu, which was prone to strong winds, and Hermann would explain that singing under such conditions might damage his voice. He would leave the ship in Corfu, free of his shipboard pretense. Until then, he strolled the main deck, gave autographs to pretty girls, warbled a few mi-mi-mi-mi-mi's and la-la-la-la-la's, and wore a scarf around his neck to protect his precious throat: the ocean air, he complained, was already making him ill.

Coincidentally, the ship's manifest included a fakir from India with three poisonous snakes. Furious when he learned that snakes that might endanger his passengers were aboard, the captain ordered that the vipers—and the fakir—be removed from the ship in Corfu, the ship's first port of call.

A few nights later, the topic of the fakir came up as Hanussen was enjoying dinner with the man on board whom he most admired: Count Montegazza. In his autobiography, Hanussen called the count "tall and svelte [and] elegant to the nth degree." Montegazza mentioned that he had gone below to watch the fakir perform. It was fascinating. Perhaps the captain would let the Indian perform for the first-class passengers? With barely two hours before the ship reached Corfu, the captain agreed. What could go wrong in two hours?

While walking toward the small stage where the fakir would perform, the count leaned over to Hanussen and whispered, "And soon, we will have the great pleasure to hear Maestro Ruffo sing." Hanussen realized that Montegazza had seen through his little game. Pulling his scarf more snugly around his neck, Hanussen moved to put some distance between himself and the count, wary of what Montegazza might do next. Suddenly, the fakir stormed onto the deck, frantic that his snakes had escaped. As the passengers panicked, only the count was calm. He and the fakir went below with a bowl of milk for the snakes. Fifteen minutes later, they returned. Montegazza was carrying the fakir's basket. Safely inside, he said, were the snakes. The crowd cheered for the brave count.

As the ship neared Corfu, Hanussen announced that the fakir finally should deliver on his promise of performing. When Montegazza protested that there was no time for a show—he and some other passengers just wanted to get off the boat—Hermann claimed an authority he did not possess and barked, "Nobody leaves the ship. Not you, Count, or you, Mr. Fakir."

After tripping the fakir as he tried to flee, Hermann picked up the basket that the man had accidentally dropped. As he tried to stop Hermann from opening it, the count whispered, "You swindler! You don't think I know what you are?"

"Count," said Hermann, loud enough for everyone to hear, "I don't mind telling everyone here that I am as much Titta Ruffo as you are Count Montegazza. I can't sing and those snakes in the basket can't bite. But to you, my dear ladies and gentlemen, I declare that there are some very special 'snakes' in this basket, indeed."

Reaching into the basket, Hermann pulled out jewelry, watches, a gold crucifix, and a diamond necklace. While Montegazza and the fakir had been pretending to catch the snakes, Hermann explained, they were actually stealing valuables from the first-class cabins. A basketful of poisonous snakes was the last place anyone would search.

As he looked closely at the fakir one day, Herman had realized that the man was using iodine on his skin to make it darker. And when he happened to be in the men's room as the fakir was washing up, he saw a tattoo on his arm identical to one on a circus performer he had heard about back in Europe. When he saw the same tattoo on the count, he realized the men were acrobats from Munich—the Pirelli Brothers, for whom police all over Europe were searching. During his work in circuses, Hermann had heard that the brothers were earning a nice living after turning to crime.

Hanussen was now a hero. But he was also as much of a phony as the count and the fakir, and the captain demanded he pay for his first-class cabin. Coming to his rescue, the passengers collected enough money to pay for the cabin.

In spirit and tone, this story is a reprise of Hanussen's operetta-and-fireworks scam back in Constantinople. Again, Hanussen turns disaster into triumph. And again, he gets the last laugh, sniggering at anyone who thought he could get the better of him. This wasn't a matter of luck. In these stories, Hanussen is invincible. No one could take advantage of him, and no one was smarter. Which is why he and Betty sailed on with the cockeyed optimism that he could handle just about anything that came his way.

★   ★   ★

Given the strength of Hermann's ambition, his devotion to Betty was unique. Betty was not just beautiful; she was the mother of another of Hanussen's children—a boy who died soon after birth. Hermann doted on her for another reason: She had tuberculosis. When doctors in Vienna said they couldn't help her, Hermann and Betty moved to Berlin, believing that treatments there were her best hope.

In Berlin, Hermann had a string of odd jobs, the first in a café on Friedrichstrasse whose ad had caught his attention: *Singing Waiter Wanted. He must amuse the guests and be a very good server. Apply to Jakob Schlesinger.* By the time Hermann got to the Nachtasyl Café, 30 men were waiting outside. Hermann was desperate. "Excuse me, excuse me," he said loudly. "I think you should let Mr. Schlesinger himself get into his office." Seconds later, Hermann was inside Mr. Schlesinger's office. He got the job.[7]

One night Hermann was asked to guide customers through a small museum in the café, really a collection of freakish oddities. Soon after beginning the tour, Hermann went into a trance. Claiming he could see the people who had owned the objects that were on display, Hanussen touched the glove of a woman who had drowned and began speaking her final thoughts as she was dying. "I talked and talked," Hanussen later wrote. "The people who were with me became silent. Horror touched their hearts and mine."[8]

That night the Nachtasyl didn't make much money. Everyone was subdued. Hermann retreated to a backroom, took off his waiter's jacket, and walked out into the cool early morning air, never to return. He was scared of the museum—and of himself.[9]

Hermann's next gig was as a magician in another café. He pulled together an entire act in less than a day with tricks he bought at a magic shop: a bag that made eggs disappear, cards that changed colors, and flowers that grew as soon as he threw seeds down on the stage. He was so bad his first night that the audience couldn't stop laughing. The café owner asked Hermann to stay on, more as a comedian who did magic than a magician who had mastered tricks.[10]

Another night, as soon as he stepped on stage, Hermann forgot a formula he had memorized to help him guess certain numbers or dates. So he started guessing. Somehow, his psychic powers kicked in, and he got every date and number right, stunning his audience and himself. "Everything started to spin," he said. "All the faces melted together. Only my mouth kept talking." Then he stopped. No one was laughing. Backstage, the manager complained that the mood Hermann had created was not conducive to selling beer. Next time, the manager yelled, throw in some jokes. Get some things wrong. Make it *funny*.[11]

The following night Hermann tried to do what the manager wanted, but his jokes fell flat and he put no one in a good mood. He was fired.[12]

With time on his hands, Hermann visited Betty in the Charité Hospital, perfecting his tricks, memorizing formulas and number patterns until they stayed in his head. A club in a Berlin suburb booked him, and, this time, Hermann was determined to rely on what he had been practicing, not on the psychic skills that had caused him so much trouble. By depending on what he had memorized, not on his intuition, Hermann stumbled and stammered and looked like an amateur. That's what people wanted—a comedian who was inept at magic—and that's what he was giving them.[13]

But in the middle of one show, Hermann started "seeing" again. This time he saw Betty in the hospital, raising her arms, calling him, blood spilling from her lips. Unnerved, Hermann started screaming at his audience. He told one woman to go home: her daughter was walking the streets. He scolded an elderly man for seeing a Gypsy that afternoon to find out how much longer his wife would live. He warned another man that his boss planned to have him arrested for embezzlement. The café owner threw Hermann out of the club. Jumping onto a streetcar, Hermann got off at the Friedrichstrasse station and raced down Karlstrasse to the hospital. He was too late; Betty was dead.[14]

After the funeral, Hermann felt empty, unapproachable, scared of himself and his "secret abilities." He "didn't want to be able to see through walls." He wanted to be like everyone else, "not someone strange and abnormal and different."[15]

One way Hermann tried to be like everyone else was by changing professions, entering a form of journalism that has always been suspect yet invariably profitable: He became editor of *Der Blitz*, a tabloid specializing in reporting on well-known Viennese who were gay, had venereal diseases, frequented prostitutes, or used drugs. It wasn't a pretty business, but it paid the bills, and Hanussen figured out how *Der Blitz* could make even more money: He would write serialized novels describing actual people in compromising situations. The stories would be based on real episodes in their lives. If they didn't pay what Hermann demanded, *Der Blitz* would publish their names—and their shameful indiscretions.[16]

In one of Hermann's "novels," the Society for the Enhancement of Virginity sends a Major Quitsch to root out evil everywhere in Vienna. Quitsch searches alleys, streets, stores, taverns, cafés, restaurants, doctors' offices, optometrists' examining rooms, shoemakers' shops—always looking for sin. If these businesses paid Hermann what he demanded, they would be mentioned favorably in his novel. If not, he would trash them.[17]

*Der Blitz* was a shady business, and Hermann seemed to relish it. But a few months later, World War I began and he joined the Austrian army, hoping it would give his life the meaning it lost when Betty died. The army was the wrong place for him. He was lazy and disobedient and "didn't care about anything." And why should he? After Betty's death, "what did I have left to lose in this world?"[18]

And yet, Hanussen later claimed, he was "incredibly popular," mostly because of the little diversions he provided in the trenches, such as reading minds the way Joe Labero, a mentalist, had taught him in Vienna. (Labero had done this while writing an article for *Der Blitz* that explained the techniques of a clairvoyant who was all the rage in Vienna.) But Hermann was still uncertain about how well he could read minds, so a friend who worked in the army's mail room helped him out, steaming open soldiers' mail so Hermann could read the latest news from home. Hermann then told the soldiers what he had learned while in a trance. That impressed the troops. It also impressed Hermann's captain, who learned through his platoon's resident psychic that his wife had given birth to a seven-pound boy.[19]

The war dragged on. The longer it lasted, the more bored Hermann got. He just wanted to "wear decent clothes without lice and go out with a beautiful girl." The best way to do that, he figured, was to be discharged. "I got myself a mental disorder," he later bragged. But he didn't get the discharge he wanted. Instead, the doctors reassigned him to Gorlice, a town in Poland that had seen one of the worst battles on the eastern front: 330,000 casualties—240,000 Russians and 90,000 Germans, Austrians, and Hungarians. Hermann's job was to bury the dead.[20]

Gorlice stank, the battlefields stank, the men working in them stank. The city was a cesspool: acres of rotting bones and decaying carcasses. Hermann stood in this mess, poking a stick into rotting, stinking clothing that covered what used to be a human being, looking for some way to identify it and trying "hard to remember that this puddle had once been a son or a spouse or a father—human beings with hearts and brains, moved by passion and pain, children of mothers like us, we who were shoveling them into boxes."[21]

As Christmas approached, Hermann gave his first real mind-reading performance in public—a fund-raiser to buy presents for the thousands of Russian prisoners of war who were doing most of the work with the dead in the stinking, rotting fields near Gorlice. Because Hanussen still was not sure of his powers, two friends offered to help him with secret signs and whispers. They confused him so much that the first half of the show flopped. For the second half, he tried "real telepathy." To his surprise, everything clicked. He didn't need his friends. He could actually read minds. He just needed to trust himself.[22]

By 1916, Hermann was performing in small towns more often than he was on the front lines. In less polite terms, he was a deserter. On one of these trips, he dazzled the man sitting next to him on a train with stories about successfully dowsing for water and entertaining the troops with mind reading. The man, an impresario named Josef "Peppi" Koller, perked up. Koller had booked the Konzerthaus Theater in Vienna for Ronny Johannson, an erotic sensation from Denmark. With four days to go before the show, ticket sales were slow. Maybe this soldier could be the grand finale for Johannson's show? But what name should he use? Worried that he would be arrested as a deserter if posters for the show used his real name, Steinschneider came up with Erik Jan Hanussen. Suddenly, he was an aristocrat from Copenhagen. Even better, by using Steinschneider's new name, Koller could pitch the show as a salute to spunky little Denmark, which was straining to remain neutral in this, the second year of the Great War.

Posters went up all over Vienna announcing this man no one had heard of—Erik Jan Hanussen—as a glorious last-minute addition to the bill. He was exotic. He was brilliant. He was a genius. The advertising blitz worked. The theater sold out. Telepaths were popular in Vienna, and one imported all the way from Copenhagen was more alluring than the home-grown variety (even if his name drew a complete blank).[23]

When Hanussen walked onto the stage of the Konzerthaus on April 30, he was slightly rattled that Emperor Karl I and many members of the royal family were sitting in the first box to his left: he was accustomed to performing before soldiers or peasants in small towns, not before royalty. Nevertheless, he stared right back at the audience; everyone wanted to know what this skinny young man had to offer. Hanussen opened with a trick called telepathic mail—delivering an envelope to someone in the audience whose name was written on a slip of paper sealed inside it. There was no applause even after Hanussen delivered two pieces of mail. He hadn't expected this crowd would be so difficult to please. Then a servant of the royal family announced that the Archduchess Immakulata wanted to send mail. For his first two deliveries, Hanussen had the person sending the mail tightly hold his wrist. Technically called "muscle reading," the method let Hanussen pick up subtle signals from whoever was sending the mail. But Hanussen couldn't ask the empress to hold his wrist as they wandered around the theater searching for the recipient of her letter. And he couldn't shout at her if she didn't concentrate hard enough, which is what he had done with his other volunteers.[24]

Realizing that this was "a complicated situation," Hanussen accepted the envelope that a servant brought down from the royal box, jumped off the stage, dashed past the first few rows of seats, then turned and paused. He started touching the shoulders of the people who were seated nearby, faster and faster, moving down one row, then another, touching, touching, touching everyone until he stopped, carefully considered what he was about to do, and handed the envelope to a distinguished-looking man with a white beard. The theater was thick with silence. No one, not even the gentleman who had received the mail, knew what to do. Finally, the one person in the theater who knew whose name was in the envelope started clapping. "Bravo! Bravo!" shouted the archduchess. "You are correct. It is him!" The archduchess had sent the letter to her personal physician.[25]

Applause thundered down on Hanussen. "The spell was broken," he wrote years later. The audience had "accepted me, and every artist knows what that means." After the show, Hanussen spent an hour in the emperor's box, exchanging pleasantries and performing more tricks as the audience stared up at him. They were so curious about what this unknown was telling their beloved emperor that they refused to leave the theater.[26]

Life was different for Hanussen after that night. He was famous. Strangers followed him down the street. They had seen his photo on posters and in newspapers. Some asked for his autograph. Others just stared at him. He stayed in Vienna for a few days after the show, in no hurry to return to the army. Finally, he dragged himself away from the drinks and good food and his new friends to discover that word had reached the army about his success. (Presumably, photos of him in the papers had alerted the military to his whereabouts.) Now, he was no ordinary deserter, not after spending an hour with the royal family in their box at the Konzerthaus. He still was locked up in the guardhouse, though he was given a clean cell, decent food, and, he would somewhat preposterously claim, even champagne.[27]

In Vienna, the impresario Peppi Koller was running all over town trying to obtain a proper leave for Hanussen so he could perform again in the capital. When Archduke Leopold Salvator told Koller that he would definitely attend Hanussen's next show in Vienna, the impresario cabled Hanussen's regiment commander: "His imperial and royal Highness, the Archduke Leopold Salvator, wishes that platoon leader Steinschneider will succeed in obtaining a leave of absence in order to perform in Vienna." Almost instantly, Hanussen was released, and soon he was regularly booked at some of the largest theaters in Vienna—delivering mail, finding small objects that members of the audience had hidden, hypnotizing volunteers from the audience. As his confidence grew, his shows grew more elaborate. His performance on November 11, 1918—billed as a "Telepathic Séance"—was especially meaningful: The war ended at 11 a.m. that day. To commemorate the cessation of hostilities, Hanussen telepathically read dates, names, and numbers that people in the audience were thinking about; demonstrated how he had divined water on the frontlines; and hypnotized volunteers from the audience so they briefly lost their memory, then their willpower, and finally pranced around the stage like graceful swans. Austria may have lost the war, but Hanussen was on his way to winning the peace. His peace.[28]

★  ★  ★

The war had been good to Hanussen. When it began, he was almost broke. When it ended, he was performing in elegant theaters before swells and royalty. His success gave him a new perspective—a deeper one—that surprised a journalist who visited him. "I came," said the reporter, "expecting the usual creep" who dabbled in the occult. Instead, he found "a small, broad-shouldered man of surprisingly athletic build." Described in the article as fun-loving, skeptical, and clever, Hanussen was then in his late twenties. Though still fairly young, he understood that magic provided a necessary illusion in our tiring, sometimes disagreeable lives. "Man walks through this miserable life dreaming of miracles," he said. "And from time to time, someone gives us the courage to believe in them." *That* was Hanussen's role: he gave people the courage to dream about possibilities.[29]

But why did they—why did anyone—trust Hanussen? And why did they trust him, as he said, unconditionally? Because, he claimed, he knew that the key to life was "pulling yourself together and not letting anyone step all over you. Performing miracles takes sharp eyes, courage and will power. Everything else is fraud."[30]

True, but believing in a fake miracle is no better than believing in no miracle. Both are follies.

# CHAPTER 3

# "A Conjuror Is an Actor Playing the Part of a Magician"

Magicians defy the laws of physics. Mind readers defy the laws of privacy, mocking the idea that our minds are our last bastion against a nosy and intrusive world. They demolish our idea that we are separate and distinct individuals. Instead, we are porous, transparent, translucent—easily invaded and with no place to hide. Mind readers easily open the vault where we store our most personal musings, brooding, lusts, and contempt—everything that makes us who we are, everything that we always figured was safe from prying busybodies. This revelation can shift the very ground of our existence: All our lives, we had assumed that our minds were our own business; now someone can plant himself inside them. Nothing is impregnable, and nothing is secure.

This was the terrain where Hanussen pitched his tent. But he actually read muscles, not minds, and he admitted this in a book he wrote in 1919: *Mind Reading and Telepathy.* (The German title was *Das Gedankenlesen: Telepathie.*) With the book, Hanussen broke one of the promises he had made before the war to Joe Labero, the mentalist who had taught him how to read minds. Hanussen had pledged to Labero that he would never teach anyone how to read muscles. His book—a step-by-step guide to muscle reading—did exactly that. Another promise he had given Labero was to never read minds in public. Hanussen had broken that vow a long time ago.

Most likely, he wrote the book not only to pick up some extra cash as his career was just taking off, but also because he couldn't resist bragging about what he knew. In time, his inability to censor himself—to stifle his urge to announce all the secrets he harbored—would prove his greatest undoing. Regardless of Hanussen's motive, the book is considered a classic in the genre. It is so detailed that in it Hanussen advises novice mind readers about the benefits of good hygiene: comb your hair, clean your fingernails, and perform only in a clean shirt and after brushing your teeth. He was just as adamant about how to choose volunteers from the audience: Pick only someone who *wants* you to succeed and has a "lively temperament—artists, journalists, . . . people with aesthetic occupations." Avoid people "whose movements are stiff" and whose skin is like "dry parchment, whose soul drowns in dust from filing cabinets." Like many people who rely on their wits, Hanussen looked down on anyone who worked in an office and had an ordinary job. To him, the mundane was suffocating.[1]

In *Mind Reading and Telepathy,* Hanussen lays down an iron-clad principle: A "telepath" can deal only with what "can be seen, grasped and reached." He can *find* a picture of the Eiffel Tower but can never guess that someone is *thinking* of the tower. He can *find* someone whose name is "Maier" but can never guess that name out of the blue. The simpler the experiment, the greater the chances it will succeed, especially for a novice. Finding a pin on someone who's in the room with you is easy. Finding a pin in a house in Berlin *is* possible even if the experiment started in, say, Vienna, though it would be a terrible nuisance: The mind reader and his subject would have to go to the local railroad station, buy a ticket to Berlin, board the train, get off in Berlin, take a tram to a certain house, and, finally, find the pin somewhere in that house. And while a telepath could never find an object that someone has thrown in the ocean, if he was clever enough, he could detect from the person who had thrown it exactly from where and in what direction it had been tossed into the water.[2]

But how do you read minds? First, says Hanussen, ask questions in a sequence that will help you determine if subjects are thinking about something concrete or abstract; if they are thinking about something that is in the same room, the same city, or even the same country; if they are thinking of a person or an inanimate object. The question-and-answer session—really more of a quick-fire, staccato exchange—between a telepath and his subject might go something like this:

"Concrete?"

"Yes."

"In this city?"

"No."

"In Germany?"

"Yes."

"A person."

"Yes."

"A sovereign?"

"No."

"A poet."

"Yes."

"A classicist."

"Yes."

"One of the greatest?"

"Yes."

The telepath would now narrow down the poets his subject was thinking about to Goethe or Schiller since, in 1919, when Hanussen was writing, they were the most renowned poets in Germany. But a good mind reader approaches the payoff to his questioning gracefully. There is no art to bluntly asking, "Are you thinking about Schiller?" Rather, Hanussen recommends proceeding in a slightly roundabout way:

"Did he die young?" (Schiller died when he was 45.)

"No."

"Was he old?"(Goethe died when he was 83.)

"Yes."

"Was he very old?" (By most standards, 83 is *very* old.)

"Yes."

"Did he live in Weimar?' (Both Goethe and Schiller lived in Weimar, but Goethe was more strongly associated with the city than Schiller. Goethe lived there almost six decades; Schiller, only six years.)

"Yes."

"Is it Goethe?"

"Yes."[3]

Cynics might dismiss *Mind Reading and Telepathy* as a classy version of Twenty Questions. But mind readers do more than fumble around for the right answers. Hanussen explains that they can also detect muscle movements so subtle that even the person manifesting these movements is not aware of them. Doing this helps the mind reader find something or someone that his subject is thinking about. To pull it off, writes Hanussen, a telepath must be in a heightened state of consciousness, stand "light and springy on his toes," and focus all his attention toward his right wrist, which his subject grips tightly. Meanwhile, the subject must have the "highest expectation" that the telepath can read his mind. And the subject can't let his thoughts wander. If the mentalist detects that his subject is not concentrating, he reminds him about this with "shouts of encouragement." If that doesn't work, he might threaten to replace the subject with someone else from the audience.[4]

The telepath then tells his subject to think only about the direction—forward, right, left—one needs to go to find the object he's thinking about. Before moving, Hanussen advises, the telepath should wait for "the soft, soft feel" of the subtle messages from the subject's hand that is firmly grasping the telepath's right wrist. And he doesn't really set off until he is encouraged by the subject's astonishment when he makes a few tentative steps in the right direction. If he starts walking in the wrong direction, he will feel "a certain something"—a slight tug or resistance from the hand grasping his wrist. Then he slowly takes a few steps in another direction, waiting for a signal from his subject that now he is on the right track.[5]

Finding a hidden object, Hanussen concedes, is difficult and complicated but "elicits a great audience response if it is performed well." It also requires considerable flair and confidence. If, for instance, a fork is hidden in a chest of drawers, the telepath starts, as usual, with the subject grasping his wrist. Then he sways back and forth—basically stalling for time while picking up faint clues about the general direction in which to go. Proceeding in that direction, he is alert to changes in his subject's stride or subtle tugs on his wrist. These indicate when the telepath should stop or change direction. If the mentalist isn't sure what to do, he says, "Think where I should turn and command me in your mind, 'Go right!' or 'Go left!'" Finally, a sudden increase in the subject's pressure on the telepath's wrist indicates they have arrived at their destination. To confirm his hunch, the telepath takes a step or two backward to see if his subject sends the same signals as before. During this whole journey, the telepath and his subject work almost in tandem: The subject *wants* the mentalist to succeed; the mentalist knows he *must* succeed. They are accomplices: two people in search of a fork.

But now that they've reached the dresser, there's a new problem: Where—precisely—in the dresser is the fork? On top of it? Underneath it? Behind it? In one of the drawers? So the telepath "swings and sways"—stalling while concentrating on the messages from his subject. Settling on the hiding place is harder than getting to the dresser. The mentalist now has to find a small object in a small, complex, and probably cluttered space: The drawers may include shirts, socks, suspenders. They might even contain other cutlery—knives and spoons—placed there as decoys.

Extending his right hand (whose wrist the subject is still holding), the mentalist slowly moves his arm from left to right, then right to left, back and forth, hyperattuned to where the subject is unconsciously guiding him. As he nears the drawer where the fork is hidden, he senses a tug from his subject, then steps back a few feet to see if the subject sends the same signal as before. If he does, the mentalist opens the drawer and finds, perhaps, three napkins, two knives, and one fork. Since the hidden item, for all he knows, could be any of these, he spreads them out on a table and, with his subject still firmly holding his right wrist, makes several sweeps over them with his right hand, sensing for signals from the subject. Through intense concentration, he eventually selects the fork. His subject is thrilled, his audience is stunned—and his booking is extended a few more weeks.[6]

The principle underlying muscle reading also explains readings from pendulums or Ouija boards: Our muscles almost have a life of their own, moving so subtly that we're not aware of them. A "magic" pendulum, for instance, slowly spells out words because the person holding it unknowingly guides it. The same is true of the pointer on a Ouija board. Muscle movement also explains Clever Hans, the equine star in early twentieth-century Germany. (Songs and books were written about him, his picture was on wine labels, and educators calculated that he was as bright as a 14-year-old child.) Hans was so smart he could count to one hundred, do basic math problems, spell words, identify people and objects by name, and even express his preference for certain music, all by shaking his head or walking over to a board and pointing with his nose to various letters. This baffled Oskar Pfungst, a psychologist who closely examined him, although the more Pfungst tested Hans, the more it became apparent that the horse gave the correct answer only when whoever was questioning him also knew the answer. Anyone questioning Hans, Pfungst realized, was sending visual cues by intensely watching the horse's hooves as he tapped out his answers. When Hans reached the correct number, the questioner raised his head, usually by less than a millimeter. The motion may have been barely perceptible to humans, yet the horse discerned it. Pfungst then took Hans's place, asking 25 people to think of a number. Just as Hans had tapped out answers with his hoof, Pfungst tapped them out with his right hand while watching the person who was thinking of the number. When Pfungst detected a slight relaxing in the other person, he stopped tapping. Invariably, he tapped out the number that was on the person's mind. In other words, Hans was only as smart as his questioner. He was also a brilliant muscle reader.[7]

Another muscle reader scientists studied was Eugen de Rubini, a mentalist who had been enormously successful in Vienna before the war, filling one of the city's major theaters, the Ronacher, for weeks on end. For one of his illusions, Rubini would ask a volunteer (who Rubini called the "medium" or the "transmitter") from the audience to hide a small object or think about someone in the theater. Simply by thinking about the object or person, and firmly holding Rubini's wrist, the transmitter would guide Rubini to the object he had hidden or the person he was thinking about. Sometimes Rubini could do this without even being touched by the volunteer. In the 1920s, Rubini was just as successful in the United States, receiving the only endorsement Harry Houdini ever gave a clairvoyant and stupefying the writer Sinclair Lewis. Without telling Rubini what he had done, Lewis hid a set of keys on his wife, Dorothy. Rubini found these by walking toward Dorothy with Sinclair mentally guiding him while walking five feet behind the mentalist.[8]

In the early 1920s, psychologists at the University of California studied Rubini, trying various ruses to isolate his senses. Rubini's abilities didn't diminish when earplugs muffled auditory clues he might be receiving as he read minds. But after Rubini balked when psychologists proposed blindfolding him, everyone agreed on a compromise: a blinder that would let him see only straight ahead and that eliminated all peripheral vision. While wearing that blinder, Rubini's performance dropped to the level of pure chance. The psychologists concluded that he was picking up "exceedingly obscure" clues, such as the posture of his transmitter or where the transmitter was standing in a room. Yet they refrained from calling Rubini a fake. Rather, they admired his "truly remarkable power." Indeed, Rubini did possess this, although his talents were closer to acute observation than to outright telepathy.[9]

Observation is indispensable for mind reading. By nature and training, Hanussen, too, was keenly observant. This helped him solve the case of the phony count and fakir on the boat from Istanbul. It also helped him and other accomplished muscle readers "read minds" with no physical contact with their transmitter. To do that, mentalists observe cues from the direction of eye movements or subtle changes in facial expression. Doing this is vastly more difficult than reading a person who is holding on to the mentalist's wrist. It is also vastly more impressive.

When done well, reading muscles looks like reading minds. That's thrilling. But no one should think these guys are really invading people's minds. If muscle readers really could read minds, they would not be wasting their time trying to find pins and silverware. They would be divining the twists and turns of stock markets, horse races, elections. Nothing would be sacred, and nothing would be private, and we would suffer from a perpetual paranoia that our brains were about to be picked.

Our muscles speak a language that we don't even know we are capable of speaking. Often we know ourselves so poorly that others can figure out our intentions before they reach our own consciousness. For this reason, we are more at the mercy of people attuned to the subtleties of the human body than we would like.

★  ★  ★

Many magicians see a danger in how muscle reading is performed. As Teller, the silent half of the mega-successful magic duo Penn & Teller, told me, "Magic is honest deception, religion is self-deluded deception, and the form of stage magic that most dangerously veers toward religion is mentalism." Mentalists are "insufficiently confident" to admit that what they do is a trick. This is troublesome. As Teller explained: "A proper stage magician is concerned with truth because the audience is watching something it knows is false. It has to reconcile what it's seeing with what it knows. Its knowledge collides with its experience, and that tension shoots off sparks. Most mentalists want to convince you that what they are doing is real. They want to be seen not as performers but as special. If it were really possible to read minds, then it would be like getting up on stage and saying, 'Look at me: I'm breathing air.' No one would pay any attention to that. You only put on a stage what is 'art,' not what is found in nature."[10]

The mature Hanussen—the performer of the early 1930s—*was* an artist. But he often mistook what he did for a phenomenon of nature. His problem was that he neglected one of the key laws of show business: Submerge yourself so deeply into your role that your personality vanishes as a sacrifice to your craft, your profession, your audience. But don't lose yourself in the process. Indeed, that was the ultimate advice from Jean Eugène Robert-Houdin, the nineteenth-century Frenchman usually considered the best magician of modern times. "A conjuror," he said, "is an actor playing the part of a magician, an artist whose fingers should be more clever than nimble." Like few others, Robert-Houdin understood the psychology of magic: Having quick hands is less important than the *feeling* that a magician creates, a feeling that emanates, he said, from "perfect simplicity of execution. The calmer the movements are, the more easy it is to produce an illusion on the spectators." Good magic (and good mind reading) demands dexterity so invisible that, in the end, audiences are buoyed by the pleasure of their own confusion. The finest magicians or clairvoyants understand that audiences are not coming to see them; they come to see what the entertainer has become. Metamorphosis is part of the act. Robert-Houdin played a magician. Erik Jan Hanussen played a clairvoyant, but Hanussen often forgot he was acting. Mistaking yourself for your transformation is the undoing of any performer.[11]

"Telepathic mail"—the trick Hanussen used to open his performance at the Konzerthaus Theater in 1919—is still in the repertoire of mentalists. Satori, a German who now ranks among the best mentalists in the world, has performed it hundreds of times, always with his transmitter holding his wrist because the mail is delivered faster that way, and you can't waste time before an audience. Privately, Satori has done it without contact (as Hanussen supposedly did at the Konzerthaus). And yet Satori asked me over coffee in Berlin, "Could the stories about how Hanussen delivered the mail at the Konzerthaus be not quite correct?" Perhaps, Satori suggested, Hanussen *did* make physical contact with someone who knew the destination of the archduchess's letter, or perhaps Hanussen's aides helped steer him toward her physician with subtle signals or a secret code? Satori has a point: Magic and clairvoyance are almost impossible to unravel even if they occur in front of us. Sometimes we are our own worst eyewitnesses.[12]

There's also the possibility that Hanussen used an old vaudeville trick: pressing on a sealed envelope with a sponge soaked in alcohol that he hid in his palm. The alcohol briefly makes the envelope transparent; since it dries almost instantly, it would have left no trace when Hanussen handed the envelope to the person to whom it was addressed.[13]

What is not in dispute is that Karl I, the last Austrian-Hungarian emperor, and his wife were both in their midforties, with sharp wits and sharper minds, and it would have been difficult for Hanussen to dupe them. Over the next few years, Hanussen would hold private séances for the emperor and his wife at their summer residence, Castle Wartholz. And Hanussen would proudly wear gold cuff links with the imperial Austrian family emblem set in rubies, a gift from Karl I for the valuable services Hanussen provided him and his wife. Kings and emperors are always in need of advice, and sometimes, apparently, it is valued more if it comes from someone who claims to commune with forces and powers unavailable to the rest of us.[14]

# CHAPTER 4

# The Iron Queen and the Jewish Samson

By 1919, Hanussen was quite a sensation in Vienna—famous, prosperous, and often recognized on the street. Which is why he was insulted one day when a passenger who boarded his tram had no idea who he was. The attractive young woman had been unable to lift her leg onto the tram's steps because her skirt was too tight, so Hanussen had bent down, swooped her up, and introduced himself. Offended that his name meant nothing to her, Hanussen asked sharply, "Don't you know who I am, young lady?" The woman was as offended as the arrogant stranger. "Wait, my dear," she thought, "I'll take you down a peg or two," and then, as blunt as Hanussen had been a moment earlier, she said, "*You* should know who *I* am."[1]

The young woman was Therese Luksch. She was quite lovely, with a confident smile, a broad, regal forehead, and brown hair that parted neatly on one side. Her figure was much to Hanussen's liking—a narrow waistline that drew attention to everything that was above and below it: her sculpted legs, her full bosom, her broad shoulders. A star herself, Therese was performing that evening in the title role of the operetta *Eva*. Therese was as accustomed to getting her way as Hanussen was. Stuck on a tram between an unpleasantly fat woman and this stranger who was full of himself, she felt trapped. "Come to the Apollo Theater," the man who had lifted her onto the tram persisted. "Then you will know who I am." "And when you should happen to have some time," Therese starchly replied, "come to the Burgertheater. Then you will know who I am." At that moment, the tram stopped and Therese got off.[2]

Hanussen did go to the Burgertheater—to ask Therese out. "From the first moment," she said later, they clicked. Hanussen was charming and told wonderful stories; best of all, he could be himself with Therese and not try to impress her with his money or his fame. After a few months of courtship, Hanussen asked Therese's father for permission to marry her. It didn't go well. He threw Hanussen out of the house, yelling that no daughter of his would marry anyone in show business. One entertainer in the family was more than enough.[3]

Their love outlasted Therese's father, who died in the summer of 1920. A few weeks later, Hanussen and Therese married in a synagogue on Seitenstettengasse. She was 27. Hanussen was 31. She was Catholic. He was Jewish. She converted. In another month, their daughter, Erika, was born.[4]

For the four years of their marriage, Therese was Hanussen's biggest fan, certain he was using his "powers" for good, like healing a boy who suffered from tremors and not charging his parents because they were poor. He also helped police solve crimes. (Therese was so proud of Hanussen that she hung letters all over their apartment from officials thanking him for his help.) Once the couple traveled to a village near the ruins of Babylon to see the Indian rope trick, the famous illusion that had stumped Westerners for decades. Taken to a small, roped-in enclosure, they were asked to face the sun, an orientation Hanussen knew had not been chosen by chance. The performers, led by a man named Abu Nasser, chanted for more than an hour on prayer rugs, a buildup probably designed to tire the audience before the trick actually began. Finally, Abu Nasser threw a rope into the air. To Hanussen, this was no rope but a "cleverly constructed apparatus cut from sheep bones... and skillfully covered with sailing cord." Twisting the flexible material turned it into "a solid stick which, like bamboo, can support the weight of a heavy man." The rope remained vertical, Hanussen figured, with the help of one or two men concealed in a sand pit.[5]

Swiftly, and "with the agility of a monkey," a young boy climbed the rope. Right behind him was Abu Nasser, a knife clenched between his teeth. At the top of the rope, they both vanished in a cloud that Hanussen was sure one of Abu Nasser's assistants was somehow producing. Screams came from the cloud as the boy's arms, legs, head, and torso dropped into a large basket lying on the sand. Everything was soaked with blood. The audience was terrified but not Hanussen. He was convinced the body parts were "stuffed rags stained with animal blood."[6]

As Abu Nasser climbed down the rope, Hanussen caught a glimpse of the boy hiding under his flowing robes. Jumping onto the sand, Abu Nasser muttered a long stream of prayers. Suddenly the boy jumped out of the basket and danced through the crowd, collecting generous tips as everyone recovered from the horror they had witnessed a few minutes earlier.[7]

No one else could have given Therese these adventures, although nothing impressed her more than the night they were relaxing in a café in Vienna. Everything was fine until Hanussen grabbed her arm and ordered her to sit in the corner of the booth. Noting the odd look on his face, she did as he asked. Soon, the couple at the next table had a terrible argument. The woman walked out; her friend remained, pulled a gun from his pocket, and fired several times at himself. One bullet missed. It hit the exact spot where Therese had been sitting.[8]

Life with Hanussen could be exhilarating; it could also be frustrating. Therese began to realize this around 1922, when Vienna found a new hero who attracted much of the attention to which Hanussen had become addicted—Siegmund Breitbart. Breitbart, a strongman, bent iron bars, bit through steel chains, pulled a fully loaded wagon with his teeth, and pounded nails into thick boards with his bare hands. But he was more than a strongman; he was a *Jewish* strongman. When performing before Jewish audiences, he draped a blue-and-white banner embroidered with the Star of David over one shoulder and announced that his mission was to defend the honor of the Jews: "If I see an anti-Semite, I give him fair warning. If he persists, I break him in half, like a matchstick."[9]

Breitbart was like a Moses on steroids—so unapologetically Jewish that musicians in a restaurant in Warsaw greeted him with "Hatikvah," the anthem of the still-dreamed-about Jewish state in Palestine; so generous he gave much of his earnings to charities; so threatening to anti-Semites that one complained that "the Jews have been more uppity since Breitbart came to town." To draw attention to the need for a Jewish homeland, Breitbart planned to reenact in Jerusalem some of the feats of the original Samson; to toughen up Jews so they could liberate Palestine from the British, who were governing it under a mandate from the League of Nations, Breitbart sponsored sports organizations in Europe and the United States. Wherever he went, Jews worshiped him. When he arrived in a small town in Poland, rabbis, teachers, businessmen, and children greeted him in the town square. "We had our share of anti-Semitism," one of those boys said later. "When Breitbart appeared, he gave us new courage." As far away as New York, a Jewish newspaper bragged about him. "It seems an anomaly to have a Jew hailed the strongest man in the world. But that is what they say of Siegmund Breitbart. He is the superman of physical perfection."[10]

In early 1923, Hanussen and Breitbart were both performing at the Ronacher Theater in Vienna. Annoyed at the attention Breitbart was getting, Hanussen told reporters there was something fishy about him. Hanussen couldn't put his finger on it, but something was wrong. "I don't know what it is," he said. "I'm only following common sense."[11]

While working in circuses, Hanussen had seen other performers do what was in Breitbart's act. He knew that a bed of nails was safe because the nails were so close together that they couldn't pierce the skin. What was dangerous was a single, isolated nail. And he knew that metal could bend if its center was relatively thin, which Breitbart's always was. Hanussen bribed some of Breitbart's aides for secrets to other tricks, but he couldn't figure out how Breitbart bit through chains. To solve that, he sneaked into the strongman's hotel room and discovered that the chains had secret links that Breitbart opened surreptitiously while raising them toward his mouth.[12]

Hanussen recruited Martha Kahn, an unemployed clothing model, for a new act. Their angle would be that he hypnotized her so she possessed superhuman strength. When Breitbart learned about Hanussen's plans, he invited him to his dressing room, demanding to know why Hanussen was stealing his show, then slammed him against the wall. Hanussen lurched into the corridor, dizzy but ready for revenge. The next day, posters all over Vienna announced that Marta Farra, "the Iron Queen," would debut at another theater in town, the Apollo. The show was a success, although one reporter had to look away as two men pounded away with sledgehammers on an anvil resting on Marta's stomach. "Why, for goodness' sake," the reporter asked the next day in *Der Tag*. "Why?"[13]

The next day, Breitbart challenged Hanussen and Marta to perform before a panel of experts—a psychoanalyst, a physiologist, two engineers, the president of the Austrian Athletic Association, the chairman of a boxing association, and an Austrian who had won two gold medals for weight lifting at the 1906 Olympics—chosen by a local paper, the *Weiner Sonn-und Montagszeitung*. Hanussen and Marta accepted the challenge; that was a mistake. The panel first attended one of Marta and Hanussen's shows at the Apollo. It didn't go well. Every member of the panel could bend the metal bars that Marta planned to turn into horseshoes.[14]

Attempting to quiet the audience, Hanussen explained that Marta was "a young girl" who didn't have the same advantages as some members of the panel who were trained athletes. Hanussen motioned for Marta to join him at centerstage. With Hanussen by her side, Marta rallied, lifting weights, throwing metal balls around the stage like they were balloons, lying down on a bed of nails. The applause for Marta got louder as the jeers for Hanussen became deafening—he was taking credit for everything Marta did.[15]

When the panel visited one of Breitbart's performances at the Ronacher, the mood in the theater was festive. Marta, the crowd knew, had barely passed the panel's scrutiny; Hanussen had proved he was a lout; and Breitbart, everyone was certain, would prove, as always, that he was the king of the strongmen. Men threw their hats in the air; women waved their scarves; the applause was so loud the building shook. One man sitting in the orchestra was brave enough to challenge the mood. Leaping onto the stage, he bet one million kronen that Breitbart couldn't bite through a chain the man had brought along with him. (At the time, one million kronen was slightly more than $62,000.) Looking closely at the chain, Breitbart realized it was steel, not iron: rock hard and unbiteable. Breitbart's manager and the theater's director tried to persuade him to turn down the challenge: it was too dangerous. He waved them away.[16]

Straining and shaking, "every muscle in his body tense," according to one paper, Breitbart bit through the chain. Facing "a sea of fists" from the audience, the man who had placed the bet donated one million kronen to the Salvation Army, and guards escorted him to a side door to avoid a beating from the crowd. A letter from Hanussen that was found on him did not help the situation.[17]

Two days later, the panel released its report. Breitbart was cited for his extraordinary strength and his "astounding performance" at the Ronacher. While characterized as shy and nervous, Marta was also commended for her strength and courage, though her act had nothing to do with a "transfer of will power" from Hanussen, and she was certainly no match for Breitbart, whose six-foot-one-inch body was one solid wedge of muscle, with 17-inch calves, 28-inch thighs, a 50-inch chest, and biceps that were 18½ inches in diameter. Marta had mettle and pluck, and her skimpy outfits were more alluring than the period costumes Breitbart wore: in a single show, he changed from a bullfighter outfit into gladiator, cowboy, and Greek god getups. It was all very entertaining, but beyond that was the genuine brawn Breitbart had been honing since he was a child. There was no way Marta could come close to that. And not coincidentally, not a single panelist had a good word for Hanussen, who was full of exaggerations, full of lies, and full of himself.[18]

Marta gave up on Hanussen and ran away with a Hungarian hypnotist, Mister Rex. That didn't stop Hanussen. At a traveling circus, he found his next Marta: Rose Presi. Rose (who adopted "Marta" as her stage name when she teamed up with Hanussen), was part British and part Italian and had so much spunk that she quickly accepted Hanussen's offer to take their act to the United States—even if they did have to leave Therese, Hanussen's patient wife, waiting for him back in Vienna. Hanussen arrived in New York in December 1923 and convinced a prominent theatrical agent, Leo Singer, to represent him. For their American premiere, Singer booked Hanussen and his new Marta into a theater in Hoboken, New Jersey. They were "worse than a total flop," Singer later griped. "The poor quality of the production, Hanussen's efforts as a hypnotist, and his accent were the worst ever seen on stage." By the time they got to New York, Singer had negotiated a new deal, essentially buying Hanussen out of the contract for $2,000 and paying Marta only $100 a week for her to continue the act—without the burden of appearing onstage with the immensely unpopular Hanussen. Apparently, Marta assumed Hanussen would adjust this disparity in their salary when they returned to Europe. "We will do the accounting in Berlin," she assured Singer. "Hanussen is not my impresario. He is my friend."[19]

Friend or not, deal or not, Hanussen would have loved to perform at the theater where Singer booked Marta—the Hippodrome, one of the biggest draws in a city that was not lacking for entertainment. Up the street, Fanny Brice was headlining the Ziegfeld Follies. Only standing-room tickets were available for *Beau Brummel,* starring John Barrymore, at the New Amsterdam Theater. You couldn't even buy tickets to hear the Egyptologist Howard Carter lecture at Carnegie Hall about discovering King Tut's tomb. And everywhere films were slowly, steadily encroaching on what had been the sacred turf of the legitimate stage: Cecil B. DeMille's *Ten Commandments* just had its 250th screening at the George M. Cohan Theater, Harold Lloyd's *Girl Shy* was in its tenth week at The Strand, and critics were saluting Norma Talmadge's *Secrets* as "an example of what can be done in motion pictures." (Maybe so, but the film was forgotten almost as soon as it premiered.)[20]

The Hippodrome was in a league of its own, attended by swells in starched tuxedoes and fine ladies bound into tight corsets, everyone slightly dusty after a carriage ride through Central Park, two miles to the north, or full from a massive dinner at Jack's, a seafood palace across the street whose specialties listed lobster fat on toast and broiled pig's feet with deviled sauce and whose decor—antlers, animals skins, and stuffed wildlife—included a stuffed pug dog that once belonged to the owner.

The Hippodrome wasn't a theater. It was a wonder, a marvel: a tabernacle in which to fire up the imagination of your customers and release them, enthralled, into the world. Its roof was constructed from fifteen thousand tons of steel, making it the heaviest ever placed on a building in the United States. Its immense interior—the Hippodrome straddled an entire block—was illuminated with twenty-five thousand lightbulbs. Cranes lifted tons of scenery like they were matchsticks. An eight-thousand-gallon glass tank could be raised from below for swimming and diving shows, with pumps so powerful they circulated 150,000 gallons a minute to simulate waves or tropical storms. The endless rows of seats (rows so wide they would swallow all of a performer's peripheral vision and balconies so high the entertainer had to strain to see the top tier) accommodated almost five thousand people, double the population of some villages in Europe where Hanussen and Marta had performed. The stage was so capacious that a full-sized circus, complete with strutting steeds and galumphing pachyderms, sometimes performed there. A few years before, Houdini made Jennie, an eight-foot-tall elephant, vanish from the stage of the Hippodrome. Not long after that, the Hippodrome mounted a mini-reenactment of the Russo-Japanese War—a production so lavish that one wit deemed it "better staged than the war on which it was founded."

The Hippodrome was so satisfying that shows there verged on the sacred. A woman from Brooklyn told the Hippodrome's owner she could attend a show there "on the Sabbath and still feel…in direct communication with God." This was theater as salvation, exaltation, deliverance, and every day, it seemed, the new Marta was becoming more enamored with her presence on the stage. As she told a muscle-building magazine, "If you have not seen me, do not picture me as an overdeveloped freak, with bulging muscles which rob my figure of all beauty of contour and a face lined and hard from years of training and persistent exertion. For the contrary is the case. I possess a face and figure [of] which any prima donna might be proud, and the good looks and form which God gave me have been enhanced by my mode of living."[21]

Critics, too, raved about the new Marta's "personality, beauty and showmanship," her "schoolgirl grace," her "shapely form." Almost everyone forgot that she had recently been performing with a man named Hanussen. One night, while trying to do a stunt she had done many times before—lifting a three-thousand-pound elephant several feet into the air by pulling on chains linked to the platform where the elephant stood—Marta strained herself. (After leaving vaudeville, Marta revealed in articles she wrote for the Hearst newspapers that she had lifted the elephant with the help of a stagehand who was hiding in the wooden frame into which she harnessed herself, with the elephant below her. As she strained against ropes and chains attached to the elephant—and with her hipbones forming a natural arch capable of sustaining an immense amount of pressure—the hidden stagehand pulled a lever that bore much of the elephant's weight, raising it a few feet in the air.) This night, Marta realized this feat was "too much for a woman." She was hospitalized, her bookings canceled. When she regained her strength, she begged Hanussen—who was still in New

York—for some cash. Instead, she ended up back in the hospital, this time with a bloody nose and a black eye. One reporter said she "looked as if she had it out with a pile driver."[22]

The tabloids in New York had a field day with the scene at the hospital. The nurses gasped, "Not the Strong Woman," when their new patient identified herself as Marta Farra. "Did the Woolworth Building fall on you?" asked an intern. "No," said the new Marta. "It was my sweetie. He got mad and knocked me down." The hospital sent for Marta's sweetie, expecting, according to one Manhattan newspaper, "a brute, a Hercules, a troglodyte, a caveman. For hadn't he knocked flat the champion strong woman of the world?" Then Hanussen walked in, "look[ing] as much like a troglodyte as Tom Thumb....Marta insisted that he hit her, cursed her, took her money away, and treated her generally like a slave. The strong girl sobbed as she told her story."[23]

Hanussen sailed to Europe before he could be prosecuted, convinced that, if he wanted a future in show business, he should return to mind reading. It was a more reliable way for him to pay his bills—and he was better at it than just about anyone in Europe.

Alone and broke, Marta appealed to Breitbart, who just happened to be performing in New York. "Through my youthful stupidity," Marta told him, "I allowed myself to be driven into this work. I was completely under the influence of Mr. Hanussen....No one on this side [of the Atlantic] cares about my welfare. I beg you to free me from this slavery. I am an innocent, helpless, sick girl. I wish I could warn all girls about what I have endured in this unsavory work."[24]

Always a gentleman, Breitbart helped Marta get back on her feet. After reviving her act for a season or two, "the Female Hercules" was rarely heard from again. One of the few times her name surfaced was when the U.S. government threatened to deport Marta as an alien and a friend suggested she marry an American. That night, she mentioned her troubles to a man she met at a party—Milton Schlessinger, a jockey. Luckily, Schlessinger took a shine to her. Three days later, they married. Just as quickly, the couple turned into fodder for New York's gossip mill, with Schlessinger complaining that, before their honeymoon was over, he knew he was in trouble—to stay in shape, Marta used him as a punching bag and carried him over mud puddles. "I didn't want to be carried," he whimpered. "Frequently, she lifted me on to buses, street cars and the like." As their marriage further disintegrated, Marta told the papers that when Schlessinger refused over dinner in a Chicago restaurant to end the marriage,

> *I knocked him off his chair. I asked him again. He refused again and I hit him again. Then we left the restaurant and we went out on the street. I asked him once and for all if he would give me a divorce. He said he wouldn't and I gave him a good beating right there on the street. He got up and ran away, but this must have had its effect. The next thing I knew, he filed for divorce. He was too tame. A lot too tame. I'm going to train tigers. Tigers would be a great relief, no matter how vicious, after a man. I'm not afraid of men and I'm not afraid of tigers. Tigers don't get on your nerves.*[25]

Breitbart returned to Europe. In August 1925, he accidentally pierced his knee with a spike during a show in the Polish city of Radom. The wound became infected, blood poisoning set in, and eight weeks later, after surgery in Berlin, Breitbart died. He was 32.

When Hanussen had returned to Europe in 1924, he had not gone to Therese, who was in Vienna with their daughter, Erika. Instead, he holed up in Paris, burning through the money he had brought back from America like a prairie fire in a bank vault. Paris has a way of parting men from their francs. Between fine dinners and fine whores, he spent his money until he was almost broke. Then a telegram arrived from Therese: "I need to talk to you immediately." Hanussen knew what was on her mind. "Never in my whole life," he rued, "have I cursed my clairvoyance more than then." After not seeing Therese for eight months, Hanussen knew that "my spouse—and who wouldn't understand her—had grown tired of having a husband who was never at home."[26]

One hour with Hanussen was all Therese needed to end their marriage. She was leaving him for a prosperous, and handsome, brewery owner who lived in northern Italy. Hanussen was fascinating, but they both knew he lacked the temperament for marriage. He was always touring and always having affairs, wasting their money on luxuries, or sailing off to be a big star in the United States. They hadn't created a home: they had created a place where he could relax while planning his next getaway. Therese needed stability—for herself, for her daughter. Perhaps Therese's father had been right. Perhaps one entertainer in the family was more than enough.

This hour with Therese was one of the more important in Hanussen's life. It freed him to be what he was. Now he could devote himself to his craft with an even greater zeal, shaping his imperfect world into something more to his liking. And he could do this in "the city I love most in the world"—Berlin. Berliners, he believed, were better than "the mawkish Austrians, the perverse French, the boring English, the stupid Americans." True, Berliners were "blunt and gruff," but for Hanussen, there was a virtue to their honesty: "You always know where you stand with them." And if you tired of their brusque charm, Hanussen said, you could always go to some of the city's famous bohemian hangouts: Café Reimann, where gays and straights sourly scanned the passing parade, or the Romanisches Café, where George Grosz, Billy Wilder, Berthold Brecht, or Erich

Maria Remarque might be discussing their latest projects and a long cast-iron railing separated these exalted patrons from the ordinary people who were strolling by. Hanussen especially looked forward to the Hotel Eden—the finest hotel in Berlin—where Marlene Dietrich and Heinrich Mann held court and service was so swift and quiet that the staff could have been clairvoyant themselves. Therese might settle with her rich Italian in his quiet town in the Italian Alps, with its spas and cures and fresh air and medicinal waters. Hanussen would take to the city in Europe that truly deserved him, the city where he felt most at home, the city that would be his prize after losing the greatest love of his life.[27]

# CHAPTER 5

# The King of Everything

Hanussen had always relied on hyperbole. But in the mid- and late 1920s he was claiming a never-ending string of even greater titles for himself: "The World's Greatest Hypnotist," "The Mental Wizard of All Ages," "Europe's Greatest Oracle Since Nostradamus." He was the king of everything: of metaphysics, astronomy, astrology, alchemy, mysticism; of ghost hunters and mind readers and soothsayers. He was a prophet, a seer, a magus. The greater Hanussen's success, the greater his boasts, although he assured audiences that he was "not a superman. I have neither divine nor devilish powers." Quite simply, he said, he was blessed with "a wonderful gift."[1]

These blandishments worked. Hanussen was such a slick salesman that, 70 years later, someone who had seen him in the 1920s still remembered him vividly. Martin Schaaff—a robust 99-year-old when I interviewed him—saw Hanussen in Berlin at the Circus Busch, Germany's preeminent circus. In 2010 Schaaff was probably the last person alive to have seen Hanussen perform. Schaaff was also one of

Germany's finest experts on circuses and vaudeville, a true connoisseur of these rare, almost-dead art forms. If Schaaff remembered Hanussen so lucidly, the clairvoyant must have been a cut above the rest.[2]

Sitting in his apartment in Berlin, the walls lined with circus photos and posters, Schaaff described Hanussen's act to me as we enjoyed tea and small cakes. Hanussen, he remembered, threw beach balls into the audience at the Circus Busch, calling out that whoever caught one could come up to the stage and participate in his show. This was Hanussen's way to screen the audience: anyone who made the effort to catch a ball, he figured, would go out of their way to help him while standing in front of a theater full of people.

Hanussen asked the volunteers to write a date on a slip of paper, and then hand it to him in a sealed envelope. Holding each envelope tightly, Hanussen said what happened on that date. Each time he was correct. Eight decades later, Hanussen's accuracy still amazed Schaaff, who was in his teens when he saw Hanussen perform. With close to a century to figure out some of Hanussen's tricks, Schaaff remained stumped.

Schaaff remembered Hanussen as "good looking in a gentlemanly sort of way," with a distinguished way of speaking—convincing, serious, deliberate, thoughtful, never condescending, and always respectful. Someone else who saw him in those days was also impressed with his voice: "Melodious, strong, sure." He "inspired trust." But for this person, a hypnotist who saw Hanussen perform in 1928, Hanussen was more of an odd duck than good looking—"small and somewhat on the stocky side," with a plump figure and dark hair and "legs not exactly perfect. Thick, bushy brows shade his eyes. . . . The man who has charmed Vienna, Berlin and Prague looked to me more like a Bulgarian tobacco dealer than a man of supernatural powers."

The hypnotist was Franz Polgar, a young man who was no slouch when it came to knowing how the mind worked. His own mind, he claimed, had changed permanently during World War I when a hand grenade knocked him unconscious. A few days later, he realized he had a new power. The Hungarian army required a soldier to look an officer squarely in the eye when being addressed by a superior. While Lieutenant Polgar reprimanded a sergeant for poor discipline, he and the sergeant stared at each other. Polgar droned on and on about the sergeant's being "asleep on his feet," then ordered him to dismiss his troops. All the men marched away except their sergeant, who stood rock still, eyes closed, seemingly at peace. Polgar's brother, who happened to be present, examined the sergeant, then told his brother, "You've hypnotized this man, Franz. Tell him to wake up immediately." With that, Polgar knew he had a new future.[3]

After the war, Polgar studied for half a year with Sigmund Freud in Vienna. Freud admired his skills as a hypnotist but didn't buy into hypnosis, calling it unscientific and "reminiscent of magic." He advised Polgar that there were better ways to understand the human psyche. After a few months, Polgar confronted Freud: "Why do you keep me here? You're against hypnosis and still you do research on it."

"Dummkopf," said Freud. "I'm also against death and do research on that."[4]

Polgar left Freud and earned a doctorate in psychology at the University of Budapest, then decided he had wasted his time. He didn't fit in anywhere. Scientists rejected hypnosis, and customers in the nightclubs where he demonstrated it called him a fake. He was confused about what to do with his life until his brother told him about a hypnotist he had seen "who was making a fortune" doing the same things as Polgar.[5]

It took Polgar ten days to find Hanussen, who was then performing at a spa in Karlsbad. After coming onstage in a white tie and tails,
Hanussen lectured briefly about the untapped powers of the human
mind and how, by concentrating and using the power of suggestion,
he could put himself "into a trance by self-hypnosis and I can see and
analyze things.... There are no tricks. There is no secret about it. I do
not want to fool you."[6]

Next, Hanussen turned toward a red-haired woman sitting in the
fifth row who was wearing a large hat. Closing his eyes, he fumbled a
bit, then gained confidence as he proceeded: "I see ... I see ... I see a broken mirror in your handbag. Your name is Margaret Steininger.... I've
never seen you before. You know that ... You live on ... You live on—"
Hanussen hesitated, letting the anxiety in the theater thicken until it
was almost palpable. How could he know this woman's address? He
had never seen her before. He had to be bluffing, perhaps hoping she
would help him in some way or her husband would blurt out their
address or some distraction would divert the audience from what he
had begun. Hanussen spoke again. In a firm, confident voice, he told
the woman, "You live on Kaiserstrasse Number ... Nein, nein, two
blocks further ... Kaiserstrasse Number 25! Is that the address?"

The woman was stunned. "You are right," she gasped. "But how
could you know this?"[7]

How, indeed? Not because Hanussen had read Frau Steininger's
mind. Rather, the hotel where she was staying had given her a free
ticket to the show. Upon arriving at the theater, she was referred to an
associate of Hanussen's who was checking the complimentary tickets.
The identifying number on each ticket tipped him off to the patron's
name and address, which he had been given by the hotel. When she
opened her handbag to get her ticket, Hanussen's accomplice had

noticed the broken mirror. Before the show began, he passed these details along to Hanussen, who had an excellent memory. Choosing this woman as a foil for Hanussen from among the hundreds in the theater was perfect: He would have no trouble spotting a red-haired woman in the fifth row who was wearing a large hat. Redheads with large hats stand out in any crowd.[8]

Next, Hanussen announced that he would hypnotize himself into a trance. An assistant blindfolded him. When he said he was ready, the audience wrote questions on slips of paper and passed them to Hanussen's assistant, who read several aloud, questions like "What happened on January 5, 1925, at Kantstrasse 132 in Berlin?" For a few moments, Hanussen sat quietly, deliberating, concentrating until he rose from his chair and began walking around the stage, still blindfolded and still in a "trance," raising his arms as he struggled to determine what happened on January 5, 1925. "A child was born," he said at last. "There were pains. There was a mother in a dark room. It was five or six in the morning."[9]

The woman who had submitted the question rose from her seat. "Correct," she said. Everyone except Polgar was impressed. He was sure Hanussen hadn't used psychic powers, although he couldn't figure out how Hanussen did the trick. Later, Polgar learned Hanussen had paid the woman in the audience 50 crowns to confirm his telepathy.[10]

During his long, successful career—after emigrating to the United States in 1935, Polgar performed at Carnegie Hall and eventually had a show on CBS-TV in the 1950s—he declared that "man has been able to control nature, but...failed to control human nature and the human mind." Hypnosis, Polgar was sure, could "help man in his age-old struggle against himself and make him master of his own nature." Hanussen did not harbor such lofty ambitions for hypnosis or clairvoyance. They were just tools to beguile and entertain. Never—not even after attaching himself to the Nazis—was Hanussen out to change the world or change human nature. That was for philosophers, from whom he kept his distance. It was also for politicians, whom he learned to tolerate and cultivate, often (or so he thought) to his advantage.[11]

CHAPTER 6

# Hitler: "There's Room for a Little Subtlety"

Throughout the last half of the 1920s, Hanussen's fame kept growing, and he was no longer sharing top billing with anyone else. He had bought a Mercedes or two and an elegant eight-cylinder LaSalle from the United States (General Motors had recently introduced the LaSalle to fill the price gap between its Buick and Cadillac lines) and gotten married for a third time, this time to Elfriede Ruehle, a beauty from a staid middle-class family. "Fritzi"—Hanussen's nickname for her—knew nothing about show business. All she knew was that she adored Hanussen. All he knew was that he adored dressing her in silk and velvet and having her on his arm as he toured from city to city. And then there were her assurances that she loved him for who he was, not for his money or fame. At this point in his life, that was a relief: he was beginning to attract too many sycophants and hangers-on, people whose motives for being with him were as dubious as their character and their integrity. Newspapers ran front-page photos of the glamour couple—Hanussen grinning in a tuxedo with wide, shiny lapels, the part through his slicked-down hair so straight he must have groomed himself with a plumb line instead of a comb; and Fritzi pouting directly into the lens, her silky blonde hair framing her perfectly oval face, her gold necklace sparkling, her white ermine fur shining. They almost floated their way through Europe—lovely, ethereal, and magical.[1]

While Hanussen's star was ascending, the appeal of the people with whom he would soon be associating was declining rapidly. In fact, the last half of the 1920s was much kinder to Hanussen than to the Nazis: It appeared that he would always remain on top as they grasped for the power that would forever elude them. Hitler had used the time he spent in jail after the beer hall putsch in Munich in 1923—more of a tragic operetta than a serious attempt to overthrow Germany's new (and weak) democracy—to write *Mein Kampf*, hoping the book would settle his debts. Instead, the barely readable screed sold only about nine thousand copies when it was published in 1925. The book was a blueprint of the Nazi nightmare. Jews, whom he deemed to be filthy, repulsive, and parasitic, would be "eliminated" through a divinely sanctioned campaign. "I am fighting," Hitler declared, "for the work of the Lord." France, Germany's "inexorable, mortal enemy," would be conquered. Austria, Czechoslovakia, Poland, and Russia would be absorbed for lebensraum, living space. Once the Nazis controlled Europe, Germany—pure, virile, and muscular—would be "the lord of the earth"—victorious and forever triumphant.[2]

By 1928, sales of *Mein Kampf* were down to three thousand a year, not the groundswell of support Hitler had expected. His party was doing no better. The times seemed to be conspiring against the Nazis: At last, Germany was enjoying some measure of prosperity, which was not to the Nazis' advantage. In 1927, industrial output was 122 percent more than in 1913, the year before the war began. In 1928, unemployment fell below one million for the first time since the war. The lower middle class—the millions of shopkeepers and workers on whom Hitler had been counting for support—now had little need for the Nazis. Most Germans preferred to think of themselves as progressive, eager to get beyond that horrible, humbling war that this Hitler, with his silly Charlie Chaplin mustache and his manic mannerisms at the podium, would never shut up about. From about 1925 to the coming of the Depression in 1929, wrote William Shirer in his monumental *The Rise and Fall of the Third Reich*, "one scarcely heard of Hitler or the Nazis except as butts of jokes." Shirer should know: he was living in Berlin at the time. The 1928 elections affirmed the Nazis' dwindling fortunes; they won just 12 of the Reichstag's 491 seats. The Social Democrats, the largest party in the country, won 153 seats. Most Germans were sure they would never hear of Adolf Hitler again.[3]

If the Nazis hadn't been so cautious about suppressing their contempt for the church, they might not have won even those 12 seats in the Reichstag. Religion, they knew, was central to German life. They had to tiptoe around the church, especially since their own ideology turned faith upside down. To them, Jesus was an Aryan sent by God to fight Jewish capitalism—"that's why the Jews liquidated Him." Hitler was just below Jesus in the Nazis' holy pantheon. Once their empire was secure, a neopagan National Reich Church would be established. The Bible would be banned, the swastika would replace the cross, and only one item would be allowed on altars: *Mein Kampf*, which Alfred Rosenberg, the Nazis' resident "theologian," called "the most sacred book...to the German people and, therefore, to God." This was the Nazis' gift to the world: a new truth, a new sacrament, a new enlightenment. Their other gift was a fairly cramped version of religious freedom. As early as 1920, Article 24 of the Nazi Party's program had espoused "liberty for all religious denominations...so far as they are not a danger to...the moral feelings of the German race." Vowing "to combat the Jewish-materialistic spirit within and around us," and determined to advance "the good of the state before the good of the individual," the Nazis embraced "positive Christianity," a phony theology that traded the "passive" Christ of the cross for the idea that God had sent him to fight the Jews.[4]

Some of these ideas Hitler kept to himself. "When I was younger," he told some friends one night during the war, "I thought it was necessary to set about matters with dynamite. I've since realized that there's room for a little subtlety." Which could be why he withheld his harshest criticism of Christianity for a private conversation with Albert Speer, the Reich's chief architect: "It has been our misfortune to have the wrong religion. Why didn't we have the religion of the Japanese, who regard sacrifice for the Fatherland as the highest good? The Mohammedan religion too would have been much more compatible to us than Christianity. Why did it have to be Christianity with its meekness and flabbiness?"[5]

Unlike Hitler, Hanussen didn't care if he offended the church. He wasn't a politician. He wasn't seeking votes. He just wanted to draw audiences to his shows. In that sense, he was bolder than the Nazis, who hid some of their beliefs (such as Hitler's idea that Jesus was only half Jewish since his immaculate conception gave him only one Jewish parent. That meant he was free of the "Jewish virus"). But the Nazis were never shy about their anti-Semitism, which, in many quarters, was acceptable, even fashionable. "Jew," "Bolshevik," and "capitalist" were used interchangeably for anything that went against the "true Germany." By the late 1920s, Jewish war veterans were banned from the Stahlhelm, Germany's largest veterans' organization, and Jews (who made up less than 1 percent of the entire population of Germany) were blamed for everything from prostitution to the increase in Berlin's rat population. Trashing Jews was permissible. Trashing the church—Protestant, Catholic, or any other Christian denomination—was taboo.[6]

And yet, as the Nazis were muffling their scorn for Christianity, Hanussen kept getting in trouble with the church. In the mid-1920s, for example, bishops in Budapest ran him out of town when he hypnotized a man into believing he was Jesus. A few years later, in the German city of Kassel, Hanussen got a standing ovation when he hypnotized a man to mimic Therese Neumann, a young woman in Bavaria who was said to bleed every Friday with stigmata just like Christ. Therese was a worldwide phenomenon: Hundreds of thousands of people worshiped her; tens of thousands made pilgrimages every year to Konnersreuth, the tiny village where she lived. Her admirers claimed that, while in a trance, she spoke Hebrew, Latin, and Aramaic, the language of Jesus, although she had been educated only in the simple German of her native village. And every day, it was said, all she ate was one thin Communion wafer.[7]

Most pilgrims who went to Konnersreuth, of course, were Catholic; some traveled from as far away as Brazil, India, Canada, Africa. In the late 1920s, the silent screen star Lillian Gish visited Therese, begging that she pray for Gish's sick mother. A few years later, Paramahansa Yogananda, the most famous teacher of Hinduism in the West, drove into Konnersreuth in his Ford. Therese told him, "I am here on earth to prove that man can live by God's invisible light, and not by food only."

Yogananda was thrilled; he was standing before a true mystic. "Can you teach others how to live without food?" he asked.

"I cannot do that," Therese stated, slightly shocked. "God does not wish it."[8]

What God wished did not matter to Hanussen, although he never said a nasty word about Therese publicly. With all the conflicting medical opinions about whether she actually did bleed from stigmata,

Hanussen probably figured that, like him, she was brilliant at conning people. But he knew he had to mute his skepticism: He couldn't risk alienating all those people who revered Therese as a saint. So in 1929 he told an audience that she was the "medium of her era." Through her, the "misery of her time was becoming visible." The blood that flowed from her stigmata was the blood of Germany. It represented the pain of the "thousands of mothers and wives crying for their killed sons and husbands" after the world war, the pain of the enormous debts imposed on Germany by the Treaty of Versailles, the pain of Germany's unbearably high unemployment. All sorrow, Hanussen said, found its spiritual counterbalance. *That* was why Therese was bleeding: she was restoring the equilibrium of the world and, especially, the equilibrium of Germany.[9]

Now that Hanussen had convinced the six hundred people in his audience that he had complete respect for Therese, he embarked on a tribute to her. A hefty coal miner named Diebel would be his volunteer. Hanussen hypnotized him, then instructed, "*You* are Therese von Konnersreuth. You have seen the Virgin Mary. You will act as Therese…I command it."[10]

What had been happening to Therese for the last seven years in northern Bavaria began occurring in the theater. With Therese, blood appeared upon the command of her Lord; with Diebel, it appeared upon the command of Erik Jan Hanussen. If a humble servant of God such as Therese could bleed as if she were one with Jesus, and if an equally humble coal miner could do the same when commanded by Hanussen, then what did that make Hanussen: a saint? an avatar? a monster? Hanussen's audience didn't care about the subtleties of theology. They applauded wildly as Diebel bled.

One of England's most reputable medical hypnotists, David Waxman, has determined that hypnotic suggestion can cause bleeding from the nose and skin. "Such phenomena," says Waxman, "bear a strong resemblance to the stigmata recognized by the Roman Catholic Church when bleeding of the skin is said to occur in sites corresponding to the wounds of Christ." Neither Waxman nor any other credible researcher has tried to induce stigmata through hypnosis. That, they say, is the domain of theater, not science.[11]

Hanussen was never a religious man, although he used religion when it helped him: A coal miner who bled like Jesus? Fine, if it sold tickets. A tribute to Therese of Konnersreuth? No problem, if his audience took it the right way. Stating, as he surprisingly did in 1930 before a small group of Jews, that he was descended from "the wonder rabbis of Prossnitz" who, Jewish legends claimed, could make themselves invisible or fly great distances? Fine, if it burnished his mystique.[12]

Wrapping himself in the cloak of these rabbis lent Hanussen an otherworldly aura, a patina derived from ancient visions and holy revelations. It also made him a bit of a throwback. Wonder rabbis dated to a world enthralled with enchantment and mystery, sorcery and séances. Hanussen was operating at a time when cynics were declaring war on anything that was irrational. He loved using his powers to frustrate all those sensible, up-to-date people. They were celebrating a different kind of wonder from what he practiced: the wonder of logic and pure, clear reason. At the same time, the Nazis were also throwbacks. They were aligning themselves with the gloomy and the mysterious, with the dim light that can barely illuminate our world, steering us backward, away from life, away from truth.

Both Hanussen and the Nazis were struggling against time and history, edging toward parts of ourselves that we thought we had discarded, the parts allied with the irrational and nonsensical. But Hanussen was merely a showman. The Nazis were champions of chaos. For all their barbarity, there was a genius to them. They understood the power of faith. ("Only faith creates a state," said Hitler. "What motivates people to battle for religious ideas? Not cognition, but blind faith.") As the Depression tightened its grip on Germany, the Nazis also understood that their frustrated and angry countrymen were hungering for a messiah who would redeem and resurrect them: rescue them from the chasm that lurked just ahead. Just one month after the Nazis took power in 1933, Walter Grundmann, a pastor in the town of Oberlichtenau, rhapsodized that Hitler was "a completely pure man!...Such a clear and truthful man does not derive from the earth, but rather out of that higher world that...Christ called the kingdom of heaven....This oneness of man with his God is a symbol of what the old church teachers intended to say with the trinity." For children, Hitler would soon supplant parents—and God. In school plays, students would declare: "My fuehrer! I know you well and love you like my father and mother. I will always obey you, like my father and mother. And when I grow up, I will help you like father and mother. And you should be proud of me, like my father and mother." Every night children in Nazi-run orphanages would praise Hitler as the source of everything good. He was their savior, their salvation, and their hope:

> Leader, my Leader, given to me by God,
> protect me and sustain my life for a long time,
> You have rescued Germany out of deepest misery, to you I owe my
>   daily bread.
> Leader, my Leader, my belief, my light,
> Leader, my Leader, do not abandon me.[13]

Hanussen could not compete with men who nursed such ambition, these masters of the universe who dreamed of usurping God and heaven and Jesus, of planting their own paradise here on Earth—small, gray, and dismal, an Eden with watchtowers and barbed wire: fascist golems along the Danube, Rhine, and Seine. Hanussen read minds. He told fortunes. This was a clever scheme for rough times. But when men are playing God, the stakes are high, and the game extends beyond the reach of mere mortals. Hanussen was mortal. The Nazis thought they were eternal—and with one thousand years at their disposal, they pretended they were as close to eternity as mere men would get.

# CHAPTER 7

# "This Man Must Be in League with the Devil"

In the 1920s, Hanussen knew nothing about Nazis. His head was in show business, rarely in politics, which he underestimated, barely comprehending that its spell could be more potent than the one he cast from the stage. One thing that Hanussen would soon understand, however, was the long reach of the law, which is why his arrest in February 1928 in the Czech town of Teplitz was so upsetting. Police had been observing him for weeks, watching him perform until they were sure he was a fake.[1]

Hanussen was interrogated six times during the next 12 days, never telling the police what they wanted to hear: that he couldn't read minds or tell the future. That his assistants used signs and a secret language to communicate with him during shows. That he invited women from his audiences to his hotel room for "free consultations," then performed "dishonest and immoral acts" with them. That he had hypnotized a 22-year-old woman from Lobositz "to satisfy his lascivious desires with her."[2]

Hanussen later compared his time in jail to a "cheap detective novel," grousing that a summons could have been sent to his house or he could have been released soon after his arrest: A brand-new car worth several thousand marks parked outside his front door proved he had enough money to pay bail. Four policemen with loaded guns didn't have to intimidate him for almost two weeks in what he called "an eerie back room." "Why," he grumbled, "was there all this dramatic hocus-pocus when everything could have been so much easier?" When Hanussen was finally released on bail, "the greatest prophet of the twentieth century" and prosecutors from a small rural district in Czechoslovakia began their journey toward what some people would call the last witch trial in Europe.[3]

The trial began 21 months later in the city of Leitmeritz, about 45 miles north of Prague. It was December 1929. The trial was expected to last four days, with both sides calling psychologists, philosophers, neurologists, and ordinary people who had paid for consultations with Hanussen. The consultations were the nub of the case against him. Prosecutors charged that he had exploited the needy and the desperate, usually charging 50 to 300 kronen for these readings, sometimes as much as 10,000 kronen.[4]

The first witness—an old friend of Hanussen's, Dr. Max Ostermann—immediately set back Hanussen's defense. Hanussen had dedicated *Mind Reading and Telepathy,* the book he wrote in 1919 in which he revealed the secrets of mind reading, to Ostermann: "Admired friend and loyal comrade . . . In commemoration of our common research." Ostermann knew Hanussen when he was still learning muscle reading, which Hanussen admitted in his book was how he read minds. Ostermann hadn't seen Hanussen for years, but that hadn't diminished his affection for him. Hanussen, Ostermann testified, was bright. He was immensely talented. But when asked if Hanussen was psychic, Ostermann hedged. "Well," he said, Hanussen was "an excellent observer." When asked the same question, this time more firmly, Ostermann responded with a circuitous explanation that meant exactly what the prosecution was seeking: "I would not want to say Hanussen was a clairvoyant." So much for an old and valued friendship.[5]

Next came a farmer named Modry, who had asked Hanussen to find a cash box his father left him. For two hundred kronen, Hanussen told Modry the box was in a small town in northern Bohemia. For another ten thousand kronen, plus 10 percent of the value of the contents of the box, he offered to take the farmer there. Modry said he would think about it. He did. He didn't come back to see Hanussen.[6]

Next on the stand was a businessman from Gablonz who had given Hanussen 375 kronen for the privilege of asking three questions:

"What shall I do if business is bad?"

"Stay open," Hanussen advised.

"I have a mortgage. Is it safe?"

"Safe."

"Should I buy a building site in Reichenberg?"

"No."

Those four words from Hanussen cost the businessman nearly 94 kronen apiece. Not satisfied, the businessman asked Hanussen to read his palm. Gladly, said Hanussen, for another 75 kronen.[7]

The rest of the day was just as bad for Hanussen. A baker from Teplitz said Hanussen told him to put an ad in the local paper's "Lost and Found" section to find his stolen watch. That advice cost one hundred kronen. And two witnesses testified how Hanussen swindled them when they sought help finding loved ones. Leo Reidel asked Hanussen to find his father, who had been missing for six years. Hanussen told him his father's body was buried in the forest where he had been killed. For three thousand kronen, Hanussen would take Reidel there. Reidel turned down the offer. And Emile Steberl said she asked Hanussen to find her husband's murderer. Hanussen said the killer worked in a local factory. He would take Frau Steberl there for ten thousand kronen. She, too, kept her money.[8]

At the end of the day, Hanussen made a request probably no other judge had heard before: he would prove his powers by demonstrating them in court. The judge tabled the motion, declaring that he would rule on it later.[9]

On the second day, a man from Teplitz said Hanussen had accurately diagnosed a relative's illness by studying a postcard from him. And two judges from the small town of Trautenau testified about testing Hanussen a few years before by randomly pulling a report about a murder from a stack of files. Without seeing it, Hanussen gave them precise details about the case. They then handed him playing cards that had a significant role in a slander case. Fingering his "golomboy," a type of rosary that Hanussen claimed helped focus his mind, he described the man who had been convicted in the case: "Tall with red hair. Wears glasses. He has blue eyes. Both his hands and feet are large. He is nervous and easily excited and speaks fast and with a lisp." The judges were amazed by Hanussen's accuracy. Asked if he had used any tricks, they firmly answered, "Absolutely not."[10]

The third day went so well that Hanussen thought he was on the verge of being acquitted. A parapsychologist said Hanussen's "perception and sensitivity [were] beyond extraordinary." A prosecutor from the town of Schonpriesen said the details Hanussen gave him about a murder helped free a man who had already been arrested. And a Dr. Heller recalled suddenly crying while having dinner with Hanussen one night in Prague. "I see a man on the floor," Hanussen said as his friend was sobbing. "He's dying—heart attack."

"No, that's not true," said Heller.

"Yes," Hanussen said. "I see a man on the floor and he's dead."

"The strange thing," Heller told the court, "is that later that night I learned that my brother had died—of a heart attack."[11]

Hanussen was thrilled. The prosecution could not possibly recover from all this. Then the judge banged his gavel, demanding order. The trial, he said, would reconvene in six weeks. He needed time to review the mountain of new material that both sides had submitted and to consider requests to call another hundred witnesses.[12]

Hanussen was furious. He had been waiting almost two years for the trial. "This stress is unbearable," he pleaded. "I'm financially ruined. I've been the victim of all kinds of libel. I've been called all kinds of names. I can't even perform because of the possibility of violence." Finally, ignoring proper etiquette when addressing a judge, Hanussen yelled, "I object to the adjournment!"[13]

Everyone was stunned. No one behaved like this in a courtroom. Hanussen's lawyer broke the ensuing silence by offering to not submit new evidence or call new witnesses if the prosecution would do the same. When the prosecutors rejected the offer, Judge Schalek adjourned the trial.[14]

The trial resumed in May, five months later. Justice moves slowly, and, after Hanussen's outburst, the judge was not inclined to quickly clear his calendar to indulge Hanussen. The suspense caused by the delay actually helped Hanussen. Weeks before the trial resumed, all the passes to the courtroom had been distributed. The day the trial reconvened, a cameraman from a newsreel company was stationed outside the courthouse. Hanussen had not enjoyed this much attention since his feud with Siegmund Breitbart seven years earlier.[15]

It was a mixed day for Hanussen. A carpet dealer from Berlin said he had been talking with a friend in a restaurant about a recent theft when a stranger at the next table leaned over and said, "The two men are at the race course in Marienbad." The merchant went to Marienbad, recognized the thieves, and had them arrested. And Alexander Rotter, a theater manager in Vienna, said that every night after Hanussen performed there in 1918, all his employees gathered in his office for a private show. One night Rotter handed Hanussen a sealed letter. Hanussen accurately said it came from Rotter's fiancée. The manager had not mentioned his engagement to anyone in the theater.[16]

Offsetting these advantages for Hanussen's defense was testimony from a man who said he had paid Hanussen one hundred kronen for a palm reading. Hanussen told him he was a farmworker; he was actually a clerk. Rosa Exner, another witness for the prosecution, had a similar experience. It cost her two hundred kronen to hear Hanussen say her husband had a liver disorder. He was actually in fine health.[17]

Two days later, the judge announced that Hanussen could demonstrate his skills in the court that afternoon. The reasons for his decision are lost to history, though the caveat he issued—"The result of these experiments will not affect the verdict in this trial in any way"—is specious: Why should Hanussen perform, if not to influence the verdict? Surely the judge was not simply seeking a recreational break during a long and difficult trial. And surely not even in a small town in Czechoslovakia is evidence allowed in a trial that is irrelevant to the verdict.[18]

People stormed the courthouse as word spread that Hanussen would perform. Minutes after the doors opened that afternoon, the courtroom was jammed. At 5:45, a large blackboard was wheeled into the courtroom, and a blindfold and Hanussen's golomboy—the heavily beaded rosary he used to put himself in a trance—were placed on the defendant's table. At 6:10, Hanussen took his seat, then the judge and lawyers and experts from both sides filed in. For the last two and a half hours, they had been meeting on the third floor, settling on the experiments Hanussen would do.[19]

Hanussen looked around. There was Judge Schalek, Hanussen later wrote, with a "kind face" and a "graceful voice that reached the smallest corners of your soul." And there were the prosecutors, all "stooped" and staring at Hanussen with "piercing" eyes. And there was Hanussen's lawyer—whose smile "had connected . . . [the two of them] during this whole trial." And beyond them were all the people who had "jumped over chairs and tables like wild animals to get a seat when the doors to the courtroom opened." Hanussen knew that reporters were prepared to telegraph news of his performance all over the world. If he failed, Hanussen told himself, "you will destroy everything you worked for your entire life. What you're about to do is insane."[20]

The judge asked Hanussen if he wanted to address the courtroom before beginning. Hanussen admitted he was nervous. "Your honor," he said, "I have smoked eighty cigarettes during the past one and a half hours while walking up and down the hall. I mention this to give you an idea of my tension." Then, with a nod to the judge, Hanussen said, "I am ready." With that, the only demonstration by a psychic ever allowed in a Czech court began.[21]

From Hanussen's perspective, "everything happened very fast, effortlessly and as if I was flying." To determine Hanussen's telepathic abilities, a Dr. Kloucek hid an object outside the courtroom. When Kloucek returned, he blindfolded Hanussen and put cotton in the clairvoyant's ears and over his eyes. Then Hanussen told Kloucek what he had said while performing in countless theaters throughout Europe: "Please firmly hold me with one of your hands, deeply concentrate and think, 'Hanussen—left!' or 'Hanussen—right!'" With that, Hanussen took a deep breath and exclaimed, "Let's go!"[22]

Hanussen and Kloucek left the courtroom. Two minutes and 15 seconds later, they returned, with Hanussen holding the keys Kloucek had hidden. The audience went wild, cheering and clapping as the judge demanded order. "What's going on?" Schalek asked when he could finally be heard. "This is not vaudeville. It is a trial." One more outburst, the judge said, and the room would be cleared.[23]

The next experiment required Hanussen to identify handwriting. Accepting a sample of handwriting from the judge, Hanussen began pacing the room, occasionally pressing one hand against his forehead, walking and walking, back and forth, until he told Schalek that the writing was by a man who "suffers from a contradiction between what he is and what he pretends to be." That was close enough for the judge. The writing was from a man who had impersonated an archbishop from the United States.[24]

After Hanussen identified the writing of Beethoven and Wagner, the judge handed him a letter. Hanussen studied it for a few minutes, then said it had been written by a woman of great wealth who was now living in equally great poverty. "This is amazingly accurate," Schalek said, not even trying to hide his admiration for Hanussen.[25]

Readying himself for the last experiment, Hanussen sat down, picked up his gomboloy, and put on his blindfold. Seven minutes later, he signaled that he was in a trance. The judge read aloud several dates. Hanussen correctly identified the birthday of a relative of a court employee, when a member of the panel that had agreed on the experiments had been promoted, and the date of a major car accident. The court was most dazzled by his answer to the last question: "What happened on February 26, 1927, at the Karolinum in Prague?"

"What is the Karolinum?" Hanussen inquired.

"The university."

There was a pause. And a beat. And slowly the answer came. "I see a room..." Hanussen said, hesitantly at first, then more quickly and with greater confidence. "I see glass...a laboratory...an explosion." But the year was wrong, he told Schalek. The explosion had occurred in 1926, not 1927.

"Amazing," thought a professional hypnotist who was in the courtroom. "Unbelievable. This man must be in league with the devil."[26]

The experiments were over. Hanussen had gotten four out of five dates correct, successfully analyzed handwriting, and found a hidden set of keys. The courtroom erupted with cheers. This time the judge didn't ask for quiet.[27]

In the coming decades, elaborate embellishments would accrue to Hanussen's courtroom performance. According to these accounts, Hanussen rattled off the contents in the prosecutor's wallet (two hundred crowns, a bus ticket, and a bill from a tailor), stated that the judge's briefcase contained two sandwiches and a book on criminal law, and told the entire courtroom that the sergeant posted at the door had a snuffbox and a comb missing three teeth in his pocket and had forgotten his handkerchief at home. Finally, Hanussen supposedly stated that a man wearing a green hat who had robbed a bank just ten minutes earlier was waiting for a train on Platform 2 of the town's railway station. The money was in his briefcase. Police raced to the station, arrested the man—and the case against Hanussen collapsed. These were great yarns. They were also impressively creative fibs—and absolutely unnecessary: Hanussen's show before Judge Schalek did not require the stretch of fiction to boggle the mind. For once, reality was more than a match for the wildest and most fertile of imaginings.[28]

After closing arguments on the day that followed Hanussen's performance in the courtroom, Schalek said he would render a decision at ten that evening. The courtroom was packed for his ruling. Letting his gaze settle on Hanussen, the judge stated, "The court does not deem itself in a position to judge whether Hanussen is incapable of clairvoyance."

The judge couldn't say another word: Applause drowned him out for ten minutes. When the racket eased, Schalek explained that he could not rule on issues that science hadn't even settled, "especially when the court has sufficient proof that the accused possesses miraculous powers of the mind." Looking again at Hanussen, Schalek concluded with the absolution Hanussen had been seeking since his arrest more than 27 months before: "There is no question that Hanussen solved the experiments and there is no way he could have faked the results. His metaphysical abilities are beyond doubt."[29]

A large crowd carried Hanussen back to his hotel, where he received "standing ovations" until dawn from the crowd below his room. Even if there had been complete silence, Hanussen probably would not have slept: Leitmeritz was the triumph of his dreams. "All the pain of the past two and a half years," he wrote, "...had now been forgotten. Like a nightmare, it all lifted off my chest."[30]

The trial was such a victory for Hanussen that as far away as America, the *New York Times* announced:

*CLAIRVOYANT PROVES POWER IN CZECH COURT;*
*JAN HANUSSEN, WITH FACE MASKED AND EARS STUFFED,*
*DEMONSTRATES WHILE EXPERTS WRANGLE.*

Not everyone was pleased. Back at the courthouse, the psychiatrist who had been the star witness for the prosecution—a Dr. Scheradcky—was telling reporters that Hanussen had been acquitted because he had hypnotized everyone in the courtroom, even the judge. But not Scheradcky; he was too smart. "Hanussen suggested everything to you," he told reporters. "He hypnotized all of you. I saw nothing. I was not hypnotized. You were all fooled."[31]

# PART TWO

# The Fuehrer, the Fire, and the Actress

Great liars are also great magicians.

—*Adolf Hitler*

# CHAPTER 8

# Triumph in Berlin

On May 28, 1930, the day after Hanussen's victory in Leitmeritz, he boarded a train for Berlin. He was returning as the curtain was going up on the season that had thrilled Mark Twain. "Germany, in the summer," Twain wrote, "is the perfection of the beautiful." But Twain hadn't been in Germany or Berlin since 1891, and both had changed immensely. The city was more elegant and cosmopolitan. Its streets, noted a Baedeker guide, were "a model of cleanliness," its squares were "embellished with gardens, monuments and fountains," its bridges were "beautified with sculpture." Three-quarters of the city's buildings were "quite modern," and broad boulevards like the Lustgarten, the Opera Platz, and the Linden were "magnificent thoroughfare[s] of the first rank."[1]

In 1920, Berlin had absorbed seven towns, 59 villages, and extensive landholdings that previously had been used exclusively by royalty. The city was now ten times the size of Paris, and it wasn't shy about this, not in this age of nationalism and chauvinism. One newspaper headline blared: "We Have 1.5 Million More People Than Paris; With

500,000 Lines the City Has the Highest Ratio of People to Telephones."
Another newspaper bragged: "We Have the Fastest Underground Rail
System in the World." And it was one of the cheapest: You could ride
the system's entire 452 miles for only 25 pfennigs—half the price of a
gallon of milk and 75 pfennigs less than a pound of beef.

For many people—the lucky ones—the city was eminently livable.
Berlin's zoo was one of the best in Europe; its film theaters were the
most up-to-date; and Luna Park, the city's most popular amusement
park, was mobbed on weekends and summer evenings. Most people
went there to cool off on the park's long water slide or to swim in the
pool whose artificial waves were almost as large as those in the ocean.
And once a week, the pool held Naked Day, so Berliners could enjoy
Germany's new fascination with nudity.

Thousands of artists and writers were swarming to Berlin: Marc
Chagall, Vladimir Nabokov, Christopher Isherwood, W. H. Auden,
Paul Klee, Josef Albers—all working furiously by day, then talking late
into the night at bistros like the Café des Westens, which—for obvious
reasons—was nicknamed the Megalomaniacs Café. With 45 theaters,
dozens of concert halls, excellent conservatories, and the most relaxed
censorship laws in Europe, Berlin was the crossroads of high-brow,
mid-brow, and the avant garde: Babylon and the Renaissance rolled
into one.

But there were two Berlins, and the city's days as a cauldron of creativity were numbered. In *Before the Deluge*, his account of Berlin in the
years leading up to World War II, Otto Friedrich wisely and elegiacally
writes that this was "a city unlike any other, we tell ourselves, not only
because of what it was but because of the fate that lay before it.... We
know that Berlin was a doomed city—as doomed as Pompeii—even at
the height of its flowering under the benevolent glare of the Weimar
eagle."[2] Away from the bright lights, the cafés where the debates never

ended about politics and aesthetics and pet projects that would change the world (or make a small fortune), and the cheap artists' garrets, Berlin was crumbling. The stone lions outside the palace at the end of the Unter den Linden were uncharacteristically quiet. The myth was that they roared whenever a virgin walked by, but it was hard to find a virgin in Berlin. As many as 100,000 whores were walking the streets. Many had moved to Berlin to be domestic servants, then realized that their wages didn't allow them to live decently in the big city. Twenty-one thousand children were crippled. Forty-four thousand veterans, sick or maimed from the Great War, were begging in the streets. Thirty-five thousand women had been widowed during the war. There was one murder every three days, and more than fifty thousand burglaries, forgeries, and swindles every year. Young girls barely in their teens were prostituting themselves after school with their parents' permission.

The slums of Chicago, the gangsters of New York, the sorrows of Dickens's London had descended on Berlin. Away from the late-night discussions about art and philosophy, Berlin was, off and on, a symphony of pain, with the economy in some years so bad that housewives burned their worthless paper currency to heat their homes, and one egg cost as much as 30 million eggs had cost before the war. Almost every day, one more person used his entire life savings for a tram ride to the other side of the city, where he threw himself off a bridge. When Wall Street collapsed in 1929 and Americans called in their German loans, unemployment tripled, then doubled again. The country was tottering, torn between democrats, Communists, and fascists, and Berlin, the capital, was crumbling under the never-ending and always-worsening crises. New to democracy, which had begun only in 1918 when the kaiser abdicated, the city—and the whole country—was breaking down.[3]

This was Hanussen's home, the city he had always championed above all others in Europe. The disabled and the widows and the homeless didn't know about him. If they had, they wouldn't have cared. Life, for them, was too much of a grind. Rather, his audience was people who enjoyed theater and spectacle and the absurdist avantgarde. And, of course, much of his following would come from the same people who were attracted to the seers and the fortune-tellers who had swarmed to Berlin after the armistice. Once the war was over, reason took a vacation. The mind could think its way out of only so much misery. Throughout Europe, the lamentations for the dead and the maimed were loud. They were louder in Berlin, which is why so many practitioners of the psychic arts—twenty thousand by one count, up from six hundred in 1900—flocked there. Hanussen knew this was his moment. What better place for him than this city of glitter, glitz, and sorrow? Hanussen was many things, but he was never cautious. The troops from the right and the left were lining up. Hanussen didn't care. He had left his trial in Leitmeritz a hero. It was time, he was sure, for Berlin to line up before him.[4]

Ever since the spiritualist craze of the late nineteenth century—when the idea that the dead could be contacted through séances and mediums became popular—Berlin had been ambivalent about the occult. People who consulted psychics were sure they were connecting with another dimension—a holier, more ethereal realm. Though a commission in 1886 essentially concluded that spiritualists were a pack of swindlers, followers still insisted that clairvoyants were proving that there was more to our lives than what we detect with our five senses. The greatest triumphs of the modern age—speedy trains, miracle medicines, inexpensive goods, mass production—had come with a cost: People were anxious and adrift. They had lost their way. The spirit world would help them find it. Cabarets and music halls all over Germany were offering telepathic acts, with ads on kiosks and billboards trumpeting the miracles that would thrill audiences. All these entertainers couched their acts as science—a genuine and subtle science that was beyond the blockheads who were attached to their formulas and calculations and their white, sterile laboratories, oblivious to the true wonders of the world. Clubs devoted to the occult, astrology, palm reading, hypnotism, and dowsing were springing up all over Germany, especially in Berlin, which had 52 such venues by the early 1930s. Members came from every profession—business, medicine, finance, the military, the arts. Some were quite wealthy. One aristocrat who had married an heiress and sat on the board of I. G. Farben, the vast chemical concern, used his fortune to build a research laboratory for psychic phenomena at his villa. He also hosted séances there, led by some of the better-known clairvoyants in Germany. While in a trance, August Machner—an untrained artist and former tanner—painted canvases that fetched top prices at a gallery on Berlin's fashionable Potsdamerstrasse. Around the same time, a butcher in Bavaria—soon known as the Alchemist of Gunzenhausen—claimed he had discovered a formula from the sixteenth century that let him turn lead into gold. The craze that was sweeping Germany would have confirmed how the German philosopher Theodor Adorno sized up the occult. Adorno called it "the metaphysics of dunces."[5]

Berlin was primed for someone like Hanussen, and soon he became a magnet—for pretty women; for the lost and confused who paid large sums to know their future; for ordinary people seeking entertainment and no more than that; and, soon enough, for the Nazis, who were plotting to seize a city that didn't know that these were its last almost-sane years.[6]

Even people who weren't sure about Hanussen approached him as an object of curiosity. In 1931, for example, Arthur Koestler, the

British journalist and novelist, visited Hanussen with an editor from a German publishing house and a reporter who considered herself an expert in the occult. They did not intend to test Hanussen's psychic abilities, which, Koestler said, "would have required a technical apparatus beyond my means." Their mission was unique: They came to test *themselves*. They wanted to know how reliable seasoned observers were when witnessing someone who claimed to have psychic powers. After watching Hanussen perform, the two journalists would independently write what they believed they had seen without discussing it with one another. The editor came along with them to give Hanussen an item from which the clairvoyant would divine the man's past, future, personality—whatever he could pick up from it.[7]

Hanussen's apartment in Berlin's Tiergarten district, Koestler wrote in his memoir, *Arrow in the Blue*, was "decorated in what one might call the lacquer-Japanese functional neo-Gothic Al Capone style." It was sumptuous but gauche, a casualty of interior decorating that the three guests tried to ignore while turning down Hanussen's offer of liquor and cigars—they wanted to remain as neutral (and as sober) as possible. And the editor was not allowed to talk with Hanussen—that might give the clairvoyant a chance "to form an opinion of the psychological lay of the land" of the editor with whom he was supposed to commune.[8]

When Hanussen learned about his guests' "puritan procedure," as Koestler called it, he was "somewhat dismayed." This was not his normal method. Annoyed, Hanussen briskly instructed the editor who had arrived with Koestler, "Give me that bunch of keys in your left-hand trouser pocket." Clutching the keys in one hand, pressing his other hand to his forehead and closing his eyes, Hanussen began speaking in a "trance-like voice." The keys, he said, were telling him about a burglary, a "severe illness and recovery," an "act of violence," the delivery of "a healthy child after much anguish," "a long-expected inheritance," and someone suffering from chronic constipation or problems with their liver.

When Hanussen finished, everyone looked at the editor. He was not impressed. "To tell the truth," he said, "no event of the kind described by the gentleman has occurred since I got these keys, which was thirty years ago. Except," he added thoughtfully, "I did have a problem with my liver around Christmas."[9]

That night, Koestler and the woman journalist wrote about what happened. Koestler's account was scathing: Hanussen was a fraud, a charlatan, and a crook. The other reporter could not have disagreed more. She had gone to Hanussen's house with "grave doubts" about his abilities. She left thinking he was spectacular. She said she could "solemnly testify and prove" that everything Hanussen had described had happened during the previous year—to *her*, not the editor. She attributed this psychic transfer to the physics of riding in a cramped taxi. On the way to Hanussen's, she had sat close to the editor in the cab, pressing against his left leg—the side of his pants where he carried his keys. "This physical contact with the keys," she wrote, "...evidently caused Hanussen to establish the subconscious psychometric nexus with me" while he mistakenly believed he was tuning into the editor.

Koestler was not persuaded. "Out of kindness to the lady," he wrote in his memoir, "the story of the Hanussen experiment was never published."[10]

Stephen Spender was another British writer who could find nothing good to say about Hanussen. In Spender's autobiographical novel, *The Temple*, which he revised over the years and finally published in 1987, a character named Hanussen owns a shop in Hamburg that sells fashionable items from England for interior decorating. While this is far from mind reading, the personality of Spender's Hanussen resembles that of the real one—both had difficulty distinguishing good from evil and truth from fiction, and both would serve masters who would darken and pollute the world. Duplicitous and unctuous, Spender's Hanussen walked with an "aggressive, sinister" air. His "prophetic eyes" blazed with an "apocalyptic vision" of immense fortresses constructed to withstand "any invader for the next thousand years" and of "blond warriors speeding across the Eastern plains in...chariots of fire," all while vast populations were destroyed by "metal and fire...[falling from] winged machines." For this Hanussen—Spender's Hanussen— death and destruction were mystical and transcendent: vehicles toward a greater good—a future ruled by the human gods known as Aryans. The skin of this Hanussen had a "high polish." His hair was "clustered on his head in golden ringlets." His eyes were "cauliflower blue." He was "a walking advertisement for ideals aggressively pure."[11]

★   ★   ★

Hanussen's shows in Berlin in the early 1930s became more elaborate, more ambitious. He was always pushing himself, trying to stay several steps ahead of the competition and at least one step of what he had done before. During one month-long engagement at the Scala Theater, one of Berlin's finest venues, volunteers from the audience hid a few small objects in the theater. Hanussen, though blindfolded, found all of them, of course. He had done this trick so often there was little chance he would fail. But knowing that some cynics in his audience were thinking, "Boring. This has been done so many times in the past," Hanussen raised the ante. "Now," he announced, "I will perform an experiment that nobody has ever done before! I would like you to think of an event that has happened in your past. Tell me the date on which this event occurred. Do *not* tell me the event itself. I will tell you what happened on that date." Aside from some nervous rustling, the audience was silent. Then a man in the rear yelled out, "December 12, 1923." For several long seconds, Hanussen closed his eyes, then he seemed to stir from a deep dream. "I see a burning house," he declared. "Three persons hurry down the steps.... Children are screaming.... In the end, they are all saved."

Hanussen walked to the edge of the stage and peered toward the rear of the theater. "Is this true, sir?" he asked. "Speak loudly and clearly. Tell me if what I saw is what really happened on December 12, 1923." From the rear, a voice rang out, "Yes, sir, it is true." The Scala thundered with applause.[12]

"Quick!" Hanussen barked. "The next date, please!" About half the audience was now shouting out dates. Choosing one date from the dozens that he was hearing, Hanussen again closed his eyes and settled into a trance. "I see Russia," he murmured. "I see endless snow.... It's cold.... I see a soldier standing at his post.... He is a private.... He is thinking of his home.... Suddenly, he has a feeling that something horrible has happened back home.... Just then, he is struck by a bullet.... At almost that same moment, at the soldier's home in the Rhineland, a woman falls to the floor with a heart attack."

"Is this what happened on that day?" Hanussen demanded to know from the person who had shouted out the date. "That is exactly what happened," came the reply. Again, the audience thundered its appreciation for this short man with the bushy eyebrows who knew everything.[13]

With no hesitation, Hanussen shouted, "Another date, please." "July 30, 1898" came from a man in the balcony. "Let me see," Hanussen said. "There is a house in a deep, green forest.... A giant is lying on a white bed.... The giant is taking his last breath.... The whole world is holding its breath.... Bismarck has died."

Slowly, a broad smile took over Hanussen's formerly blank, almost expressionless face. "My dear sir," he said with slight condescension, "if you want to test the clairvoyance of Erik Jan Hanussen, do not forget that he is also an historian. I did not ask for historical dates. I asked for dates in your life."[14]

Now the audience completely adored Hanussen, and people were shouting out dates almost faster than he could respond. His answers were so quick and so accurate that a journalist who was in the theater that night—a Jew who would flee Germany in a few years—wrote: "The audience nearly stopped breathing." And every time Hanussen—a clairvoyant whirlwind on the stage of the Scala—gave an answer, he would ask, "Is this true? Is this what happened?" And every time, the person who had thrown out the date would respond, "Yes, that is correct."[15]

Hanussen was bringing awe and wonder to a city that needed it. Each year, the fighting and the tensions between Communists and Nazis and other demagogues of the right and the left were verging more and more on the apocalyptic. Everyone was preaching that the political end of days—the revolution that would end capitalism or end democracy, depending on who led it—was nigh. The Communists' attitude toward the occult was obvious to anyone who knew how Karl Marx belittled religion and faith as fantasies and illusions that dispense false hope and empty distractions. "Man," said Marx, "is the world of man—state, society." And religion was "the sigh of the oppressed creature, the heart of a heartless world, and the soul of soulless conditions. It is the opium of the people." The attitudes of the Nazis were less evident and less consistent. Though Hitler denied he was superstitious, he appreciated the power certain words, dates, numbers, or stars had on *other* people. Foolish, weak men used these as a crutch but not Hitler; he equated superstition with ignorance and stupidity yet valued it, not because it made sense but precisely because it did not. Horoscopes, for example, he called a swindle, so he got great pleasure from the story of British newspapers during World War II that tried to prove that an astrologer who predicted a German victory was a quack. And when in 1941 an officer on Hitler's staff—"some imbecile," muttered the fuehrer—attributed the difficulties on the eastern front to Germany's invading Russia on June 22 (the same date that Napoleon began his own disastrous Russian campaign in 1812, the aide noted), Hitler correctly countered that Napoleon's invasion began on June *23*.[16]

And yet, while Hitler loved portraying himself as the most sensible of men, occasionally he lapsed. In 1934, the year after he became chancellor, Hitler was persuaded by his lifelong fear of cancer to hire a dowser to scan the Chancellery for signs of cancer-causing "earth rays." He also believed that people's hands revealed their character, intelligence, and soul as much as the shape of a skull revealed personality to a phrenologist. When Hitler met someone for the first time, he looked closely at their hands: their length and width, the shape of their nails, the structure of their joints and knuckles. Generals and diplomats often wondered why Hitler might begin a conversation cordially, then grow cool and frosty until abruptly walking away. They later learned that their hands had displeased the fuehrer.[17]

(The book about hands was in Hitler's library, as was *The Art of Worldly Wisdom* by a seventeenth-century mystic, Balthasar Gracian, which could have been a blueprint for how Hitler seized power. *Worldly Wisdom*'s principles blended a high moral tone with Machiavellian shrewdness and duplicity. "The truth, but not the whole truth," counseled Gracian. "Not all truths can be spoken." Hitler followed this faithfully. Although he respected another rule in *Worldly Wisdom*— "Mix a little mystery with everything, and the very mystery arouses veneration"—Hitler blithely ignored two others. One was "Begin the conflict with command over your temper....Every excess of passion is a digression from rational conduct." The other was "Wage War Honorably—Gallantry wins all men's praise: one should fight so as to conquer, not alone by force but by the way it is used." Hitler's temper was legendary, and his conduct was never synonymous with *gallant*. He would have been smart to study Gracian more.)[18]

Hitler, it seems, often retreated into fantasy—and a conviction that he operated in a realm beyond that of ordinary people. Bearing this in mind, a spirited conversation between Hitler and Hanussen about supernatural powers might have illuminated fascinating qualities about each man. As a teenager, for instance, Hitler had swooned over Stephanie Jansten—a tall, slim girl with thick, fair hair that she always pulled back into a bun. Hitler threatened to jump off a bridge if she didn't notice him—"I will make an end of it!" he told a friend—and he wrote a series of romantic, overwrought poems for her that he never sent, including "Hymn for the Beloved" in which Stephanie was a fair damsel dressed in a flowing velvet robe, riding on a white horse through meadows, her long tresses falling over her shoulders as a bright spring sky filled her with a pure and incandescent happiness. Teenage boys always have crushes on girls, and they often write poetry to them. Hitler's crush (and his poetry) are particularly ludicrous because he never said a word to Stephanie. He never even met her. He just admired her from afar on the street, once declining a friend's offer to introduce them and explaining that eventually "everything would be clear [between the two of them] without as much as a word being exchanged." Why bother speaking when Hitler was sure that he and Stephanie were already communicating—by their eyes alone. "For such exceptional beings as himself and Stephanie," one of Hitler's friends later said, there was no need to communicate through words. "Extraordinary human beings would understand each other by intuition." For Hitler and for Hanussen, intuition was the royal road to power, fame, and a Svengali-like control over others.[19]

Both Hitler and Hanussen imposed themselves on others through the power of their stares, that gleam from the subterranean of their unconscious: Hanussen's dazzled his audiences; Hitler's frightened the world or, as the British historian H. R. Trevor-Roper said, he "seduced the wits and affection of all who yielded to his power" simply with his eyes, the "eyes of a hypnotist." Both Hanussen and Hitler believed they had superhuman qualities: Hanussen thought he operated out of time and space, and Hitler not only thought he was a god but convinced an entire nation he was one. As Christ was being nailed to the cross at the passion play in Oberammergau one year during the Third Reich, a woman in the audience sighed, "There he is. That is our Fuehrer, our Hitler." Making a holy man out of this former tramp from Austria was fairly common: one of Hitler's economic advisers—not an unsophisticated man—told friends in London that Hitler communicated directly with God. And from Switzerland came a diagnosis from a man congenitally fascinated with people who claimed they were divine—Carl Jung, who diagnosed Hitler's power as magical, not political. Hitler's "exceptional access to his unconscious," said Jung, let him behave "like a man who listens intently to a stream of suggestions in a whispered voice from a mysterious source, and then acts upon them." Most of us are too rational, too sensible, to obey these orders from another dimension. But not Hitler, who, Jung noted, "obeys, and he listens." Jung's verdict on Hitler applied just as much to Hanussen, though Hanussen simply wanted to make a buck, not control the world.[20]

Two of the fuehrer's closest advisers had even stranger ideas than their leader. Heinrich Himmler, the head of the Gestapo and the SS, believed in the world ice theory, which posited that the solar system was formed millions of years ago when a massive block of ice collided with the sun. Molten material from the explosion formed the planets, and the gravitational force unleashed by three moons orbiting the earth created a race of supermen—the Aryans—who were killed in a slave rebellion. Through careful, scientific breeding, Himmler believed, the Nazis would restore the Aryans to their rightful place as the rulers of the earth. And Hermann Goering, the commander of the Luftwaffe, was sure that the earth was hollow, an idea he picked up from an old friend—the World War I flying ace Peter Bender. Bender said that the entire human race was living on the *inside* surface of a huge sphere that contained the entire universe. By inverting all accepted facts about physics and astronomy, the hollow earth theory turned the universe into an optical illusion, shriveling some heavenly bodies to less than the size of a peanut in an attempt to explain how they appear to our unaided eye. The moon, according to Bender, was 955 meters across, the sun 2.5 meters, and all the stars were 2 millimeters. Poor Pluto was the size of a bacterium. To Goering, a hollow earth represented paradise. If the whole universe was cradled inside the earth, and if the Nazis soon controlled most of the planet, then they would control the cosmos, with all its galaxies, star systems, and nebulae: the ultimate dream of a pack of misanthropes. Goering was so enamored with the hollow earth theory that he sent navy ships to the Baltic Sea, where they pointed special cameras *upward*—across the planet's empty, concave center—to (they hoped) photograph British ships in the North Atlantic. (When Hitler learned about this, he had a tantrum that strategic resources were being squandered at a crucial moment of the war.)[21]

Compared to Himmler and Goering, Hanussen was a model of sanity, although what he claimed to do—read minds and tell the future—resonated with all the craziness that was sweeping through Berlin, a city falling to the bizarre, the bogus, and the creepy. What Hanussen did, and what some Nazis believed, was part of the spectrum of irrationality that was gripping Germany. These men recognized that Germans were looking for something beyond themselves, and each offered a salvation that could not be found elsewhere. Hanussen, though, was almost blind to what was occurring beyond his immediate sphere. Paying scant attention to the lunatics and thugs who were filling the capital, he was primarily concerned with selling out the best theaters in town when he performed in them—and making a lot of money. After his trial in Leitmeritz, in fact, Hanussen became enormously wealthy, owning a small publishing empire, several apartments in Berlin's best neighborhoods, and a luxurious yacht, the *Ursel IV.* He was so popular that, while sailing the Baltic, he could stop at almost any resort along the coast and get booked into its theater that evening. At one of these shows, Hanussen predicted that, in 50 years, everyone would be telepathic and able to "peep around the corner in a time-and-space sense." Of course, he already possessed this power. The rest of the world just had to catch up with him. Other than that, he would say to these audiences, he was completely normal: He loved to eat well and drink well, and he loved women. He also loved being rich—and he loved flaunting it. Almost every night in Berlin, his chauffeur would pick him up in one of his limousines and drive Hanussen to a café or nightclub. Invariably, Hanussen had a good-looking woman on his arm, and most likely she wasn't his wife. Hanussen didn't need the hollow earth theory. He was the center of his own universe, and, for now, it was functioning enormously well.[22]

CHAPTER 9

# An Alliance of Scoundrels

Despite the welcome Hanussen received in Berlin after Leitmeritz, he was in trouble in the German capital before his trial in Czechoslovakia even ended. On April 1, 1930—about six weeks before the second half of the trial began—Hanussen sued the *Berliner Herold* for libel. The paper claimed Hanussen "read minds" with the help of assistants who scurried around the theaters where he performed, gathering information about audience members and passing it to Hanussen through codes and signals. The trial convened soon after Hanussen was acquitted in Leitmeritz. He didn't do as well with the German judges as he had with the judge in Czechoslovakia who had been so fond of him. The judges who Hanussen now had to confront refused to rule whether Hanussen was real, partly because clairvoyance was so poorly defined. But they also found that skepticism toward clairvoyance was not unusual and that skepticism toward Hanussen, in particular, was fairly common—journalists and scientists were always questioning his powers. And anyway, they said, he "had not been insulted enough" to win his lawsuit.[1]

Sitting in the courtroom was the man who would haunt Hanussen for the rest of his life: Albert Hellwig, the director of the regional court in Potsdam. Since 1904, near the beginning of his career, Judge Hellwig had been fascinated with how the law treated superstition and the occult, especially since some criminals claimed that a "higher force" was giving them permission to commit crimes. Around 1910, as films were just becoming popular, Hellwig attacked what he called "smut movies"—films that were influencing people to commit crimes they had seen on-screen. This new entertainment had to be censored to make it more wholesome and less harmful—new standards were necessary for the new medium. Always, Hellwig's concern was the frauds and baneful influences that were leading people astray. These had to be constrained: too many people were susceptible to their power. If Hanussen—one of the premier clairvoyants of the day—had been more honest about how he operated, Hellwig might have given him a break. "People want real occult experiences," Hellwig acknowledged. "They also want the truth. It would be very nice if Hanussen would call himself an 'artist' and not pretend to be something else."[2]

Hellwig was not a man to be trifled with. His severity surfaced in the courtroom as well as at home, where he had little patience with his one child, a son named Gerhard. Hellwig had too many things on his mind to be a good parent. Tillman Hellwig, who never met his great-uncle, says family lore has passed along an image of a "very dominant and very busy" man, a combination "which does not make for a good family life. The day only has 24 hours." As severe as he was, Hellwig's courage cannot be dismissed. He possessed an old-fashioned Prussian sense of right and wrong and refused to be intimidated. Around 1935, when someone asked why he had close working relationships with Jews, Hellwig said he "preferred a Jewish scholar to an Aryan charlatan." Hearing about this, *Der Sturmer* (the infamously anti-Semitic Nazi newspaper) denounced Hellwig as an unreliable citizen. Hellwig and his wife marched to the local office of the Nazi Party and demanded a retraction. They got one. Even the Nazis backed down before Albert Hellwig. He must have had the strongest backbone in Potsdam.[3]

Hellwig became obsessed with bringing Hanussen down after the clairvoyant began boasting that he had helped the police solve one of the worst serial murder cases in German history. Although Hanussen was one of many clairvoyants who were offering to help the police—in fact, there were so many that a name was coined for them: *kriminaltelepathen*, or criminal telepaths—he was the most flamboyant and the most famous. Some had been tried for fraud, as Hanussen had been in Leitmeritz. Some were convicted; a few were acquitted. But none of them drew headlines like Hanussen. And most were never heard from again. Hanussen's refusal to disappear—his supple resilience—was a goad to Hellwig, whose commitment to truth and justice equaled his contempt for trickery and deception.[4]

Further driving Hellwig was a report he acquired from a psychological institute in Czechoslovakia. In 1928, Hanussen had asked the institute to test his powers. It found that Hanussen had a "high intelligence...appropriate for attending a college or university." His "general knowledge" was very good. His short-term memory was superb. But he failed every test that gauged psychic powers. The institute concluded that Hanussen was using his "intelligence and cleverness" to convince audiences he was clairvoyant. In that regard, stated the report, Hanussen was "no different from any good vaudeville performer."[5]

Hellwig's campaign was in the vanguard of the attacks against Hanussen that would soon be mounted in Germany. The combination of assaults from the political extremes—right *and* left—and the sensible middle (embodied by Hellwig) would force Hanussen to seek allies wherever he could—a quest that got more dubious as Hanussen became more frantic.

*   *   *

For several years, criminal telepaths had been pestering police all over Germany to let them solve crimes. With the economy constantly wavering, much of the country was a wreck, and hardly anyone felt safe. By the mid-1920s, robberies had doubled, thefts had tripled, and, in Berlin alone, murders had more than quadrupled from a decade before. Inflation was driving city residents to the country, where they stole anything they could get their hands on. "Light bulbs are screwed out in corridors," wrote one German, "brass plates are removed from entrance doors, even the dustbins left outside for the waste collection disappear."[6]

The police were desperate for help. The hundreds, perhaps thousands, of criminal telepaths who came to their aid were often compared to police dogs in their ability to track down crooks, killers, and thieves. Sometimes these psychics actually helped. In 1921, for example, prosecutors—stumped after the murder of a forest warden near the town of Mugeln—sent to Leipzig for Louise Diedrich, a clairvoyant. In four sessions with investigators, Diedrich provided the murderer's address and part of his name, information about his accomplice, and where the men hid the murder weapon. She was correct on every count. But sometimes the *kriminaltelepathen* were a pain in the ass. At first, while investigating the "Dusseldorf Monster"—the case that formed the basis of Albert Hellwig's contempt for criminal telepaths and, especially, for Hanussen—police were happy to get anyone's help. Once they realized that much of what the psychics were telling them was useless, they shooed them away. "No police force," Hellwig wrote, "should rely on these frauds and publicity seekers. This is dangerous and irresponsible and does not make any sense."[7]

Nor did it make any sense to the police in Dusseldorf, a city that, for much of 1929 and 1930, was under a reign of terror. In February, there were two murders. In August, six women and three girls were strangled, drowned, or stabbed. In September, a servant girl was raped and killed. The next month, two women were pounded to death with a hammer. In November, a five-year-old girl was strangled, then stabbed 36 times with scissors. The variety of victims and murder weapons persuaded police that more than one killer was involved. The public turned in more than 900,000 names to the authorities as potential suspects—more than twice the population of the entire city.[8]

The break in the case came in May 1930, when a woman was enticed to the home of a friendly stranger, who then led her to a nearby forest on the pretense that he was taking her to a women's hostel. After he attempted to rape her, he let her go when she assured him she had no idea where he lived. A few days later, Maria Budlick led police to a three-room flat on the fourth floor of 71 Mettmannerstrasse—the home of Peter Kurten, a man so ordinary and so peaceful that his neighbors protested his arrest. Psychiatrists found that Kurten suffered from an unrestrained narcissism. "Kurten," one doctor wrote, "dearly loved himself. The kernel of his tragedy, perhaps, was that he was unable truly to love any other human being." In September 1931, Kurten was sent to the guillotine.[9]

At the height of the manhunt, four hundred telepaths, graphologists, and astrologers offered to help. Hanussen joined them. His open letter to the killer was published in several newspapers. "I am on your track and I will find you," Hanussen warned. "You should confess to the police. Do not put more guilt upon yourself with another murder." Hanussen offered to come to Dusseldorf to help solve the murders. There would be no fee; the reward money would be sufficient—15,000 marks. The police turned him down. So, not wanted in Dusseldorf, Hanussen hit the lecture circuit, telling an audience in Stuttgart that there would be a total of 14 murders (in truth, there were nine) and listing 26 details about the murderer—all wrong. The killer was not, as Hanussen said, a young adult who read a lot, came from a family of intellectuals, and never smoked. When caught, the murderer turned out to be 47 years old; heavily addicted to tobacco; from a lower-class, poorly educated family; and read only articles about himself and his crimes. And yet after Kurten was arrested, Hanussen told one audience that he had helped solve the case. Dusseldorf's police chief was outraged. "Hanussen was of no assistance," he told newspapers. And in Potsdam, just outside Berlin, Judge Hellwig was furious. Hanussen could strut his stuff on stage. That's where he belonged. But keep him away from honest cops who were doing their best to solve crimes that were paralyzing a city. Hanussen was a danger to the public, a threat to their confidence in the police, and a danger to the civic order. He had to be stopped.[10]

At least with these cases, the police could act as a buffer between Hanussen and the public. Hellwig was more concerned about people who were ill or desperate or needy. Who would protect them from Hanussen when they sat down with him for his expensive private consultations? These sessions, Hellwig worried, were making people irresponsible. They were letting Hanussen make important decisions about their own lives. It was too late to help anyone already "under Hanussen's spell," Hellwig said, but perhaps he could deter new customers from these consultations. This is why Hellwig sprang into action in late 1931, when he heard that Hanussen was planning to turn a castle in Godesberg into a spa.[11]

About 360 miles west of Berlin, Godesberg is one of the oldest towns along the Rhine, ringed with castles and proud of its promenade with a lovely view of boats wending their way along the river. It was famous throughout Germany for its many spas, which drew thousands of people every year for cures and comfort. Hanussen had never tapped this market. Now he wanted his share of it.

The people of Godesberg were alarmed, especially its doctors. One physician wrote Hellwig, "We must protect the people. How stupid some of them are." He was frantic that some people would be desperate enough to pay Hanussen 30, 50, perhaps as much as one hundred marks for private consultations. The controversy was more about Hanussen than whether spas helped anyone. The efficacy of spas was firmly embedded in German culture: That same year, a booklet about spas distributed abroad by the German government bragged that there was "hardly a disease" that spas could not cure or prevent. Gout, paralysis, diabetes, "diseases of women"—you name it; spas cured it. People didn't need to be saved from the spas; they needed to be saved from Hanussen. Hellwig warned the mayor of Godesberg that this "vaudeville artist" would "hurt the reputation" of this town whose economy relied so heavily on visitors who came to Godesberg's many spas for cures and solace. Worse, perhaps, was that people would be "damage[d]...psychologically and emotionally." From Berlin, the German Society Against Medical Fraud weighed in: Stop the spa! From Potsdam, Hellwig offered to give a lecture in Godesberg. The topic? Stop the spa! And in Godesberg itself, local judges demanded: Stop the spa![12]

Hanussen hired an architect. Before his plans were even approved, he was distributing flyers touting the powers of the mineral spring on his property and the efficacy of the magnet therapy he would conduct there. (The curative power of magnets was then in vogue in Germany, with practitioners usually claiming they could relieve migraines and arthritis and improve blood circulation. One magnetist, as they were called—Balthasar Wehdanner—even announced that he commanded the same forces that Christ had used to resurrect the dead.) Five months later, Hanussen canceled his project in Godesberg. Nothing had ever been built for it, though many brochures about Hanussen's grand vision had been distributed. Hanussen yielded because the pressures against him were too great: for once, the stars were not aligned in his favor. Godesberg was safe, and German medicine was safe. Until the next January, when Hellwig received a letter from the Society Against Medical Fraud informing him that large posters had been spotted on kiosks in Berlin advertising Hanussen's services for treating diseases. He was at it again. Could this man never be stopped?[13]

★  ★  ★

Hanussen was more resilient than Judge Hellwig anticipated. And he was involved in so many projects that it was hard to keep track of them all: his stage career, and his private consultations, and his newspapers, and, soon, his associations with some of the more unsavory characters in German politics. And then there were his predictions. As 1931 ended, Hanussen forecast that the new year would be full of "extraordinary changes." A famous German academic would die. A German boxer would be defeated. Auto sales would decline but only slightly. Crime would rise but only for a few months. Overall, Hanussen saw a Germany on the move. Industry would revive, and personal spending would increase. There would be a greater demand for military equipment, and inflation would end. An economic partnership between France and Germany—never great friends—would trigger much of this prosperity. All this would be guided by a politician who would rule Germany with such "an iron hand" that he might even suspend the Reichstag.[14]

Hanussen didn't name the politician; he didn't need to. "The world will not become bolshevist," Hanussen stated in his prediction for 1932. "To the contrary, it will become fascist." Despite their instincts, Hanussen said, once the Nazis were in power, they would respect democracy. Their brief reign would be a bitter but necessary path to a stronger, wealthier Germany. Thanks to the Nazis, Hanussen said, "future generations will say, 'It was only then'"—in 1932—that Germany ceased suffering from the emasculating Versailles Treaty that had ended World War I, only then that Germany began to recover its self-respect.[15]

If nothing else, Hanussen understood the mood of the country. Germany was desperate. Almost 30 percent of Germans were unemployed. In Berlin, more than 700,000 people were out of work—more than 10 percent of the total unemployed population in the entire country. Hunger and cold were eating away at people, sapping their strength, both physical and moral. Sizing up the situation, Joseph Goebbels, the Nazis' propaganda genius, kept urging Hitler to run for president, but his fuehrer kept vacillating. "The eternal waiting is almost wearing me out," Goebbels whispered into his diary. Finally, in late February 1932, Hitler announced he was a candidate, glowering at his opposition, "I know your slogan. You say, 'We will stay [in office] at any cost.' And I tell you: 'We will overthrow you in any case!'"[16]

★　★　★

On March 12, *Der Angriff*, the Nazi newspaper in Berlin that Goebbels had founded five years earlier, proclaimed, "Tomorrow Hitler will be president of the Reich." The paper was wrong. Paul von Hindenburg was reelected president, and Hitler won only 30 percent of the vote. The setback did not matter; there would be other elections and greater triumphs. Hardly anyone noticed that Hanussen, the prophet, had not mentioned these reversals in his predictions for 1932. Either he was smart enough to know that it was wise not to offend Hitler—or he had no idea what he was talking about. In any case, Albert Hellwig should have been worrying about Hanussen's cheerleading for the Nazis, not about the psychic's plans to build a spa in a tiny town in central Germany.[17]

Until the early 1930s Hanussen had never needed a protector. He was slippery enough to fend off skeptics, prosecutors, debunkers, and crusaders. But soon after his victory in Leitmeritz, he began cultivating a relationship with a rising Nazi named Count Wolf-Heinrich von Helldorf. Their friendship was mutually beneficial. Berlin was a dangerous place, the number of Hanussen's critics was growing, and Helldorf was an increasingly powerful man. His clout enveloped Hanussen in a protective cocoon as the Weimar government—Germany's perennially crippled democracy—slowly withered away, making a parody of the words "freedom," "justice," and, most important, "self-rule."

Helldorf has been called "one of the most contradictory figures of the Third Reich," "an SA hooligan," "a military profiteer of the worst sort," a "drunken, vainglorious lout," and "a sinister adventurer." These were from two historians, a German journalist, and the French ambassador to Germany. Eventually, even Hitler called him "a scoundrel," but that was after Helldorf participated in the July 20, 1944, plot to kill the fuehrer. By the end of his life, Helldorf had few friends and many enemies. In that sense, he was similar to Hanussen. And yet Hanussen selected Helldorf wisely. At his core, the count was weak, rash, and pliable, a man who was inclined to be dependent, financially and psychologically, on a strong and forceful personality—on someone just like Hanussen.[18]

Outwardly, Helldorf was the ideal Nazi: a blond, blue-eyed descendent of generations of landed German nobility. For centuries, his family had been living in Saxony, about 20 miles west of Leipzig, prospering through farming and public service. Well-chosen marriages tied the Helldorfs to other prominent families. Helldorf joined the army soon after the First World War broke out. On his eighteenth birthday, his regiment arrived on the front line, where he served bravely and honorably—he commanded machine gun units in some of the worst battles of the war—and was decorated with the Iron Cross. Other than recuperating in a hospital from venereal disease for three months, Helldorf served in the army almost non-stop for four long, miserable years.[19]

Not long after the war ended, the Weimar government alienated Germany's aristocrats by terminating their special privileges and cutting back on the high positions in the military and civil service that were traditionally reserved for them. The army had been one of the few German institutions to which Helldorf was dedicated. Now he was barred from it. As a release from his frustrations, he found a parallel career in the Freikorps—ultra-nationalistic ex-servicemen who fought the Communists, argued against the Versailles Treaty and tried to overthrow the government. In 1920, Helldorf had to flee to Italy after a coup he organized failed. When he returned a few months later—Weimar was a very forgiving government—he married and received his inheritance: an 80-year-old manor surrounded by extensive lands.[20]

Helldorf should have been set for life. He wasn't. He devoted most of his time to recruiting more troops for the Freikorps and meeting with close colleagues of Hitler. After serving for four years in the Landtag—Prussia's parliament—as a Nazi, he returned to farming in the late 1920s and early 1930s. His timing was bad—crop prices were sinking. His behavior was worse—he was always overspending, like paying five thousand marks he barely had on his son's baptism. Between his income dropping, his gambling debts ballooning, and his exorbitant spending, Helldorf lost his estate. His sole source of income was now his racehorse, Narcissus, who did quite well in 1929 and 1930, but didn't earn a single mark in 1931, the year Helldorf declared bankruptcy. With no farm, no land, and high debts, Helldorf wasn't sure how to make a living. The Nazis were glad to help him out.[21]

In the fall of 1931, Helldorf was named head of the storm troopers in Berlin, officially known as the Sturmabteilung, or SA for short. This was only a few days after he led a pogrom down one of the city's most elegant boulevards, the Kurfürstendamm, on the Jewish new year of Rosh Hashanah. Chanting "Jews Out" and "Kill the Jews," a thousand SA members roamed the street in packs of 50 or more, smashing the windows of Jewish-owned shops, attacking anyone who looked remotely Jewish. A 63-year-old man was one of their victims, slammed over the head with brass knuckles, as were two Armenian students who were sitting at the Café Reimann. And all the while, Helldorf rode slowly up and down the boulevard in a chauffeur-driven car, shouting encouragement to his goons. At one intersection, a policeman asked Helldorf what dirty business he was up to, then ordered him to move along. Ignoring him, Helldorf had his driver block a car as the count yelled, "Bank Jews! Bank Jews!," referring to the Nazis' incessant gripe that the Jews controlled Germany's financial institutions. A policeman who ran over to help the people trapped in the car turned to ask Helldorf for identification. "What?" Helldorf protested. "We have to identify ourselves to these bank Jews?" He was arrested and taken to a nearby police station.[22]

After some backstage negotiations by Goebbels, Helldorf was acquitted of starting the riot and fined a hundred marks for insulting the "bank Jews." With his new criminal record, Helldorf was a certified Nazi, so proud of his jail time that he added it to his listing in *Who's Who*, burnishing his new résumé by exaggerating from six weeks to two months the time he waited in jail for his trial.[23]

Now that Helldorf had proved himself to the Nazis—he was an anti-Semite, just like them—they really put him to work, exploiting his elite credentials as a calling card to the conservatives they were courting. After Chancellor Franz von Papen met in August 1932 with Helldorf and Ernst Roehm, who commanded the entire SA in Germany, the chancellor muttered that Roehm "looked remarkably like a bulldog." And, indeed, he did: short and stocky, with closely cropped hair, a round face, and a scar on his cheek that could have been mistaken for a wound incurred while upholding his honor in a duel but really had been caused by a bullet during the last war. In another battle, the upper part of Roehm's nose had been shot away. He was not a pretty man. Keeping his distance from Roehm, von Papen gravitated toward the count. He had known Helldorf for years and felt comfortable with his "most aristocratic appearance," a regal contrast to Roehm's. The two men "monopolized the conversation," ignoring poor, fat, disfigured Roehm.[24]

By 1933, Helldorf had the confidence of the highest levels of the Nazi machine. When Hitler heard rumors on January 29, the eve of his appointment as chancellor, that a coup was imminent to prevent him from forming a cabinet, he entrusted Helldorf to secure Berlin by putting the city's storm troopers on alert. Soon Goering was smoothing the way for Helldorf to be appointed police chief of Potsdam (though he was still head of the SA in Berlin). In another two years, Helldorf was promoted to police chief in Berlin (where his first act was to close Jewish-owned ice cream parlors early for an entire week). One of the prime reasons Helldorf was made police chief in the capital was that the Nazis knew he would do their bidding. The previous chief, the former rear admiral Magnus von Levetzow, had never fully acquiesced to the Nazis' brutality or their anti-Semitism. For the three years he was in office, he had tried (usually unsuccessfully) to limit SA excesses and occasionally rebuffed Nazi mobs from attacking Jewish-owned businesses. In July 1935, after Jews protested *inside* a theater featuring an anti-Semitic film, Goebbels and Hitler ditched von Levetzow and installed Helldorf as police chief. At a press conference, Helldorf declared that clearing the streets of Jews would be his main job. Goebbels was jubilant. "Levetzow sacked," he wrote in his diary. "Helldorf appointed. Bravo!"[25]

As Helldorf's career was advancing, his personal life was a shambles: his marriage was coming apart; he was estranged from his mother; creditors were hounding him. Luckily, a friend had introduced him to Hanussen, who was always there to bail him out. All Helldorf had to do was sign another IOU. Soon, these were piling up in the safe in Hanussen's office. Hanussen began spreading around his protection money—some to Helldorf or other top SA men or for supplies and even a car for the men in their ranks. Hanussen was the storm troopers' angel when they most desperately needed one: They were almost broke. The two national elections during the six months leading up to Hitler's becoming chancellor in 1933 almost wiped out the Nazi Party's bank accounts. The Nazis poured vast resources into the July 1932 election, when they had their best showing yet—almost 14 million votes, up by 13 million since 1928. With 230 seats, the Nazis were now the largest party in the Reichstag. But they were still short of a majority in the 608-seat parliament, and they did even worse in the next elections, which were held in November. As Goebbels wrote, "Money is extraordinarily hard to obtain. All the men of 'Property and Education' are standing by the government." Even the party faithful were tired of the never-ending campaigning. The Communists picked up 11 seats in the Reichstag, bringing their total to 100. The Nazis lost 34 seats, reducing their total to 196 delegates. Throughout the Nazi organization, morale was down, especially among the storm troopers, whose leaders were desperate for money. Things were so bad in eastern Germany that one commander had to pawn his own typewriter and duplicating machine to provide supplies for his troops. The SA was so strapped for cash that it revived its fund-raising drives. It had tried to raise money a few years before, mostly by selling the sort of gear used by gangs and thugs (brass knuckles and daggers) or by selling brown shirts, swastika armbands, and military caps to new recruits. Now it began endorsing products—razor blades, margarine, and the Sturm brand of cigarettes. Nazi symbols and slogans were printed on the cigarette packages, and the SA got a percentage of the sales. In return, manufacturers expected some marketing help from the storm troopers, like "show[ing] a little energy" to discourage tavern owners from selling competing brands of cigarettes. The deal with Sturm was a bonanza for everyone involved: in some parts of Germany, sales went up tenfold; an insider said many SA leaders "could make a living as . . . representative[s]" of the cigarette company; and some SA units were making as much as 1,200 marks a month from commissions. And still the storm troopers were short on money. Which is why Hanussen's deep pockets—and his friendship with Helldorf—were a blessing. For most of the second half of 1932, the Nazis were sinking into despair. Hanussen's generosity gave the SA desperately needed supplies and kept Helldorf a few steps ahead of his creditors. In return, Helldorf made sure no danger came to Hanussen as Berlin sank deeper into anarchy.[26]

★　★　★

Clever enough to keep his religion a secret from Helldorf, Hanussen had begun getting friendly with the count within a year after he returned to Berlin from his trial in Leitmeritz. Helldorf was an interesting character to know; with political tension and violence escalating in the city, it was wise to have an ally with some muscle behind him. But Hanussen

was even more motivated to ally himself with the Nazis in 1932 when a
Communist newspaper, *Berlin am Morgen*, began what would turn into
an eight-month campaign against him. Hanussen was a logical target for
the paper: a celebrity and the most famous mentalist in a city teeming
with them, he was a friend of powerful Nazis. In this increasingly dangerous environment, Hanussen was among the fascists' more visible—
and unabashed—sympathizers. Exposing him might weaken the Nazis.

This was a pivotal moment for Hanussen, the crucial juncture
when he would irretrievably cast his lot with some despicable men. It
reveals misjudgments on all sides: by Communists, who thought they
could defeat Hitler by taking down Hanussen; by Nazis, who trusted
a man whose secrets were labyrinthine, even by their standards; by
Hanussen, whose political innocence could not have served him worse.
This inadequate acumen by three parties was indicative of the desperation simmering in Berlin, a city fraught with rumors, intrigue, suspicions, and paranoia, all fed by everyone's certainty that the Weimar
Republic was dying and by fear about what would replace it. Germany
was on the cusp of losing its sanity. We know that now. At the time,
the political jockeying simply appeared to pit one bad faction against
another. No one could foresee the degree of depravity that lay ahead.
What was apparent in the short run was that only the Nazis would
benefit from the phenomenon known as Erik Jan Hanussen, tolerating
his pronouncements about their glorious future so long as he was useful
to them. They were good at that.

★   ★   ★

The *Berlin am Morgen*'s crusade against Hanussen began when its new
editor, Bruno Frei, ordered his reporters to provoke the clairvoyant
into a lawsuit. Any sensible judge, Frei hoped—especially a judge more

sensible than the one who had ruled in Hanussen's favor in Leitmeritz—would rule that Hanussen was a fake. This, Frei believed, would topple not only Hanussen but Hitler too. Like many other people in Berlin, Frei was sure that Hanussen's contacts with the Nazis went straight to the top and that he was advising Hitler on his oratory and who was trustworthy in his inner circle as well as assuring him that astrological charts were in his favor. "Comrades," Frei told his staff, ". . . not everyone who believes in Hanussen believes in Hitler. But we have to get to the root of the problem. The basis of all religion . . . rests in believing in miracles."[27]

In May 1932, *Berlin am Morgen* began its series—"Ein Scharlatan Erobert Berlin" ("A Charlatan Takes over Berlin"). This was more about simply exposing a fake; the articles equated Hanussen and Hitler. By exploiting the irrationality sweeping Germany, both Hanussen and Hitler were capitalizing "on people's stupidity in shameless ways," using "unscrupulous self-promotion which passes off untruth for truth." Hanussen was "Hitler's counterpart." "We will not rest," Frei said, "until Berlin is cleansed of the last bit of this clairvoyant scum."[28]

As a Communist, Frei had contempt for religion—"human idiocy," as he put it. "Great magicians," Frei firmly told his staff, "show the decay of society." Cagliostro, an Italian occultist, was part of the decay of Versailles; Rasputin was part of the rot of the czars. Hanussen was Hitler's weak spot. When Hanussen fell, Frei said, Hitler would fall. "People who believe in Hanussen," Frei explained, "also believe in Hitler. . . . You have to eradicate evil where it starts to grow. Part of our anti-fascist battle is ending this belief in wonder."[29]

By November, Frei's attacks were rattling Hanussen—not good for someone who needed his full concentration onstage. Shaken by the articles in *Berlin am Morgen*, Hanussen further solidified his friendship with Helldorf, providing women for him and perhaps drugs and often taking him for cruises on the *Ursel*. Berlin was full of gossip about these cruises. People knew naughty things occurred on them. They didn't know *how* naughty.[30]

Soon, Hanussen also turned his newspaper, *Erik Jan Hanussen's Berliner Wochenschau,* into a pro-Nazi organ. The paper was sold throughout Germany and had a circulation of about 200,000. Hanussen's support was an opportunity for the Nazis to expand the reach of their propaganda while gaining the seal of Germany's most famous clairvoyant.

Hanussen's paper blended news, horoscopes, film reviews, humor, and advice for the lovelorn. An issue in April 1932, for instance, featured a vivid front-page story of Rasputin's murder during the final days of the Czars. Inside was a review of a club where women were hypnotized and ads for a private detective and for a café opposite the Scala Theater (where Hanussen often performed). The drawing in the ad for the café was overtly racist—a half-dressed African man with a bone through his nose on the verge of doing something wicked to a defenseless but eager white woman. Almost every issue had ads for Hanussen's cure-all for nerves, timidity, laziness, stuttering, insomnia, and smoking: a gomboloy, the same kind of 12-beaded rosary he used onstage to help him concentrate. For only two marks, you got a booklet by Hanussen, "My System for the Control of Nerves," and a *free* gomboloy—"the rope of pearls from the Orient." Another regular feature was an advice column. When a Mrs. G. of Aussich inquired in September 1932 whether she should purchase a hotel, she was told, "Do not buy a hotel now. It is not the best time for such a purchase." It is not known if she followed the suggestion.[31]

As Bruno Frei's Communist newspaper increased its attacks on Hanussen, all this was relegated to the inside pages of the clairvoyant's newspaper. By July 1932, the front page of every issue was reserved for stories about Hitler and for large photos of the fuehrer: Hitler in a Nazi uniform bestowing a Nazi flag on a proud, beaming boy. Hitler marching at the head of an endless line of storm troopers, goose-stepping toward the New Germany. Hitler, kind, fierce, benign, virile: savior of the Fatherland. In the buildup to every election—and there were many in 1932 and early 1933—the paper predicted a Nazi victory: "Hitler Will Win!" "Government Will Have Hitler." "Hitler Will Defeat Communism." Eventually, Hanussen's paper became no more than a Nazi rag, with swastikas strategically placed in the top corners of every front page. In one issue, an astrological chart with a German army helmet in its center stated, "Without Hitler, there is no Germany." In another issue, a story titled "Hitler Awakens Germany!" was illustrated with a photo of a decrepit tank from the Great War, a symbol of Germany's decline—and of Hitler's resolve to restore the nation to its past glory.[32]

Hanussen had chosen the Nazis for his refuge: The political center was disintegrating, centrists like Judge Hellwig were contemptuous of psychics and the occult, and the left was crusading against the mentalist. For more than a year, Hanussen had been ingratiating himself with Nazis like Helldorf. Now those maneuverings were paying off. Politically, Berlin was splintered like no other city in Europe. It was there, on the extreme right, that Hanussen thought he had found a safe and impregnable haven.

Unsettled by the Communists' crusade, in November 1932 Hanussen hired SA members to ensure order at the Bachsale Theater where he was performing. Although his performances had not been disrupted, he wanted assurances that, should trouble occur, whoever caused it would be removed quickly from the theater. The last thing a clairvoyant needs is his mind split between his act and the fear that an audience member will rattle his concentration.

Briefly, the shows went better. Hanussen regained his confidence—until the next month, which was a near disaster. Once again Hanussen overplayed his hand, announcing that his newspaper would shift from a weekly to a daily. This meant it would compete directly with Goebbels's paper. To get even, *Der Angriff* ran a story about the "Czech Jew Hanussen," supported by details of Hanussen's parentage obtained from Ernest Juhn, a disgruntled former employee of Hanussen's. Hanussen's patron, Helldorf, was understandably shocked at the news and demanded an explanation. Hanussen—clever as ever—invented a new history for himself on the spot: He had been adopted by a kindly Jewish couple after his parents—Danish nobles—died in a mountain-climbing accident in Moravia. This accounted for his smattering of Yiddish and his affinity for Jews. Two days later, *Der Angriff*—pressured by Helldorf—retracted its story, calling Hanussen "a great man and an important force in the new Germany." Barely missing a beat, Frei's Communist paper followed by revealing that Hanussen's uncle was a famous Austrian rabbi, Daniel Prossnitz. A week later, Frei published another bombshell on his front page: a handwritten letter from a rabbi in Rumburg, a small town in northern Czechoslovakia, stating that on January 1, 1928, he had officiated at a wedding between Hanussen and Elfriede Ruhle, Hanussen's third wife. Hanussen had always skirted around the fact that he was Jewish. Now his cover was being blown.[33]

Hanussen secured two injunctions against Frei's newspaper. One forbade the paper from calling him a charlatan, swindler, or fraud. These were harming Hanussen's business, and German law considered clairvoyance a legitimate business. The other injunction forbade the paper from repeating its claim that Hanussen was related to a famous rabbi. Again, this was bad for business, especially with anti-Semitism increasing in Germany. Why needlessly remind customers that a businessman was Jewish?[34]

Nevertheless, Hanussen's problems with the press didn't stop. In late December, he sued Alfred Hurtig, the editor of *Welt am Abend*, another Communist newspaper in Berlin. The previous spring, Hurtig's paper had blamed Hanussen for the death of a race car driver. Hanussen had predicted that a Czech prince, George-Christian Lobkowicz, would die in the German Grand Prix. A few days before the race, Hanussen had told its organizers, "I see a serious accident happening to Prince Lobkowicz. He shouldn't be allowed to race. If you can stop him, please do so." The officials did nothing. The night before the race, Alfred Neubauer, the manager of the Mercedes racing team, was at a bar with some friends. Hanussen was there too. Neubauer challenged Hanussen to predict the winner of the race. Hanussen wrote two names on a piece of paper, sealed it in an envelope, handed it to the bartender, and instructed him not to open it until the next evening. "One of us at this table will win tomorrow," Hanussen told the small group. "Another will die. The two names are inside the envelope." The next night, Neubauer opened the envelope. Inside Hanussen had written the name of the winner: Manfred von Brauchitsch. He had also written the name of the driver who had died on the first lap at the race: Prince Lobkowicz.[35]

Police blamed the crash on a mechanical defect. *Welt am Abend*, blamed Hanussen, stating that his prediction had rattled the prince, who had somehow heard about it.[36]

If racing organizers stopped every driver from racing whenever a clairvoyant sensed danger, no one would ever get past the starting line: danger is endemic to racing. But Hanussen did have a point: the prince's 300-horsepower, 1,100-pound Bugatti was a runaway colossus, purring at 90 miles an hour *in first gear*. Years later, Phil Hill, a legendary race car driver, tried a Bugatti Type 54, the same model the prince raced. Hill called it the scariest car he ever drove.[37]

Hanussen withdrew his libel suit soon after the trial began in Berlin—he had just learned that the defendant was not the person who had edited the issue of *Welt am Abend* that blamed him for Lobkowicz's crash. Hanussen should have checked sooner; when he presented his passport to the judge to identify himself, his real name slipped out, the one hardly anyone in Berlin knew: Hermann Steinschneider, clearly a Jewish name. And when he introduced himself to the judge, he hoped to ingratiate himself by saying, "I represent the interests of the right-wing German parties." That did not impress the judge, who did not sympathize with the Nazis.[38]

The next day—Christmas Eve—Frei's paper ran this headline: "Hanussen Makes an Eternal Fool of Himself." The story began: "The guy's name is Hermann." Hanussen or Steinschneider—or whoever he was—did not have a good Christmas.[39]

★  ★  ★

It's uncertain how Hanussen was able to predict Lobkowicz's crash the previous summer. Did he sabotage the Bugatti? Unlikely. Hanussen associated with thugs and sociopaths, but he was not a violent person. He left that to others. Did a saboteur confide in him? Unlikely. Lobkowicz had no known enemies, and sabotage has never been suspected in any grand prix. The sport is perilous enough. Which may lead us—reluctantly and cautiously—to the possibility that, by 1932, Hanussen had developed some psychic abilities. Doubtless, for much of his career, he had elevated fakery to an art. And a living. Yet during the many years that Hanussen was honing his concentration for his act, he may have inadvertently developed skills that surprised even him, unintentionally becoming the beneficiary of his own swindle. This was a gift he had not earned, since true clairvoyance—not the show biz/show-offy kind—requires a deep, cleansing humility, and Hanussen despised humility. To Hanussen, humble people were meek and cowardly. He was strong and proud. It went against his nature to be humble, but occasionally this may have been useful for his act—humility opens us up to the obscure and the elusive and the mysterious. Hanussen's entire act—his entire life—was predicated on rarely, if ever, revealing a single flaw or a smidgen of vulnerability. So whatever abilities or powers he possessed surfaced without the requisite interior preparation, which is one reason many people didn't take him seriously: he strutted too much to be genuine. If he had been less of a peacock, he might have been more believable. And if Prince Lobkowicz had actually heard Hanussen's prediction about the crash, there's a chance he might have taken it more seriously and been more cautious that lovely May afternoon at the Avus track. Then again, maybe not. No matter how credible Hanussen was, most likely the prince would have jumped into his Bugatti and turned its outrageously overpowered engine loose on that first lap. People race cars to beat their fate and frustrate the gods, even when a seer says they are doomed.

# CHAPTER 10

# The Noose Tightens

Hanussen needed to get away from Berlin. The tensions, the pressures, the political jousting, and the lawsuits were exhausting. During the last few months of 1932, even as lawsuits were being filed (and dismissed), and as Hanussen was conclusively identified as a Jew, he went to Denmark, France, and Italy. And still while traveling farther and farther away from the German capital, he couldn't escape a premonition that followed him like a shadow: catastrophe was imminent. His best refuge, perhaps his only refuge, were the skills he had been honing for decades. Boldness and cleverness had taken him this far; surely they would not fail him now.

In Copenhagen, Hanussen stayed at the Dagmar, a hotel a notch below the city's finest—the Palads, which was only two blocks away and boasted that every one of its 175 rooms had "modern conveniences." Still, with the Dagmar's rates for a double room eight kroner below the Palads', it was wise to occasionally economize, even for Erik Jan Hanussen. After all, it was 1932, the depths of the Depression.[1]

One Danish newspaper referred to Hanussen as Copenhagen's "hottest topic." Every evening his shows at the Concert Palace were selling out, and every day from 11 a.m. to 5 p.m. private consultations were keeping him busy in his hotel room. The consultations were Hanussen's big mistake. His nighttime shows were considered entertainment; his lucrative daytime consultations were deemed probable frauds in which he crossed the line from showman to personal adviser whose insights and premonitions, he promised, would guide his clients to happier and better lives. When one paper complained that no "scientific testing" had been done on Hanussen's powers, reporters were delighted to dig up an exposé about Hanussen that had been recently published in the German journal, *Archiv für Kriminologie*.[2]

The article was by Albert Hellwig, the judge in Potsdam who had been on Hanussen's trail for almost two years now. It cataloged all of Hellwig's complaints about Hanussen: He was a fake. He couldn't cure anyone. He couldn't read the past, predict the future, or even state with any certainty when his own magazine, the *Other World*, would be published. (The first issue was scheduled for summer 1931. "Economic problems" had delayed it until late that fall.) And Hanussen, Hellwig claimed, had never solved a single criminal case. Experts, the judge wrote, "who are not 'supernormal' do a better job than [Hanussen]."[3]

Armed with Hellwig's article, reporters and police in Copenhagen began looking into Hanussen's private consultations, the same kind that had gotten him into trouble in Leitmeritz a few years earlier. A reporter visited Hanussen's room at the Dagmar just in time to overhear a young couple debating whether "to pay for a look into the future" and Hanussen's secretary telling them, "There are no guarantees. We do not give guarantees." The couple paid to have their fortunes told anyway. When they left, Hanussen and his assistant began counting their profits—it "took a long time," the reporter wrote, because there was so much cash. The reporter inquired about the fee for a consultation. "One hundred and fifty kroner for the easy ones," Hanussen's secretary answered. "Business men seeking information about the stock market pay 500 kroner. Business moguls pay 1,000." Knowing that Hanussen had done about one hundred consultations that day, the reporter calculated that the psychic had made roughly fifteen thousand kroner—about $44,000 at the time—in roughly six hours.[4]

The police in Copenhagen were not ready to move against Hanussen—there was no conclusive proof that he was a fake or that he was exploiting the people who paid him for the consultations. An ad for Hanussen's show did not endear him to the authorities, however; it included this unexpected endorsement: "The Chief Investigator says, 'Hanussen is not and cannot be a fraud!'" A few hours later, the city's chief investigator told reporters inquiring about the endorsement that he had enjoyed the one performance by Hanussen he attended: "I know for a fact that people were present who Hanussen did not know beforehand, but whose thoughts he still read." While the chief was not pleased that Hanussen was quoting him in the ads, he emphasized that he was primarily concerned about Hanussen's *private* consultations. That's where the real mischief lay. There, quite likely, Hanussen was leading people astray regarding some of the most personal issues in their lives.[5]

Hanussen had survived his trial in Leitmeritz; he might not be so lucky this time. Police in Copenhagen were investigating him, and local papers were mocking him. One ran a cartoon of a blindfolded Hanussen divining the contents of two sealed envelopes. "I think one is from the police," read the cartoon's caption, "and the other is from the tax collector." After about two weeks, it was time for Hanussen to close up shop. His secretary now told customers that he was not seeing anyone. Come back next Wednesday, she said. It was Friday. By Wednesday, he was gone.[6]

Hanussen tried to enter Norway but was turned back even after promising not to do any private readings. The kind of people who attended his type of show, Norwegian police said, were "psychologically weak," "easily swayed," or "under psychological stress." Hanussen had such a strong personality that "people would just give themselves blindly" to him. Some "might be psychologically damaged."[7]

Hanussen returned to Berlin, where he found it difficult to relax. As the Communists continued to expose him in their newspapers, the Nazis were privately deliberating about what to do with him. To them, it didn't matter if he was a fraud as a clairvoyant; it *did* matter that their ally and financial supporter was a Jew. And overall, Hanussen could see, this city was exhausted, beaten down as it was witnessing the death of democracy. People were beginning to leave. Berlin was no longer the new Athens, with artists and intellectuals arguing about arcane points of aesthetics for half the night, not with all the street fights between Nazis and Communists and wagons rumbling through the streets loaded with guns, rubber hoses, daggers, brass knuckles, iron rods, and dynamite for blowing up buildings. Berlin was a war zone, chosen carefully by the Nazis, who knew that after Moscow, the German capital was the largest Communist stronghold in the world, headquarters to a party with 250,000 members, 4,000 cells, 25 newspapers, and 87 affiliated organizations. The Communists had an efficient courier system, a network of informers, and a sophisticated surveillance operation. The Soviet Union was pouring vast funds into the city, teaching party members how to forge signatures and passports, churn out propaganda, infiltrate rival organizations, and run covert operations. Beating the Communists here would make the Nazis the saviors of capitalism.

At first, the Nazis were no match for the Communists. They soon made up for that with contributions from bankers and industrialists, with Goebbels' genius for propaganda and Hitler's for stirring passions, and with street fights that kept ordinary civilians inside, huddled and frightened. In 1932, 84 Nazis were killed in street fights; in the first half of 1933, 75 Communists were killed. Both sides were engaged in violence full throttle, turning bars, taverns, meetinghouses, apartments, streets, and bridges into battlefields. Communists fired from speeding cars into taverns frequented by SA members. In a nighttime rumble in the neighborhood of Reinickendorf, one Communist was shot and a Nazi was stabbed, both fatally. A Communist who stumbled into a bar frequented by the SA staggered out a few minutes later, a knife wound in his abdomen. He died two weeks later.

Berlin was not the only German city wracked by violence. When seven thousand Nazis marched through a Communist neighborhood in Hamburg, the Communists responded with snipers shooting from windows and rooftops. By the end of the day, 18 people were dead. In Potempa, a small village in Upper Silesia (a province in Poland that Germany claimed it possessed), five SA men barged into the apartment of a Communist, dragged him out of bed, and stomped him to death in front of his mother. The Nazis had such a tight grip on certain cities in Germany itself that many people who disagreed with them were too terrified to leave their homes. As a Communist told party members in Berlin, "there are streets [in Brunswick, a city in northwestern Germany] in which our comrades dare not be seen after dark. A Brunswick comrade reported to me that...he and his family could only leave the house after dark in disguise."[8]

After Hanussen had been hounded out of Denmark and refused entry to Norway, he had hoped Berlin would be his refuge, that he was clever enough to balance Nazi against Communist, that the Nazis would still depend on his largesse to the SA, that they would ignore that he was a Jew. But the city, and Germany, was a disaster. As quickly as possible, Hanussen left for an engagement at the Empire Theatre in Paris. Perhaps the City of Light could dispel some of the darkness descending on the clairvoyant who had brought awe and wonder to so many people.[9]

The Empire, one of the finest theaters in Paris, featured classy song-and-dance men like Maurice Chevalier and novelty acts like Keith Clark, a dapper man with a pencil-thin mustache, brilliant timing, and a routine he called "Silks Supreme"—a large scarf materialized out of thin air, then divided into another scarf of equal size. When Clark tied them together, somehow a third scarf appeared out of nowhere, then a fourth, and a fifth, and a sixth until 18 scarves manifested from the "fourth dimension" and the audience was as charmed as it was mystified.[10]

Hanussen was no Keith Clark and definitely no Maurice Chevalier. But he did negotiate a fairly decent deal for himself: a guaranteed minimum of 5,200 francs a day, plus 30 percent of ticket sales until they reached 30,000 francs. The Empire called his act "Les Merveilles de la Telepathie"—the Marvels of Telepathy. The problem was that it wasn't marvelous. The audience was bored with its languid pace: Everything Hanussen said had to be translated into French. This was no way to establish rapport with the twelve hundred people in the audience. The critic who called Hanussen mediocre was kinder than the one who called him horrible. Hanussen lasted three days at the Empire.[11]

Before leaving Paris, Hanussen did one more show—at the Club du Faubourg, really more of a salon devoted to ideas than a cabaret with pretty girls and smooth song-and-dance men. The Faubourg hosted discussions three times a week, usually about politics, medicine, or literature. Leo Poldes, the socialist who ran the club, hated fascists yet sometimes invited them to speak: He wanted to transcend ideology—or, at least, to understand it in all its forms. The Faubourg was about seeking truth, not defining it. Occasionally, a night was devoted to the occult. That's where Hanussen came in. Before the show, Poldes thought he would have some fun. Walking up to Hanussen backstage, he held out his palm and asked Hanussen what he saw. Hanussen stared at Poldes's palm and refused to answer. Poldes insisted that Hanussen tell him. "Sir," said Hanussen, "you will die a violent death." Amused, Poldes took Hanussen's palm. "And you, sir," he said, "will be murdered."[12]

Poldes died in 1970 of natural causes; Hanussen would die almost four decades before him.

★  ★  ★

Hanussen's life was always marked by urgency. Now he was almost manic: a fantasist losing control of his fantasies. Copenhagen had been a disaster. Paris wasn't much better. Berlin was where he had a life and a wife and a career and friends, and fancy cars and a fancy apartment. It was also where Nazis and Communists were waiting for him. Like them, Hanussen believed in manipulation, that all it took to reach your audience was hammering away at a few points again and again, appealing to their emotions, not their intellect. The Nazis did this brilliantly, with a venom that reduced Hanussen's theatrics to childish, useless entertainments. Hanussen had spent decades mastering a certain playfulness: For him, everything was ironic. Nothing was taken too seriously. But the Nazis did not understand irony, and they took everything immensely seriously. They were also beginning to dislike Hanussen intensely, with all this talk of his being a Jew and the nephew of a rabbi. So before boarding the train to Berlin, Hanussen needed to make one more stop, one that might save him from ever seeing that city again.

Hanussen had not seen Therese, his second wife, since their divorce in 1924. She was now living in northern Italy with her second husband and with Erika, the daughter she had with Hanussen. Therese didn't miss life with Hanussen, but she was still fond of him.

Therese lived in a salmon-colored, three-story house in Merano, a prosperous town cradled in a deep valley in the Italian Alps. She often sat on the balcony, watching her daughter play in the family's large yard. Therese was content amid this beauty and domesticity. Now Hanussen was on his way. Why, Therese wasn't sure, but that rascal, she thought with some affection, was always up to something.

Hanussen stayed for eight days at the Hotel Meranerhof, one of the best hotels in town, with a spacious garden in the rear with palm trees and cedars of Lebanon and a patio where breakfast was served in the fresh morning air. The hotel was an easy walk to Therese's house, about ten blocks away. Hanussen went there every day. He played with Erika, then 12 years old and fond of white, lacy dresses and high-button shoes. He hadn't seen her since she was four. He spoiled her with toys and candy and bought her a camera and other presents that made her feel special and loved. He was getting to know his daughter, to whom he essentially was a stranger. He hoped that if he could not directly convince Therese to do what he wanted, perhaps he could convince her through their child, who was the one thing they truly had in common at this point.

"You know, Risa," he said to Therese one day, using his nickname for her, "I have had many women, but there has been only one Risa." She laughed. Another day he proposed that he leave Fritzi (his wife who was waiting for him in Berlin) and that Therese leave Fuchs (who was busy running his brewery) and they run away to New York—the two of them and Erika: again, a family. Therese blushed, amused that Hanussen had come this far to ask *that*! He hadn't changed; he was as lovable as ever. But he deserved only one answer, which was the one she gave him. "Oh, Hanussen, you're still the same. You always want the other man's wife." Her best offer was that Hanussen could take Erika "on a little cruise in your yacht, but you can't have me."[13]

Hanussen returned to Berlin. Somehow, he hoped that neither the Nazis nor the Communists would deter him from living the life he had always imagined for himself here. His cleverness—and his obliviousness to politics and the sinister motives of some people with whom he was associating—had taken him this far in life. He was sure it could take him further. And yet the worse life got in Berlin, the more he would romanticize what might have been had he remained in Merano with Therese and Erika.

A few weeks after returning to Germany, Hanussen sent his daughter some photos of his yacht and a note:

> *My dear girl Erika,*
> *Do you think of me sometimes? Well then, please write me a letter from*
> *time to time. How is your bike? Can you ride it well? For Christmas,*
> *I will send you the photos that the two of us took and something else*
> *that you will like. My regards to everybody!*

In the left-hand margin, he scribbled: "In summer, we will sail on my boat."[14]

There would be no summer for Hanussen.

★ ★ ★

In one letter to Therese, Hanussen advised that he had a new address in Berlin—Lietzenburgerstrasse 16 in the desirable neighborhood of Charlottenburg. Given the political situation, moving about a mile was providential. Hanussen's previous apartment at 17 Bendlerstrasse had been adjacent to the Bendlerblock, the epicenter of the German military. Hanussen's letter to Therese was dated February 4, 1933—the day after Hitler met in the Bendlerblock with Germany's high command to lay out his plans for lebensraum—living space. In Hitler's scheme, Germany would secretly rearm, then conquer the enormous lands to the east for farming and homes and so Germans could psychologically stretch themselves: they felt like the Versailles Treaty was choking them. But it would take more than a one mile move for Hanussen to distance himself from the Nazis: any Jew in Berlin would soon discover that Jews needed their own version of living space, and that there was never enough. The city was closing in on everyone the Nazis deemed undesirable. It was especially closing in on Hanussen.[15]

These were not good times. Hanussen's plans for a spa in Godesberg had fallen through; Albert Hellwig and the German Society Against Medical Fraud were on his trail; Communists and Nazis were watching every move he made; and many cynics were saying he didn't read minds—he just read signals that he was getting from his aides about some people in his audience. The best decision he had made recently was moving to an apartment that was so large he didn't have to do his private consultations elsewhere. Until now, he had held his consultations in a room at the Esplanade, one of the city's more elegant hotels. The kaiser, before the war, held exclusive, men-only dinners at the hotel, and, in the 1920s, film stars like Charlie Chaplin and Greta Garbo stayed there when they were in town. Holding his consultations at the Esplanade had given Hanussen a certain cachet—a celebrated address for a shady line of work. Of all the people who went there to see Hanussen, one that he never forgot was a wealthy American who, Hanussen knew immediately, would disregard everything he told her. Before she even opened her mouth, he told her, "You want to ask me if you should sell that stock you got from your husband. This will cost you one thousand marks because you are a rich woman and because you will make a lot of money if you follow my advice. You will pay me the thousand marks. You will listen to my advice. And you will not follow it."

The woman paid, she listened, and she ignored Hanussen's advice. She also lost a lot of money.[16]

Hanussen liked that he could now hold his consultations in his large new apartment on Lietzenburgerstrasse. He didn't like the attacks on him, which were becoming more frequent and more shrill. To defend his honor, he issued a challenge in February: 10,000 marks to anyone who could prove he was receiving secret signals from his aides or that during his shows he read the minds of people he already knew. For this challenge, Hanussen sold out the Beethovensaal Theater, a massive hall usually reserved for the Berlin Philharmonic.

At the start of the show, Hanussen assured his audience that he had never met anyone he was about to call on. And indeed, everyone he did call on confirmed this: the gentleman who Hanussen said was worried about someone who was missing, and the man who Hanussen said had attempted suicide, and the woman who had made a complete recovery from what doctors had mistakenly diagnosed as an incurable disease.[17]

Other than the man who said Hanussen was "half right" about him and another man who said the clairvoyant was entirely wrong, Hanussen did quite well. No one went home with the reward and at least one person—a writer—left the theater enthralled. By proving "his skill in an atmosphere similar to a court trial," he wrote, Hanussen's victory "will live on as the enemies of the occult fall into their graves." But this writer, a columnist for an occult magazine, was one of Hanussen's faithful.

Ominously, another newspaper, *Die Wahrheit*, wasn't convinced Hanussen was anything but a showman. *Die Wahrheit* noted that when Hanussen invited a woman from the audience to the stage to write down the name of someone he had to find, Hanussen turned away so he couldn't see what she was writing. But he turned back before she finished and also before she sealed the note in an envelope. The impression that Hanussen had glanced at the name, *Die Wahrheit* reported, was reinforced when Hanussen asked her "if she had written the first letter in a unique way, say a 'D' that resembled a 'B.'" Presumably, Hanussen did this to gain more information about what he had briefly seen. After she put the slip of paper in an envelope, Hanussen told her to firmly hold his wrist—Hanussen was still muscle reading 17 years after Joe Labero taught him how to do it—and they began walking toward the person whose name was sealed in the envelope. If *Die Wahrheit* speculated correctly that most people wrote the name of someone who sat with them, maybe even of someone who sat right next to them, then this improved Hanussen's chances of knowing where to go since he had seen where the woman was sitting.[18]

At the end of the first act, Hanussen asked the audience to jot down dates on slips of paper during the intermission. They could give these to his aides in a small room just off the lobby. When the show resumed, he would announce what occurred on each date. As the audience was milling about the lobby, *Die Wahrheit* reported, some people were bragging that *their* date would stump Hanussen; some people—even more foolishly—were telling their friends what had happened on that date. It was remarkable, the paper noted dryly, "that only those ladies and gentlemen who... [were] talking rather loudly" were allowed in the room where Hanussen's assistants were accepting the slips of paper with dates. And since only one person was allowed in the room at a time, all that was necessary for Hanussen to match a date with an event was to hire assistants with good hearing and an excellent memory.[19]

That *Die Wahrheit* was leading the charge against Hanussen was not a healthy sign. The paper was rabidly anti-Semitic. If such a rag was calling

Hanussen a liar and a swindler and revealing his secrets, then surely he had not impressed every National Socialist. Every day Hanussen's life was becoming more of a balancing act, with Communists and socialists crusading against him and the Nazis increasingly disgusted with him because he was a fake. Or a Jew. Or both. Running away to New York with Therese and Erika had never looked so good.

*Hanussen demonstrating his clairvoyant abilities by finding an object that had been hidden near the Potsdamer Platz in Berlin, April 29, 1932. (Imagno–ullstein bild/The Granger Collection)*

*Hanussen using his hypnotic powers at an elegant ball at the Berlin Zoo, 1932. (ullstein bild/The Granger Collection)*

*Prince Lobkowicz (right) inspecting his Bugatti Type 54 the day before the 1932 German Grand Prix. As Hanussen predicted, the prince died in the race. (© Science & Society Picture Library)*

*Dr. Albert Hellwig, the Potsdam judge who persisted in exposing Hanussen from the late 1920s onward. "People want real occult experiences," Hellwig said. "They also want the truth." (Courtesy of Dr. Tillman Hellwig)*

*Street fighting between Nazis and Communists, Berlin, early 1930s. As tensions mounted, Hanussen sought protection by financing and socializing with the Nazis. (Photo Archive, Yad Vashem, Jerusalem)*

*Count Wolfgang Heinrich von Helldorf, Hanussen's prime patron among the Nazis. First the head of the storm troopers in Berlin, then the capital's police chief, Helldorf counted on Hanussen to bail him out of his many debts. Helldorf also organized some of the worst pogroms against Berlin's Jews. (ullstein bild/The Granger Collection)*

*On January 30, 1933, Nazis celebrated Hitler's being named chancellor with a vast torchlight parade in Berlin. Hanussen had predicted this would be "a fortunate day. Good for all kinds of undertakings." (U.S. Holocaust Memorial Museum)*

Hitler and Ernst Roehm, close friends since 1920. Hitler had Roehm assassinated in 1934 during a power struggle. Hitler, Heinrich Himmler, Hermann Goering, and the army were on one side; Roehm and his storm troopers were on the other. (Library of Congress, Prints & Photos Div., 3rd Reich Collection)

*Almost certainly, the order to kill Hanussen originated with Roehm, who commanded the storm troopers throughout Germany. Here, Roehm's homosexuality is ridiculed in a caricature in a German exile magazine in 1933. (U.S. Holocaust Memorial Museum)*

*Karl Ernst, Helldorf's successor as head of the Berlin storm troopers, ordered SA Major Wilhelm Ohst to kill Hanussen. When Ohst protested, Ernst glowered, "Are you going soft on me?" (Photo Archive, Yad Vashem, Jerusalem)*

*The storm trooper prison on General Pape-strasse where Hanussen was killed. To this day, the upper levels are used for offices, and the basement level is divided into cells where prisoners were tortured. (Arthur J. Magida)*

*Hanussen's tombstone in the Southwest Cemetery near Berlin. (Arthur J. Magida)*

# CHAPTER 11

# The Fuehrer's Court Jew

By January 1933, as President Hindenburg was nearing his decision to name Hitler chancellor, every issue of Hanussen's newspaper, *Erik Jan Hanussen's Berliner Wochenschau,* was cheering Hitler on to the finish line: "Hitler Takes the Offensive." "Germany Will Rise to Power." "Hitler Doesn't Give Up Before the Big Decision." Lavish photos showed the fuehrer surrounded by fawning storm troopers or accepting a bouquet from a child, her eyes a blend of curiosity, fear, and adoration. When Hitler finally became chancellor on January 30, Hanussen's paper crowed, simply and jubilantly, "Hitler on Top." A large photo showed a stern Hitler. Under it was this quote: "My power will be unlimited." The words were Hitler's.[1]

Hanussen had predicted that January 30 would be a "generally fortunate day. Good for all kinds of undertakings." Not, as it turned out, good for unions, liberals, Communists, socialists, intellectuals, Jews, gays, Gypsies, writers, scientists, or clergy, for anyone with a good heart and an open mind. But a great day for the brown-shirted goons who rushed to the grandest boulevard in Berlin—Unter der Linden—and marched for hours, each thug carrying a torch. The parade of fire passed under the Brandenburg Gate in disciplined formation, then down Wilhelmstrasse, where the marchers paid homage to feeble old Hindenburg, who watched them from a window of the presidential palace, and then past the Chancellery under the proud, triumphant eyes of their fuehrer. That night, one Nazi said years later, "Everyone felt the same—that things will get better." Edgar Mowrer, an American in Berlin at the time, was less sanguine. Hitler's victory, he said, was "the rejection by Germany of 1,000 years of civilization."[2]

Until that night, the Nazis had rarely felt comfortable in Berlin. It was never their stronghold, not with a majority of residents consistently voting for the Communists or Social Democrats. Hitler saw the city as a hotbed of modernity, capitalism, socialism, and Jews—though the city's 160,000 Jews made up barely 4 percent of its population. Feeling that they had seized the capital from their enemies, the Nazis made preparations to overhaul Berlin politically and physically, planning eventually to rename it Germania and carving vast, oversized boulevards throughout the city, with one—the Konigsplatz—bordered by the fuehrer's palace on one side (to be completed in 1950—these people planned ahead) and a great hall on the other side that could accommodate 150,000 people, all gathered under a 954-foot-high dome to hear Hitler speak in a space 16 times larger than St. Peter's Cathedral in Rome. Three miles to the south would be a great arch—two and a half times taller than the Arc de Triomphe in Paris—etched with the names of the 1.8 million Germans who had died in the Great War. Germania would be the grandest city in Europe, a testament to the man who had raised the nation from angst and shame and established it as the paragon of the world.[3]

The night that Hitler became chancellor, people gathered to celebrate in Hanussen's apartment. Nazis—some still dependent on handouts from this clairvoyant Jew, some still uncertain about how anti-Semitic they needed to be in the new regime—strutted about in their uniforms. Even the dethroned royalty who were there, like the fourth son of the kaiser, were joyous about the Nazis' victory, believing that Hitler would restore the monarchy. Some second-rate writers were celebrating their belief that their ordinary and uninspired prose would come into fashion under the Nazis. Everyone was elated that Hitler was chancellor: thanks to him, Germany was on the threshold of a new and thrilling glory. But they were also there to pay homage to Hanussen: after all, the clairvoyant had predicted Hitler's success, worked for it, and convinced millions of people that it would happen, that it *had* to happen, that the stars and fate and destiny were all aligned to make it happen. On this night, Hanussen was their guru, their sage, their prophet. He knew the future, and he knew it would flower under the swastika.[4]

While Hanussen loved the obeisance, he was smart enough to know that he could trust people in the room only so far. Late in the evening, when his guests had drunk too much, he reportedly photographed Count Helldorf hugging a beautiful Jewish woman. Several guests wanted the photo: What a lark! Helldorf and a Jewess! Hanussen allegedly sent it to a friend in Holland the next day for safekeeping, along with instructions to publish it if something happened to Hanussen. As he went to bed, he thought to himself, "I'm now the most secure Jew in Germany."[5]

But no one was safe in the new Germany—not the rich, the poor, the left, the right. Not even the allies of the Nazis or the Nazis themselves. Some were already plotting against each other: the Nazis were less a unified political organization than a loose alliance of scheming paranoids—a Germanic gaggle of cabals, with conspiracies and back-stabbing as essential as intrigue and ideology. Jews, of course, were in the most precarious position. Although Hanussen thought he had been assiduously playing all the angles with the Nazis for almost two years, the many recent newspaper articles that focused on his being a Jew were ruining this moment for him, now that Hitler was actually in office. Hanussen had never denied that he was Jewish. In fact, each of his weddings had been held in synagogues, and his divorces had been Jewish divorces. And adopting a stage name like Erik Jan Hanussen was no different from the many entertainers who masked their religious identity or simply wanted a classier name when they performed. Despite all the work he had been doing for the Nazis, Hanussen's Jewishness was a liability now, and he knew it.[6]

But Hanussen was not the only Jew who was pro-Nazi or who believed some good could come from Hitler. As far away as Salonika in Greece, a Jew who ran the local branch of a German firm raised a flag with a swastika over the heads of his 15 Jewish employees. In Berlin, the head of the Association of German National Jews defended Hitler from the "despicably false" charges of anti-Semitism and praised him for a "revolution so bloodless and so quiet as has not been seen in centuries." In Frankfurt, Max Warburg, a Jewish banker who would soon be helping the Nazis bring economic stability to Germany, pleaded for the protests against Hitler in other countries to end. "Please let us settle our internal problems," he begged his friends who lived abroad. "... We Germans will settle our problems if only we are left alone." Even some socialists were sure that sensible Germans—and a sensible world—would realize that Hitler and his claque were psychotic and would force them out of office in no more than six months. The optimism wasn't limited to Germans. A veteran observer of Germany stationed at the U.S. embassy in Berlin cabled back to Washington that "there is much reason to believe that the Chancellor, Mr. Hitler, does not approve of the indiscriminate and general action that has been taken against Jews.... He is believed to be very moderate in his views in this respect." A reporter from the *New York Times* agreed. "Hitler," he wrote, "will abandon his anti-Semitic stand."[7]

The most bizarre of the pro-Hitler Jews in Germany was Max Naumann, a lawyer who ran the League of German Nationalist Jews. The league attracted solidly middle-class Jews—doctors, lawyers, bankers—who were obsessed with assimilation. Naumann wanted Jews to be invisible. Those Jews who had emigrated from eastern Europe and "looked Jewish" should be expelled. They were an embarrassment. The Zionists who were kvetching about a homeland should shut up. They were annoying the gentiles. And Hitler? A misunderstood idealist who had outgrown his youthful anti-Semitism. Naumann urged Jews to celebrate Christmas as a national holiday and observe the Sabbath on Sunday like everyone else. "We reject Yahweh, the old tribal God of the Asiatic nomadic horde," Naumann exhorted. "We have a German god." Naumann's league sickened the few foreigners who knew about it. One American imagined these Jews shouting, as they marched out of their meetings, "Down with us! Down with us!," their arms stiffly raised in the Nazi salute. Naumann died of cancer in May 1939, his faith in Hitler still intact.[8]

Hanussen was different from those sycophants. He was not middle class. He was not a nationalist. Nor did he did run an organization or an institution. Like many entertainers, he had always resided along the fringes of society. Pleased that he had been smart enough to choose the winning side in the political wars that had shaken Germany, and aware that Hitler would rule with an iron fist, Hanussen's primary concern was staying on the right side of that fist.

With that in mind, Hanussen's predictions about the Nazis in early 1933 became more glowing than ever. They also became more desperate. In six years, Hanussen said, not a single Marxist would be left in Germany. This was four years ahead of Hitler's own timetable for getting rid of them. And when dead bodies were found on the streets of Berlin—the victims of homicides and street fights—Hanussen immediately knew who the killers were. "Look around the labor unions," he advised the police. "The Socialists are killing their own comrades to make martyrs and gain sympathy." When the government seized the headquarters of the Communist Party, Hanussen was relieved that Germany had been liberated from "the red plague." The Communists, he wrote, "didn't have a glorious end. . . . It was more like a bully getting his bottom smacked after bothering peaceful people for too long. For years, I have dreamt of this day. Hitler will make sure they don't come back."[9]

And in an open letter to Hitler published in Hanussen's newspaper a few days after the Nazi became chancellor, Hanussen declared that his "only mission" was "to say what my second sight tells me—I foresaw your coming and I truthfully spoke of it." For this, Hanussen had been ridiculed as a "Nazi prophet." His only comfort, he assured Hitler—almost groveling now—was "knowing I was in good company: yours!"[10]

Hanussen reiterated what he had said in so many of his predictions: There were "no coincidences." Hitler's destiny "had been long written." Those torches at the rallies in Berlin the day Hitler became chancellor "did not illuminate only . . . [Hitler's] sober and serious face. They have been glowing in the hearts of millions of Germans since the day they realized: Hitler it is!" The river of torches the night that Hitler ascended to the chancellorship had redeemed the honor of every German killed in the war, stanched the threat from Moscow, and brought hope to millions of Germans who were hungry or homeless or had no jobs. Hitler would return Germans "to their place in the sun" while governing with wisdom and justice on behalf of "any decent person who honestly wants the best for Germany"—all of which can be read as a plea for mercy if Hitler turned on Hanussen, for surely Hitler was a "decent person" who wanted "the best for Germany" and, implicitly, would not harm anyone.[11]

In one way, Hanussen deviated publicly from the Nazi party line: he didn't buy their obscene fantasy about ruling for a thousand years. Hitler's reign, Hanussen said, would end as soon as Germany was strong and stable and an equal in the family of nations. A conservative and more democratic government would follow the Nazis. Was this Hanussen's hedge against repercussions if Hitler was thrown out of office? If that occurred, Hanussen could claim that he had only been arguing that a few years of Hitler was the medicine Germany needed to get back on its feet.

Hanussen closed his letter to Hitler as abjectly as it began. "Mister Reich Chancellor, stating this again and again"—celebrating Hitler and his cause—"is my purpose in life, one that reached its fruition the moment you happily became chancellor."[12]

★ ★ ★

All that remained was for Hanussen to wish that Hitler actually read the letter. And pray that the fuehrer did not recognize a fellow con-artist, although there were other similarities between the two men. Both had strained relations with their fathers: Hanussen thought his was a failure—a "poor devil" and a wretch who "worked all his life for nothing"; Hitler thought his father was a brute. (Alois Hitler often beat Adolf with a whip.) When they were about the same age, both Hitler and Hanussen tried to run away from home. Hanussen was quite successful: his life on the road was the beginning of his life as an enter-tainer. Hitler didn't get too far: his father caught him and locked him in his room. Both men idealized their mothers, who died when they were fairly young. Both overcame poverty, hardship, deprivation, and barely any formal education. And both believed they communed with forces beyond themselves. In 1914, for instance, while serving in the

Austrian army during the Great War, Hitler left his regimental commander's tent just minutes before British artillery smashed into it, killing three men and seriously wounding Hitler's commander. Clearly, Hitler later concluded, he was being saved for another day. And when he began speaking in public after the war, Hitler was sure he was tapping into a dimension that even he did not understand: "I'm now and then aware that it is not I who is speaking, but that something speaks through me. . . . Now and then, ideas, concepts, views occur to me that I read nowhere, heard nowhere and never before thought." Hitler's epiphanies and revelations and sermons—some early Nazis called him a priest—swept his audiences toward a collective salvation and a soothing, if desperate, redemption.[13]

With Hitler, as with Hanussen, speech, gesture, drama, and a colossal sense of anticipation in their audience helped them sell the illusions they were peddling. But unlike Hanussen, Hitler didn't have to sell himself as a clairvoyant. He let others do that for him.

Hitler and Hanussen were similar in another way: early in their careers, each knew his own shortcomings and began figuring out how to compensate for them. Hanussen didn't really hypnotize Marta so she would have superhuman strength, but she was a good enough actress to convince audiences she was under his power. And Hitler, a naïf at first when it came to speaking in public, was brilliant at learning the stagecraft of speech making: when to glower, stare, pause, or peer into the distance, searching for a meaning that only he could grasp. He learned when to gesture with one hand or with two hands; when to hammer in the air or on the podium with one fist or two fists; when to beseech the crowd before him with outstretched hands or appeal to the heavens with one arm raised skyward as his eyes gazed toward the holy and mysterious firmament, the realm from which Hitler had descended, according to the mythology that was evolving about him. All this took time and effort, and Hitler—and his Nazi friends—were brilliant at it, shaping the myth early on in his career that he was a demigod, chanting incantations at the podium that reduced grown women to tears and stirred brave men to action. In time, Hitler grew into the myth. And as he did, many Germans accepted the illusion that he was inevitable and unstoppable, a holy gift for a people who needed the comforting rumor that a messiah had been sent to lift them from their suffering, their pain, and their sorrow.[14]

And yet the plot thickens: Why did Hanussen need to write a letter to get a message to Hitler, especially with half of Berlin certain Hanussen not only knew Hitler but that the clairvoyant had been advising the fuehrer for years about how to give speeches and whom to choose as his closest aides? Some rumors even claimed that Hanussen, the savant of black magic, exorcised evil spirits that were blocking Hitler's route to power. Were all those stories bogus—efforts to discredit both Hanussen and Hitler, tarring one man for associating with a monster and the other for associating with a Jew? The truth, while slightly more nuanced than the rumors, is enormously disturbing since anyone—especially a Jew—who helped Hitler was an accomplice to the worst atrocities of the twentieth century.

But how did the two meet in the first place? One story had Hanussen and Hitler meeting as far back as a dinner party at the home of a wealthy socialite in Berlin in 1919. There, Hanussen reportedly told Hitler, a newcomer to public life, "If you are serious about politics, Herr Hitler, why don't you learn how to speak?" Under Hanussen's tutelage, according to this story, Hitler worked hard, sharpening his power to deliver words that went straight to the heart of his listeners, filling them with fear, loathing, and hope. Hanussen taught Hitler hypnotic hand gestures that let him appeal directly to the subconscious of audiences. With each speech, thanks to Hanussen, Hitler drew larger crowds. He also became increasingly adept at stirring them into a full, barely controlled frenzy. By the mid-1920s, a new Hitler—Hanussen's Hitler—was striding into massive arenas. Wearing a trench coat and followed by his entourage, he took to the podium. As his right arm went out in the Nazi salute, the music swelled and flags passed beneath him, carried on glittering standards as storm troopers stood bolt upright while their leader's words spilled out in a torrent and his gestures held his audience spellbound, mesmerized by the human cyclone in front of them. When interrupted by applause, Hitler extended his hands theatrically; when stressing certain words and themes, he drove his audience toward hate and venom; when attacking the Jews, he stopped just short of foaming at the mouth. *This*, it was said, was oration—Hanussen-style. *This* is what Hitler had learned from the master, Erik Jan Hanussen.[15]

Another version of this story appeared in the July 5, 1933, issue of *Vu*, a French magazine. The journalist Francois Lassagne claimed that Hitler and Hanussen initially met in the early 1930s in the home of a mutual friend—Hans Ewers, a second-rate novelist. Hitler had seen Hanussen's show, liked it, and knew that Hanussen admired the Nazis. Hanussen and Hitler began talking and found they shared a deep faith in the occult. Hanussen then read Hitler's horoscope and his palm. They were consistent: Hitler's power and fortune would only increase. Hanussen soon became valuable to Hitler, teaching him how to use his eyes—habitually small and sunken—and widen them in the manner of fakirs from India: all knowing, all seeing. Hanussen showed Hitler how to summon the full force of his personality; how to release everything thatwas within him and withhold nothing; how to show his country, his enemies, his friends, and even himself the depths and the many complicated levels of his soul.[16]

But Hitler didn't need a coach. Even when he first started speaking in public not long after the Great War, people called him magnetic and "a force of nature." Hanussen had fierce concentration and a persuasive manner—useful skills before an audience. But his voice was strident and a bit reedy, and the speed and intensity of his speech—he often over-pronounced words or rolled his *r*'s semi-operatically—became tiresome. Hanussen was adamant and direct, qualities Hitler certainly cultivated. But he cultivated them on his terms, not Hanussen's. Hitler didn't need anyone to tell him how to express his furies, and his maniacal rants were nothing like the measured, controlled presence that Hanussen displayed onstage. Hanussen sought respect from his audience; Hitler sought fear. Surely, though, one quality they both shared was an appreciation of the power of suggestion. Initially, Hitler had relied in almost equal measure on the power of his personality and on the specifics of his political agenda to sway audiences. Given its radicalism, Hitler had been foolishly candid in *Mein Kampf* about his long-term goals. His speeches were another matter: with these, he was cagier and more oblique, aware that he could use his hypnotic ranting to convince Germans that he would rescue them from their pain and deliver them to their dreams. Hanussen, too, knew the power of persuasion: how to convince an audience that his powers were not mere stagecraft but the stuff of reality. And of mystery.

It's also improbable that Hanussen helped Hitler orchestrate his rallies. Hanussen's aesthetics didn't extend to the virile showmanship of the Nazis. This was beyond him. It was beyond almost anyone except the fascist messiah and his overcompensating stagehands, all stoked on their fanaticism and their warped, oversized sense of theatrics.

Slightly more probable are the stories that Hitler's photographer introduced Hitler and Hanussen sometime in the 1920s. Heinrich Hoffman had known Hitler since 1922. They were quite close. Before Hoffman was involved with the Nazis, he had moved in a vaguely bohemian crowd in Munich, once photographing the young French artist Marcel Duchamp. And soon after they met, Hoffman wrote in his memoir, Hitler confessed to him that he feared he had limits as a speaker: "In a small, intimate circle, I never know what to say. I should only disappoint.... As a speaker either at a family gathering or a funeral, I'm no use at all." So perhaps Hoffman took this as a hint to find Hitler a speaking coach.[17]

Yet there is nothing in Hoffman's memoir, *Hitler Was My Friend*, about Hanussen. In the book, Hoffman drops a lot of names and is often frank, even cruel, about Hitler's aides and associates. Eva Braun, for instance, was "a simple, pretty and inconsequential girl." Surely, if Hoffman had introduced Hitler and Hanussen, he would have bragged about it: after all, in 1955, when the book was published, Hoffman was totally unrepentant about anything he had done as Nazi Party member #427.[18]

There was yet another story about how Hitler and Hanussen met, and this version has the ring of truth. It is set in the early 1930s in Berlin. By then both Hanussen and Hitler were quite famous, and, thanks to Hanussen's friendship with Helldorf, both moved in similar circles. They met in the restaurant of the Kaiserhof, the hotel where Hitler was then living. Warmly telling Hanussen that his experiments with clairvoyance fascinated him, Hitler assured him that the Nazis would research the occult extensively and offer serious courses devoted to it in universities when they ran Germany. After that, Hanussen and Hitler were often seen conferring in whispers at the Kaiserhof, the clairvoyant giving the Nazi his latest predictions, assuring Hitler that the entire universe—stars, moons, and planets—was aligned in his favor: all of creation was rooting for this man who would set the world right. Herr Hitler, Hanussen would say, you are no mere politician who kisses babies and gives speeches until you are hoarse. You are the destiny of Germany: the final alchemy of history, a salve for a noble and suffering people, a blessed redeemer and a heroic savior. Hanussen's blandishments were another voice in the choir that had clustered around

Hitler, all assuring him that his long years of wandering in the political wilderness were nearing their end. Hitler may have been skeptical of psychics, but, for now, he was not inclined to turn away anyone who was optimistic about his future—and surely not the celebrated Erik Jan Hanussen, who was influencing millions of people every week through the predictions in his newspaper. Hitler was a master tactician. Indulging Hanussen was another way for Hitler to sway the masses and convince them that a Nazi takeover was inevitable.[19]

These meetings at the Kaiserhof would have occurred before *Berlin am Morgen* published a letter from a rabbi confirming that Hanussen was Jewish. Whenever they occurred, Hitler must have always had a terrible cold: he was supposed to be able to smell a Jew ten miles away.[20]

*  *  *

There were innumerable other stories about how the relationship between Hanussen and Hitler evolved as Hitler marched toward his domination of Germany. Consider the one about Hitler summoning Hanussen in December 1932. Jittery about his future, Hitler asked Hanussen what lay ahead. Hanussen cast a generally favorable horoscope—only a few minor obstacles stood between Hitler and power, and they needed to be removed. Hanussen volunteered to do this by plucking a mandrake (a root in the shape of a man) from the yard of a butcher in the town where Hitler had been born. Returning from this bizarre mission on New Year's Day 1933, Hanussen presented the mandrake to Hitler along with this oblique prediction that he would be chancellor by the end of the month:

> The way to the goal is still blocked,
> The right helpers not yet gathered,
> But in three days—from three countries,

*Through the bank everything will change!*
*And then on the day before the end of the month,*
*You stand at your goal and a turning point!*
*No eagle could carry you on your path,*
*The termites had to gnaw your way!*
*To the ground falls what was rotten and withered.*
*It already creaks in the beams!*[21]

This story and poem appear in *Adolf Hitler*, a biography by the Pulitzer Prize-winning historian John Toland. Hitler, Toland notes, "must surely have been startled" by the poem's allusion to an important meeting in three days—that was when Hitler was secretly meeting with a banker who planned to pressure Hindenburg to make Hitler chancellor. How did Hanussen know this? Easily, says Toland. Hanussen was "a clever fraud who based his predictions on information from reliable sources." And the phrase "through the bank" in the fourth line of the poem—in German, "durch die bank"—may have been a way for Hanussen to cover several possibilities, since the phrase also means "across the board" or "in its entirety." When substituting that meaning, the line now reads "Everything will change radically," a goal clearly synonymous with Hitler's ambitions.[22]

How plausible is any of this? There is no record that Hanussen ever used mandrakes to exorcise anything, that he even knew how to do this, or that he wrote predictions in poetry. Or—and this may be key—that Hitler was so superstitious that he would collude in such an adventure.

But perhaps the most ludicrous story about Hitler and Hanussen was set in the days leading up to January 30, 1933, when Hitler became chancellor. Sensing that Hitler was about to gain the political post, Hanussen requested a meeting with him. Certain that the Nazis would persecute the Jews, he hoped for assurances that his service to Hitler would save him. Don't worry, my good friend, Hitler said affectionately. Anointing Hanussen an "honorary Aryan," he handed him a note warning that anyone who bothered the distinguished Erik Jan Hanussen would feel the feel force of Hitler's wrath. "Was du mir geleistet hast, Erik," Hitler assured Hanussen, "werde ich dir niemals vergessen." "I will never forget, Erik, what you have done for me." "Tears came to the soothsayer's eyes," according to this story. "Hanussen wanted to kiss the Fuehrer's hands, but Hitler raised his bent head and embraced him. Appreciatively, Hanussen raised his right arm: 'Heil Hitler.'"[23]

These stories—and more—form a larger story: Many people wanted Hanussen to know Hitler, and some would go to any lengths to prove this. They knew that Hanussen and Helldorf were friends. Extending that link to Hitler ratcheted up the improbability of a Jew associating with Nazis. Yet during a French television show about Hanussen in 1971, only one of the five participants expressed the belief the clairvoyant had known Hitler. The one holdout was an author, Pierre Mariel, who was certain that Hanussen had taught Hitler hypnosis, although Mariel offered no evidence to support this notion. Strongly disagreeing was a left-wing German editor who had waged a campaign against Hanussen in 1932 and 1933. The editor had intensely disliked Hanussen and now he was sure that the clairvoyant "never gave advice to Hitler. He never saw Hitler. In the 1930s, the German people were hoping for a miracle. ... Hanussen did on a small scale what Hitler did on a large scale."[24]

That should settle the question about Hanussen's working closely with Hitler. It doesn't, partly because after discrediting Hanussen from the 1930s through the early 1970s, the editor wasn't about to give him any slack. Also, many other people—credible people—said they saw Hanussen and Hitler at the Kaiserhof. Hanussen's aides supported these stories by saying that the psychic was always running off to see Hitler or that the two men often spoke on the phone.

Hanussen was many things, but he wasn't stupid. If it was true that Hanussen and Hitler met and that Hanussen helped the fuehrer, Hanussen was more than incredibly naive: Anyone with half a brain would have known not to test the Nazis with only wit and cunning. Yet these were Hanussen's only weapons. Somehow he believed he could survive the Nazis' vitriol, perhaps even change or moderate it. A man on a fool's errand, quite possibly Hanussen believed he was operating in a long (and not necessarily noble) tradition in Europe: the tradition of the court Jew—bankers or financiers who lent money to Christian nobles in exchange for social privileges. If, indeed, Hanussen helped Hitler in any way, then maybe he was operating under the assumption that he would be Hitler's court Jew, safe from the worst anti-Semitism in history.

Another way to view Hanussen's behavior regarding Hitler is by remembering that, for him, all life was illusion: the illusion that he could read minds, the illusion that he knew the future, the illusion that he could influence Hitler. In this way, Hanussen was elevating himself as he had always done. His fantasies and his imagination had served him well in the past. But walking into a cage of wild animals in a borrowed lion tamer's costume when he was a teenager would prove safer than being in the same city, let alone the same room, as Nazis. He couldn't slap Hitler across the face with his whip as he had slapped Sultan, the rebellious lion. When that worked decades before, Hanussen had proudly purred: "In life, the bolder one always wins." In 1933, no one in Germany was bolder than Adolf Hitler, and even Hanussen, with all his powers and all his fame, was no match for him. Now that he had returned from visiting Therese and Erika, Hanussen was more determined than ever that nothing would budge him from Berlin. What he didn't understand was that the noose in which he had placed himself was tightening every day.

# CHAPTER 12

# The Fire that Killed a Country

In early February 1933, Hanussen started laying the groundwork for a show in Merano, the town in northern Italy where Therese and Erika lived. That way he could spend more time with both of them while earning some money. It would also give him a break from Berlin. While he loved the city, he knew—almost paradoxically—that he needed a breather from the pressure of being targeted by Nazis, Communists, and, still, that pesky jurist from Potsdam, Albert Hellwig. Hanussen was already booked at a theater in Germany's capital for all of March and at one in Vienna for the second half of April. Between those engagements, he suggested to Therese in a letter, perhaps she could produce his show in Merano, handle advertising, and guarantee his fee. Anticipating that she would balk at the amount he proposed, Hanussen tried to sweet-talk her, referring to himself in the third person (for that, of course, is how important people speak about themselves) and assuring her that the figure was his usual minimum: "You have to say how much you can guarantee because without guarantees, nobody of distinction would travel from Germany to Merano. The clairvoyant Erik Jan Hanussen usually receives a guarantee of 2,000 Reichmarks for an evening like this. And he does get it."[1]

Hanussen asked Therese to book him into the Teatro Puccini Stadt Theater—only two blocks from the Hotel Meranerhof, where he had stayed the previous fall. The theater appealed to Hanussen: regal and palatial, outside its columned entrance was a small fountain with water streaming out of the mouth of a statue of Bacchus, and bas-reliefs on the exterior depicted Roman gods playing flutes and cymbals and scampering through the woods. Hanussen would have felt right at home.

Hanussen's letter to Therese wasn't all business. He wanted to know how much he owed her for a camera he had asked her to buy for Erika. And he was "terribly excited" at the prospect of seeing his daughter again. A letter he had received from her had made him feel "very strange." Its first two words—"Dear Father"—had opened up odd and unfamiliar emotions in him. "I haven't been addressed like that in my whole life," Hanussen confessed to Therese. "I shook my head and thought, 'There are things in life…'" He was unable to find the words to complete his thought.[2]

With Hitler now chancellor, Berlin was more dangerous than ever, especially for a Jew. But if Hanussen had been able to outsmart those judges in Leitmeritz, how hard could it be to outsmart the Nazis? None impressed him as being very smart. A hypnotist friend of his, Fred Marion, agreed but still couldn't understand why Hanussen had thrown in his lot with the Nazis. Marion asked him about this one day. "They'll come to power, as we both know," Marion said. "But surely a man with your psychic gifts realizes that they will fall."[3]

With a quick grin, Hanussen agreed with Marion. "I know," he said. "I'm making a hell of a lot of money [from shows, private consultations, and publishing ventures].... Once I make more, I'm getting out of this country and going to America. I can write a book there about the inside story about what's happening here and make a million dollars."[4]

Faced with this "blatant example of the perfect double-cross," Marion couldn't think of anything to say. He had been worried that Hanussen was misusing his magic, taking what Marion called the "left-hand path" of magic—the sinister, demonic route. Now he was sure of it. Hanussen, he wrote, was becoming "a black magician. I warned him earnestly against the frightful dangers which attend those who strive to control the powers of darkness.... Let there be one slip, one lapse from the chosen path, and the black magician becomes overwhelmed by the powers he has employed."[5]

Marion considered Hanussen a gifted entertainer who could have had "a pleasant and comfortable life." There was no need for him to pursue the path of the devil. For that, Marion blamed Hanussen's greed, which Marion called "a consuming fire."[6]

Fire. There would be much fire in Hanussen's life in the coming weeks. For now, the fire that bothered Fred Marion—the fire of greed—drove Hanussen to use his splendid new apartment on Lietzenburgerstrasse as a snare for Berlin's power elite. For weeks, carpenters, painters, and craftsmen had been swarming to realize Hanussen's vision: a mishmash of mystical-astrological goofiness and strident neo-fascism. Scattered about were four massive statues of the Buddha. Stars and astrological signs were painted on the ceilings, rainbows on the floors. Fountains and aquariums gurgled everywhere. Greenhouses held lizards and snakes, exotic plants, and chirping birds. Several globes were as large as a man. Giant couches and massive desks, everything immense and oversized, mimicked the megalomaniacal interior decorating favored by Hitler and Mussolini. Indirect lighting, mostly yellow and green, created an eerie aura. The great centerpiece of all this was a large, circular table with a frosted glass top lit from above and below. The table was large enough to accommodate ten people, with Hanussen elevated slightly above them in a chair whose headrest was illuminated from behind. This was his throne, and that was his halo. Hanussen called this den in his apartment the Palace of the Occult.[7]

The palace was not inexpensive, and Hanussen's demands that contractors complete their work by the announced date of its opening— February 26—only boosted the costs. Its premiere was well attended, with some real royalty (one or two princes and a few counts) and some fake royalty (a woman who claimed to be Princess Anastasia, the lone survivor of the murdered Russian royal family). There was the manager of the Scala Theater, where Hanussen was scheduled to perform for all of March; and Hans Ewers, a failed novelist who pleased the Nazis by writing a biography of their martyr Horst Wessel, who had been killed by a Communist in 1930. Filling out the crowd were assorted actors and singers and comedians and Nazis—lots of them—in uniform. Loyalists, royalists, sycophants, and knaves—all awed by Hanussen's palace. "When you enter the apartment," wrote a reporter who was there that night, "you don't know what to say. You might even lose your power of speech. After ten minutes, you know that, in here, the most elaborate film has become a reality."[8]

Around midnight, the guests sat down in rows of chairs, the lights dimmed, and a séance began. Hanussen assured them that the woman in the room who called herself Anastasia was truly the daughter of the last czar of Russia and that they were all honored to be in her presence. (Most likely this particular Anastasia—there were several—was a Polish factory worker, Franziska Schanozkowska. Her DNA, tested after her death in 1984, proved she lacked a single drop of Romanov blood.)

Turning toward his good friend Count Heldorff, Hanussen assured him that Hitler, now in his fourth week as chancellor, would prove wise and effective, an inspiration to everyone. "And now," Hanussen asked, "who will volunteer for some mind reading?" No one raised their hand: they were reluctant to have someone poke around in their heads. Hanussen spotted Maria Paudler, a popular actress who had just arrived from the theater where she was performing. The choice of Paudler was convenient: She was sitting on the end of an aisle. She was famous: everyone knew who she was. And everyone liked her. When Hanussen asked for her help, she couldn't turn him down. "I didn't want to be a spoilsport," she later wrote in her autobiography.[9]

Paudler sat down in a comfortable chair in front of the other guests. Hanussen stood over her. Someone handed her a glass of champagne. A bit nervous, she finished it in almost one swallow. "Then," she recalled, "this small man...waved his hands around my head, trying to pierce me with his eyes." Paudler let out a little laugh. This must have irritated Hanussen: when hypnotizing someone, he demanded their complete concentration. But he wasn't ready to give up on the actress. To help her relax, he began stroking her face with his fingers. At first, she recalled, "I found this extremely unpleasant." Then, closing her eyes, she began to float away.[10]

From far away, Paudler heard Hanussen ask if she saw red circles. Yes, she answered, realizing later that it was not surprising she had seen circles: all the zodiac signs in the room were brightly lit—and Hanussen's voice, soft and soothing, was extremely persuasive. Continuing with this theme of red, Hanussen led Paudler down a path she did not necessarily want to follow. Was the red actually flames? he asked. Were they "coming out of a big house?" Hanussen kept taking her back to the red and the flames and the house as Paudler "unmistakably felt this whole scene was going beyond a normal parlor game and I was being used as more than an object of entertainment by this gentleman. I really did not want to be used in this manner."[11]

"So what does a lady do at a moment like that?" Paudler asked in her memoir. "She faints! After all, why shouldn't I take advantage of my womanly prerogative?"[12]

Hanussen's assistant caught Paudler as she fell toward the floor and offered her a glass of water. Everything, she recalled, "worked out marvelously," as the palace returned to its joyful mood. Despite Hanussen's obsession with flames and Paudler's fainting spell, the evening was a smash. As one newspaper noted, amid "declining economic order, people with the most extreme and contradictory worldviews can join together under the roof of a clairvoyant." If it took a psychic to bring such people together in the first weeks of the Third Reich, then perhaps Hanussen really did have powers.[13]

★  ★  ★

The next day, February 27—a Monday—Berlin's papers were full of news about the fancy party at Hanussen's palace and the glamorous guests and the weird decor and, especially, his odd fascination with flames. No one paid much attention to the conflagration Hanussen had conjured up. Over the years, he had talked about many weird things. Some were true. Many were false. For all the talk that Hanussen was the Nazis' favorite shaman, most people laughed him off as an entertainer—a good one and a slick one but really no more than an upscale sideshow.

By Berlin standards, the day was fairly comfortable, with temperatures slightly above normal. The evening was no less pleasant. Rudolf Diels, the head of the Gestapo, described it as "ein regnerischer Vorfruhlingsabend"—a drizzly, pre-spring evening. People went about their lives with no apprehension that a sea change was about to occur. That night, Bella Fromm, a Jew who was a social columnist for the highly respected liberal newspaper *Vossische Zeitung*, attended a party at the Hotel Esplanade along with many foreign diplomats and German officials. Suddenly an aide to Berlin's military commandant, Colonel Ernst von Schaumberg, rushed in and whispered hurriedly to his superior. Schaumberg stood up and politely excused himself. "I am sorry," he explained. "The Reichstag is on fire!" Schaumberg dashed out of the hotel, followed by many of the guests, who raced in their cars to the Reichstag, the massive German parliament barely a mile away. No one wanted to miss the excitement.[14]

Around the same time, Franz Hollering, the editor of the liberal newspaper *12 Uhr Blatt*, was taking a nap in his office, exhausted from the strain of trying to run a paper under the Nazis. On Sunday, an editorial he had written warned that the Nazis could not win the Reichstag elections scheduled for March 5 "unless something unforeseen happens." Hollering had no idea what that unforeseen event might be, but he didn't put anything past Hitler. Now a reporter's shout from the next room roused Hollering: "Fire in the Reichstag." Figuring that there had been an electrical short circuit, Hollering rolled over and went back to sleep. Then there was a second shout and a third and a fourth. Hollering jumped up. The Reichstag was on fire! The unforeseen had happened.[15]

A few minutes before, a young theology student walking home from the State Library heard glass breaking inside the Reichstag, where he saw a man carrying a torch. Sprinting toward a policeman, the student blurted out what he had seen. The officer immediately called the fire brigade. It was 9:10. By 9:23, eight fire trucks had raced to the Reichstag. More were on the way, and firemen were already scrambling up the sides of the building. At 9:24, a 24-year-old Dutchman, Marinus van der Lubbe, who may (or may not) have been a Communist, was arrested inside the Reichstag. At the same time, a fireman, Waldermar Klotz, fought his way past the lobby into the Grand Chamber where the deputies met; the hall was full of thick smoke. About all Klotz could see was a glow in the chamber's northeastern corner. At 9:30—20 minutes after the first call had gone out to the fire department—the phone rang in Franz Hollering's office. It was Hanussen.[16]

"How much of a fire is there at the Reichstag?" Hanussen asked.

"Where are you calling from?" Hollering replied. He was wary of Hanussen: the man associated with Nazis.

"From my apartment"—which was miles from the Reichstag.

"How did you find out about the fire?"

Hanussen avoided the question. "As a matter of fact," he said, "I want to warn you—all of you. Be on your guard tonight. No one knows what may happen. The Communists have set fire to the Reichstag."

"The Communists? Ridiculous! They wouldn't dream of it. They don't want to commit suicide. . . ."

"Wait and see! And you better be careful."[17]

As Hanussen hung up, Hollering remembered the stories about Hanussen's obsession with flames at the Palace of the Occult the night before. Now that there actually was a fire, Hanussen knew about it from the other side of town. And he was blaming the Communists. Hanussen's blunder (first concentrating on a fire the night before at his Palace of the Occult, then calling Hollering minutes after it broke out) was that he had beaten the Nazis to their own script *if*, indeed, the fire—and whom to blame it on—was part of a plot that had been conceived at the highest levels of Hitler's regime. Such a plot has been central to the conventional wisdom regarding the fire for almost 80 years. The Reichstag fire remains one of the great unsolved mysteries of modern history, although Hanussen's involvement from the sidelines firmly implicates the Nazis in one of history's most momentous conflagrations.

That night, Hitler was enjoying dinner with Goebbels and his wife at their home in Berlin—relaxing, telling stories, listening to music on the gramophone, discussing plans for the elections that would be held the next week. In deference to Hitler, a dedicated vegetarian, there were no meat dishes, although a large carp was served. When it was offered to Hitler, he refused. "I thought you ate fish," said Frau Goebbels. "Fish isn't meat, you know." Smiling, Hitler answered half-sarcastically, "I suppose, then, that fish, dear lady, is a plant."[18]

These pleasures were interrupted by a phone call from Ernest Hanfstangl, the head of the new government's foreign press department. "The Reichstag is on fire!" he shouted into the phone. "Tell the Fuehrer!"

"Stop that nonsense," responded Goebbels, annoyed at the practical joke. "It is not even funny."

"But I am telling the truth."

"No more of your stale jokes. Good night." Goebbels slammed the phone down, but Hanfstangl called again.

"What I am saying is true. It is your duty to tell the Fuehrer. If you do not, I guarantee there will be trouble." If Hitler and Goebbels did not believe him, Hanfstangl added, they should go to the Reichstag and see for themselves. Then it was Hanfstangl's turn to slam the phone down.[19]

When Goebbels passed on the news, Hitler immediately shouted, "It's the Communists! We'll have a showdown over this! I must go at once! Now I've got them!" Jumping into the chancellor's Mercedes, Hitler and Goebbels "raced 60 miles an hour down the Charlottenburger Chausse toward the scene of the crime," Goebbels later said. What they saw stunned them: Flames were shooting out of portions of the building as the great cupola, the pride of the last kaiser, collapsed in a crash of glass and copper. Police had cordoned off the building to keep the crowd away, and almost every fire engine in Berlin, assisted by fire boats on the Spree, was pumping water onto the blaze. Goering, who had been informed that a Communist had been arrested inside the Reichstag, was there, too, shouting, "This is the beginning of the new Communist revolution! We must not wait a minute. We will show no mercy. Every Communist official must be shot wherever he is found. Every Communist deputy must this very night be strung up."[20]

Picking up the chant, Hitler raged to Sefton Delmer, a British journalist he had known for several years, "God grant that this be the work of the Communists. . . . You are witnessing the work of a great new epoch in German history. This fire is the beginning. . . . You see this building? You see how it is aflame! If the Communists got hold of Europe and had control of it but for six months—what am I saying?—two months, the whole continent would be aflame like this building."[21]

Almost like an apparition, Franz von Papen, the vice chancellor, appeared before Hitler. Seizing him by the arm, Hitler exclaimed, "This is a God-given signal. . . . If this fire, as I believe, is the work of the Communists, then we must crush this murderous pest with an iron fist."[22]

The next day, Hitler persuaded President Hindenburg to sign the Reichstag Fire Decrees "for the Protection of the People and the State." Suspending the sections of the constitution guaranteeing individual and civil liberties, the decrees placed "restrictions on personal liberty, on the right of free expression of opinion, including freedom of the press; on the rights of assembly and association." Privacy in letters, telegrams, and phone calls ceased; warrants for searching houses or confiscating property could extend "beyond the legal limits [unless] otherwise prescribed"; and people could be arrested without charges.

When the Reich government deemed it necessary, it could completely take over the individual states in Germany, and the death sentence was now extended to a number of crimes, including "serious disturbances of the peace" by anyone who was armed. Storm troopers were sworn in as "auxiliary police." Four thousand Communists, socialists, and liberals were arrested. In the few days until the March 5 election, meetings of the democratic parties were broken up, and only the Nazis and their allies could campaign unhindered. And yet, while the Nazis won 288 seats (more than any other party and 92 more than they secured in the previous election), 56 percent of Germans voted for other parties, and even the Communists managed to place third. The Nazis still did not control a majority of the Reichstag's 633 seats, but the Reichstag fire the previous week had served as pretext for a major power grab by them, both politically and legally, and somehow Hanussen had been squarely in the middle of it.[23]

Standing in front of the burning Reichstag on February 27, Goebbels and Hitler had screamed "Communist." Now the Communists were screaming "Nazi," with their delegates to the Reichstag, which was now meeting in the Kroll Opera House, insisting that they could prove that Hitler had caused the fire. Germany was quickly disintegrating into chaos, with shouting matches between the right and left and the very head of the government—Hitler—accused of burning down the building that housed the nation's highest legislative body. A few months later, the brawl extended beyond Germany when an international best seller explained (with somewhat tortured logic) how the Nazis set the fire to panic Germans into believing that a red takeover was imminent. *The Brown Book of the Hitler Terror and the Burning of the Reichstag* was translated into 24 languages and published in more than 55 editions. (In the United States, *The Brown Book* was published by the prestigious publisher Alfred A. Knopf.) For decades, the book set the standard for explaining the Reichstag fire. It claimed that Marinus van der Lubbe—the love slave of Ernst Roehm, the homosexual chief of the SA—was a halfwit with a knack for arson. He had already tried to set fire to several buildings in Berlin; now he would turn the Reichstag to ashes in some twisted Nazi plot to incriminate the Bolshevists. Assuming that it would take more than one man to do the job, Goebbels and Goering ordered the SA to enter the Reichstag with van der Lubbe through an underground tunnel from Goering's official residence as president of the Reichstag. To further implicate "international communism," the Nazis arrested Ernst Togler, the head of the Communist delegation to the Reichstag, and three Bulgarian Communists who just happened to be in Berlin. *The Brown Book*'s premise was that the Nazis were sure the fire, the arrests, the specter of a worldwide red conspiracy would terrify voters and deliver Germany—legally—to them in the March election.[24]

What *The Brown Book* did not mention was that the World Committee for the Victims of German Fascism—the book's putative author—was a front for Willy Munzenberg, the former propaganda chief of the German Communist Party. Munzenberg had slipped through the Nazi dragnet the day after the fire and fled to Paris, where he concocted his revenge on the Nazis with the help of some very creative collaborators on the Left Bank. One of them, the journalist, author, and, at the time, card-carrying Communist Arthur Koestler, later admitted that *The Brown Book* was a collage of "isolated scraps of information, deduction, guesswork and brazen bluff.... We had no direct proof, no access to witnesses.... We had, in fact, not the faintest idea of the concrete circumstances." In other words, this book that solved the fire of the century was a piece of fiction. Even Munzenberg told a friend that much of *The Brown Book* was pure fantasy.[25]

Whether van der Lubbe was a lone arsonist or was aided by as many as 20 storm troopers and whether he was a Communist or a fascist or a dunce, he was a gift to the Nazis. He gave them an excuse to declare a national emergency, to throw thousands of Communists and socialists into concentration camps, to terrorize the whole country with apocalyptic visions of a red menace. But history wasn't finished with van der Lubbe, not even after the Nazis beheaded him in January 1934. (The four men accused of being his co-conspirators were acquitted the previous month.) In 1939, Sefton Delmer, the British journalist who had talked with Hitler as the Reichstag was burning, concluded that van der Lubbe had acted independently and alone. Delmer had reviewed the police investigations (they had even gone over van der Lubbe's route inside the Reichstag with a stopwatch); their efforts to track the man's trail since leaving Holland; and his confessions: "I did it alone. I was there. I know." To Delmer, all these made more sense than the Communists' fantasy that the Nazis set the fire or the Nazis' equally crazy idea that a vast Communist conspiracy was behind it. But Goering and Hitler, Delmar noted, had to cling to their narrative. "The fire," he wrote, "had to be the work of a gang—a Communist gang. If it was not, the whole moral foundation of their new police state was undermined."[26]

Lost amid all these machinations (the fire was a Nazi plot, a Communist plot, a deranged plan by a lone arsonist) was the testimony from Count Helldorf—Hanussen's pal—at the Reichstag fire trial in October 1933. Helldorf told the court that, on February 27, he had been dining at a restaurant on Rankestrasse with a friend when an aide phoned him about the fire. Helldorf calmly told the aide to get to the Reichstag as quickly as possible and let him know if he was needed there. Helldorf then went to his apartment on Nurnbergerstrasse. A phone call at 10 p.m. told him his presence at the Reichstag was not necessary. It is very odd that Helldorf received news of the fire with such equanimity, unless his aide simply confirmed what he already knew was going to happen. Otherwise, a fire in the Reichstag, especially after rumors had been sweeping the capital about an imminent Communist uprising, should have so alarmed Helldorf that he would insist on seeing it firsthand. Instead, he sent his deputy, even as Hitler, Goebbels, and Goering were racing there themselves.[27]

Which takes us back to Hanussen and the vision of flames at the opening of his palace and his phone call to the editor at the *12 Uhr Blatt*—a man Hanussen barely knew—on the night of the fire. With that call to Hollering, Hanussen became the Nazis' messenger boy. No Nazi could call a liberal editor and say the fire was the work of Communists. That would have been too transparent. It was wiser for someone who was not-quite-a-Nazi (and who was Jewish) to call the editor to ensure that the panic-inducing news of a Communist plot was in the next day's paper. Whether the Nazis instructed Hanussen to do this or if he just couldn't keep his mouth shut (as he had proven the night before when he tried to steer Maria Paudler into talking about a "big house" on fire) is entirely open to conjecture.

Neither Helldorf nor Hanussen was his usual self as the Reichstag was burning: Helldorf was preternaturally calm; Hanussen was politically assertive. So questions remain: Why? And how did Hanussen know about the fire? Perhaps he was a genuine psychic, although little in his history suggests this. Or perhaps *The Brown Book*—that masterpiece of Communist propaganda—somehow correctly guessed that Helldorf was one of the Nazis who planned the fire. And, if so, then how did Hanussen learn about it? One theory is that the two men conferred privately at the opening of the Palace of the Occult. Hanussen was worried that if Hitler lost the upcoming election, any new government would frown on Hanussen's associations with the Nazis and his career would end. To calm him, Helldorf told him what would happen the next night at the Reichstag. Hanussen was so relieved that he couldn't restrain himself during the séance with Maria Paudler a while later.[28]

History is messy. The Reichstag fire is messy. And politics is always messy, particularly its cavalier attitude toward truth. With the fire, each side—the left and the right—devised a narrative that suited its purpose. Both narratives, to some extent, were preposterous. But what should be remembered is that stories—or parts of a story—are not necessarily untrue simply because they occur within the broader framework of propaganda. Elements of both the Nazis' and the Communists' versions of the fire may be correct. Although van der Lubbe was a disillusioned Communist, he still may have been opposed to fascism; and his enthusiastic call for action while standing outside a welfare office in a Berlin suburb—"the revolution should start with some big fire"—a few days before the Reichstag fire may have reached some Nazis who helped him torch the building without van der Lubbe's even knowing they were helping him.[29]

In the accounts about Hanussen and the Reichstag fire that eventually were written, he was a better clairvoyant than even he claimed. By the late 1930s and during most of World War II, German refugees writing about Hanussen in American magazines vastly overstated what had occurred at the Palace of the Occult. In these tales, he had not tried to put words into Maria Paudler's mouth about flames—a vain manipulation that proves fire was on his mind, not on hers. These fables tell of Count Helldorf passing Hanussen a note at the séance with the date of February 27—the night of the fire—and asking what would happen then. Hanussen fell into a trance and had a premonition of the fire in a vision so clear and so detailed that he stopped just short of naming the building that would burn or giving its address. Sinking into a deep reverie, Hanussen spoke in a distant, hollow voice.

"I see troops on the march! German troops! The Fuehrer is leading his men to glory!...The world bows down before the German leader. Germany is like a magnet, attracting five, ten nations to its side. All the world comes to Germany! The Fuehrer is like God—he commands and rules the universe."[30]

Now with more passion—almost shouting, in fact—Hanussen said:

> *I see flames! A great fire...an enormous building...a great German government building is on fire! The flames lick their way to the top of a great dome! The flames mount rapidly...I can hear them crackle as they rise higher and higher!...They reach the spire! The dome bursts into flames! The entire neighborhood is lit up! It is here, here in Berlin! I see a row of statues....It is on the Siegesallee! A majestic building at the end of the avenue is on fire....The Fuehrer's enemies have set it on fire! A dastardly crime! We must stamp out the vermin who try to steal victory from the Fuehrer and set up Bolshevism in his place.*[31]

According to these versions of the séance, Hanussen tore the blindfold from his eyes, exhausted. Some guests left, too upset to stay. Everyone understood what Hanussen meant: the only "majestic building" on the Siegesallee with a row of marble statues of German warriors and heroes was the Reichstag.[32]

Doubtless, these versions of how Hanussen predicted the Reichstag fire were anti-Nazi propaganda. In almost all of them, Paudler disappears and Hanussen commandeers center stage, offering details of the fire, the building, the culprits, and Hitler's divinity. As propaganda, these tales were better than talking about a clairvoyant who did his best to seduce a pretty actress into some vague prophesy about flames in a "big house." And they implied that Hanussen—and, therefore, Helldorf (and, by implication, other Nazis)—knew about the fire before the first match was struck. But the Hanussen myth did not need to be massaged this way. His strained effort for Maria Paudler to see flames, his telephone call to the editor of the *12 Uhr Blatt* in which he blamed the conflagration on Communists—all his actions strongly suggest that he knew what the Nazis were planning and how they wanted the fire to be interpreted. Hanussen's crime was that he didn't tell Germany—and the world—what he knew. The Nazis, though, were furious that he blurted out even a fraction of their plan.[33]

Most likely, the Reichstag fire will never be solved. The details are too murky, too fuzzy. What is clear is that Hanussen's intrusion into the story line compromised the Nazis' insistence that they were innocent. Equally puzzling is why Hanussen could not silence himself about the fire during the séance. Blabbing about it—or trying to get Maria Paudler to do so—sealed his fate. His life was now meaningless to the Nazis.

# CHAPTER 13

# A Ride to a Wild Prison

Despite everything, business remained good at the Palace of the Occult. Hanussen was charging bigwigs several thousand marks for private consultations, while his assistants, who charged less, spared him the bother of meeting with less important people. These lowly clients—when told that the master was busy—would settle for Hanussen's aides. He had taught them how to speak in broad, sweeping generalities—"On that date in 1917, there was an attack in the West. I see blood. A general dies. An Iron Cross is awarded"—and the visitors would leave, astounded by the abilities of these strangers to distill truths, transcend time, and know secrets about them that they hadn't told anyone.[1]

These aides were doing "cold readings"—offering truths based on intuition, on information that the people they were reading were unconsciously feeding them and relying on a talent for cautiously treading the line between the obvious and the probable. Someone doing a cold reading might make an observation that is universally true but that the person who had come to see them would conclude applied exclusively to them, such as "I see you in high school. You're walking with the other children, but you feel like there's a certain separation between you and them." Another classic technique is conflating two opposite and commonplace observations so they seem unique while erasing any apparent contradiction between them. "You're naturally a very trusting person," a psychic might say, "but this has gotten you into trouble at times. So you're now more reserved." The person who is being read is flattered (he's a trusting individual who thinks the best of people) as he is being sympathized with (people have taken advantage of his faith in them). He leaves thankful that he has met someone who understands him so deeply. He's also completely puzzled that this person—whom he never met before—knows him so well. This is part of the pleasure—and the frustration—of consulting with a psychic or, indeed, enjoying any type of magic: We cannot figure out why our normal thinking, which comes in handy the rest of our lives, is now so useless. Everywhere we turn, it seems, the psychic is one step ahead of us.[2]

Since no one did cold readings better than Hanussen, he kept the wealthier or more famous paying clients who came to the Palace of the Occult for himself. Once past its front doors, they would be ushered through two small rooms where Hanussen's assistants would stare at the visitors, a ruse that made it seem as if the newcomers were entering a mystical and otherworldly realm. The assistants' real job was to dig up information on the customers, who were kept waiting while Hanussen's crew phoned anyone who could shed light on visitors. When the crew finally gathered sufficient information, they briefed Hanussen, who then allowed the visitors to be ushered into his inner sanctum. Just as they were entering Hanussen's lair, he might be wrapping up a call with one of the notables he frequently advised—or so he would tell them. It was all so convincing, and so calculated: a theater not of the absurd but of the gullible.[3]

Hanussen's consultation business stayed as lucrative as ever. But as he began losing his standing with the new regime, he also began losing his leverage with the theaters where he was performing. In March, at the end of the first week of a month-long engagement at the Scala and just about a week after the Reichstag fire, Hanussen went to the manager to collect the bonus they had negotiated if he exceeded certain ticket sales. Sure that they had a hit on their hands, Hanussen expected a large check for the extra business he was bringing to the theater. The manager disagreed. Yes, he said, the public loves you. And we love you. But as good as ticket sales are, our projections for the entire month that you'll be here indicate you'll fall short of your bonus.

"You tricked me," Hanussen shouted. "I refuse to perform any longer."

"Do you want us to tell the public that you did not foresee you were making a bad deal?" asked the manager. "'What a fine clairvoyant,' people will say."[4]

Hanussen had been outswindled. He stayed at the Scala, worried about where to get the money he needed to meet the expenses for his staff and his fancy apartment and his yacht and his fleet of limousines. Performing at the Scala was great for his reputation; it wasn't that great for his wallet. But he was so busy that he barely had time to think about other ways to earn money. His last attempt to increase his income—turning his newspaper from a weekly into a daily—had infuriated Goebbels, who would brook no competition for his own paper. But when Hanussen learned that the Nazis wanted to acquire the massive Mosse publishing empire, he began scheming about ways to profit from the sale.

The Mosse family was Jewish. They had owned the publishing firm for three generations, specializing in fine books and taking great pride in the company's newspapers, the *Frankfurter Zeitung* and the *Berliner*

*Tageblatt*, the most liberal dailies in Germany. The papers reflected the Mosse family's sensibilities. The Mosses were cultured and well educated, patrons of the arts and defenders of the Enlightenment. Family members lived in several mansions: One was on 32 acres in the village of Schenkendorf, 40 minutes south of Berlin. It had eight bedrooms, each with its own bathroom—an unheard-of luxury in those days. A second mansion on Berlin's Leipzinger Place was modeled on an Italian Renaissance palace, with a courtyard encircling a fountain with statues of dancing maidens. Inside, a library with first editions of Goethe and an art collection that included a fresco depicting Rudolf Mosse (the head of the second generation of Mosse publishers) and his wife and daughter in Renaissance costumes and seated at a banquet table in an Italian setting, talking and making toasts and having a fine time. Another Mosse residence, this one in Berlin's Westend, had four bedrooms on the second floor, two ornate sitting rooms on the first, a large dining room decorated with Medici tapestries, and a concert hall where famous musicians performed. A minimum of six servants were assigned to each of these mansions—cooks, butlers, chambermaids, nannies, governesses, and, for the country house, stable hands. Live-in tutors from France or Ireland taught the children French or English. Some were quite close to the Mosse children—sometimes so close that their shy, distant mother was jealous.[5]

The family established homes for orphans and hostels for poor women; commissioned the modernist architect Erich Mendelsohn to design a luxury apartment building and a major theater complex on the Kurfürstendamm—Berlin's Fifth Avenue; and contributed generously to the Berlin Philharmonic. Although Hans Lachmann-Mosse, who became the head of the family after his father-in-law, Rudolf Mosse, died in 1920, called religion humbug, he never rejected Judaism. He simply wanted to be a modern Jew. With that in mind, he joined

Berlin's largest Reform congregation, a sanctuary of rationalism, and campaigned to revolutionize synagogue music, which he deplored as "universally bad." With the temple's musical director, he selected music by Schubert, Beethoven, and Handel to accompany the liturgy and paid for a recording featuring the Philharmonic, top opera singers, and a choir of one hundred voices. The records were played in Reform temples throughout Germany, ensuring that their music was as inspiring as the rest of the service was up-to-date.[6]

Professionally and personally, the Mosses placed their trust in reason and common sense and the discriminating power of a well-developed mind. They were confident Germany would repudiate Hitler. This was, after all, a civilized nation.[7]

Or was until January 30, when Hitler became chancellor. Hans Mosse fled to Paris; the rest of his family quickly followed. Mosse left his company in the hands of Karl Vetter, the firm's general manager, whom he trusted completely, although most of his family didn't. They thought Vetter was an opportunist. One even called him an "evil genius." Vetter would prove they were right.[8]

To Hitler, the Mosses symbolized what was wrong with Germany: They were elegant. They were cosmopolitan. They were powerful. They were Jews. They were part of the rot that was suffocating Germany. To silence them, the Nazis offered two million marks for their publishing house. Vetter asked Hanussen, who was a friend of his, for advice about how to negotiate. As Hanussen knew the Nazis well, surely he had insight into how they thought. "Two million," said Hanussen, "is not a bad price, but you can do better." Hanussen went to his safe and pulled out a pile of IOUs. Most were signed by Helldorf. Mention these to the Nazis, Hanussen instructed, and tell them you want six million marks. These people, said Hanussen, will do *anything* so the public doesn't learn that Helldorf is not only good friends with a Jew but that the Jew has been bankrolling him for years, paying most of his bills and making sure he doesn't go bankrupt again. Hanussen and Vetter would split the take from the Nazis, with a token amount going to Hans Mosse, who was far away in Paris. Everyone would be happy.[9]

A clever plan, Vetter assured Hanussen. Quite brilliant. What Hanussen didn't know was that some members of the Mosse family were right: Vetter could not be trusted. His next stop was Helldorf. "Sir," he said, "I understand you're low on money. Here's a check for 10,000 marks. Consider this a present." Helldorf gratefully pocketed the check, asking almost as an afterthought, "How did you know I'm low on money?" Vetter explained Hanussen's idea about using Helldorf's IOUs as blackmail to triple the price for the publishing company. The blackmailer had been outsmarted.[10]

Hanussen was already in trouble with the Nazis for revealing their plans for the Reichstag the night before the fire. Helldorf was appalled that Hanussen planned to use those IOUs against him. Helldorf, Hanussen's friend and protector for more than two years, was through with him. Hanussen was on his own.

On March 21, the Nazis officially took over the Mosse publishing company. Hans Lachmann-Mosse had returned to Berlin secretly at the invitation of Goebbels to discuss the future of his business. Assuring Mosse that he would be safe, Goebbels even hinted that some Jews who had been fired from the firm might be rehired. But the Nazis had not invited Mosse for a friendly chat over warm brandy. While Mosse was at the meeting, Wilhelm Ohst, a major in the SA and the Nazis' point man in their campaign to take over the firm, stood over him, brandishing a revolver and ordering Lachmann-Mosse to sign over the publishing house to a foundation that aided war victims. The foundation was really a front for a conglomerate that eventually controlled almost every newspaper in Germany. Few takeovers gave Goebbels as much pleasure: a decade before, the paper had turned down his application for a job.[11]

As Mosse's signature was drying on the agreement, Ohst—who knew nothing about publishing—became the head of what had been Germany's finest and proudest publishing firm. (The Nazis let Lachmann-Mosse leave Germany unharmed after signing away his empire. He settled in France. When the Nazis invaded, he emigrated to the United States and died in Oakland, California, in April 1944— bereft of his homeland, his fortune, and his wife, who had divorced him, convinced that his poor sense of politics and business had undone everything her father had created.) A few days after Ohst was installed as head of the Mosse enterprise, he would have a hand in Erik Jan Hanussen's final act. Ohst would not find this distasteful. It was to Ohst that Hanussen had said about Hitler, "Adolf looks more like an unemployed hair dresser than a Caesar." In the new Germany, such words were blasphemy.[12]

★   ★   ★

People were disappearing in Berlin in those days. Some were fleeing the Nazis. Others had been caught by the storm troopers, who moved fast and asked questions later. So at first, no one knew what to make of Hanussen's disappearance on March 24. Around 10 p.m. at the Scala Theater, the acrobats and singers finished performing, and the orchestra was playing a short fanfare as a buildup to the headliner— Hanussen—who had the second act to himself. Hanussen's aides were settling into place to help him find items that members of the audience hid or to steer him toward people who were burning to ask what had happened on key dates in their lives. Of course, Hanussen would get everything correct. He always did.

The stage manager was getting nervous: it was almost curtain time, and Hanussen hadn't shown up. The manager sent his staff to search the bars and cafés where Hanussen usually hung out. No one had seen him. Then the manager called Hanussen's apartment. No one answered. He called the café next to the theater where Hanussen often went before his show. A waiter told him that, about 45 minutes earlier, two men had approached Hanussen as he was picking up his hat to leave. "Mr. Hanussen," they said, "we need to talk with you." They escorted Hanussen to his car and drove away. "He really should be back at the Scala by now," the waiter said encouragingly. The manager called the police—none of the officers had seen the car Hanussen used that night: a gray limousine, the same one, as it turned out, he had lent Helldorf in September 1931 so he could ride up and down the Kurfürstendamm, urging on the SA during one of the first anti-Semitic riots in Berlin.[13]

The Scala's audience was restless—booing and clapping rhythmically every few minutes. Finally, the stage manager announced that Hanussen had a "sudden, unexpected illness" and the show was canceled. Their tickets could be exchanged for a show another evening.[14]

As the theater was emptying, the director of the Scala showed up and called an old friend from the Great War, a Herr Fleischer, who was now a bigwig in the SA. "Please do me a favor and come over here fast," he said. "We're worried about something. I can't talk about it on the phone." Fleischer went to the theater immediately. When he learned that, earlier that day, some storm troopers had asked the theater's stage porter about Hanussen, Fleischer called SA posts all over Berlin, asking if anyone knew who had been doing the questioning. Fleischer learned nothing.

"Maybe," Fleischer said, "we should drive over to Hanussen's apartment? Maybe he really is sick and no one is with him?" The SA man had his own ideas about what had happened, but he didn't want to worry his friend.

The doorman at Hanussen's apartment building told them that the showman had stopped by the building earlier that night with two men. The three of them had gone upstairs for about 15 minutes, then drove away. Hanussen had looked very pale.

"Did they drive toward the Scala?" Fleischer asked hopefully.

"No," the doorman told him. "Toward Halensee"—the opposite direction.

Fleischer and the director of the Scala looked silently at each other. In the new Berlin—the Nazis' Berlin—a ride in a car with strangers never ended well.[15]

Hanussen had been taken to a prison on General Pape-strasse—about four miles south of his apartment. This facility was among the 150 or so improvised prisons that the storm troopers began running after the Reichstag fire. The day after the fire, a national emergency was declared and, almost instantly, thousands of people were arrested—Communists, socialists, democrats, and anyone brave enough to openly dislike the new regime or unfortunate enough for the Nazis to dislike them. They had to be put somewhere. Ordinary prisons were already packed and, anyway, these "enemies of the revolution" needed lessons they couldn't get in the existing facilities—lessons beyond the law and the morals and the rules of the established prisons. To staff these prisons, the most vicious storm troopers were chosen, men hardened by years of street fighting or who were naturally sadistic. These places were concentration camps (on a small, almost experimental scale) before that term was invented—crude prototypes of the Nazis' factories of death: the beginnings of the Nazi terror that, in a few years, would be hammered into the minds and the hearts of every German in every city and town and village in the Reich.[16]

Hitler's horrors commenced in these prisons. At the Nuremberg trials in 1946, Herman Goering minimized their brutality. "Of course," he told the tribunal, with impeccable and sensible reasoning, "in the beginning, there were excesses; of course, the innocent were also hurt here and there; of course, there were beatings here and there.... I naturally gave instructions that such things should not happen.... It was important to me to win over some of these people for our side and to re-educate them."[17]

For Goering, the prisons were established to reform and rehabilitate, not to kill and torture. But the storm troopers were having a fine time settling old scores and inventing new ones. These prisons sickened even Rudolf Diels, the first head of the Gestapo. Diels called them "wild camps"—uncontrollable and beyond the law. (Apparently he was fine with sadism that *he* ordered.) By August 1933, Goering, fed up with the prisons, ended the SA's power to arrest people—a power that he had given them in the aftermath of the Reichstag fire. Then he shut down the wild prisons one by one. The most troublesome prison was in Papenburg, near the Dutch border, where SA members opened fire on Goering's police as they entered the prison. Goering had to ask Hitler for army artillery to smash through the storm troopers' resistance.[18]

Most of these prisons were improvised affairs—one in Berlin's Charlottenburg neighborhood was in a seized Communist meeting center; another was in Friedrichstrasse 234, a combination apartment-and-office building that had been donated to the SA by Nazi sympathizers in 1932. Hanussen was taken to an abandoned military barracks built in the 1890s. The Treaty of Versailles banned the use of the barracks, a stipulation that was part of the Allies' effort to demilitarize Germany after World War I. The storm troopers had seized the barracks in mid-March, just a few weeks before Hanussen was taken there, turning its upper floors into a residence for Nazi bullies and the basement into a prison. Many of these storm troopers had been unemployed or homeless; they appreciated having a roof over their heads. Some were criminals or psychopaths. All liked having a place where they could terrify anyone they didn't like.[19]

At Friedrichstrasse 234, prisoners stood for hours in a cellar filled with water. A resident who lived near the prison later said, "For several days during the week after the elections [for the Reichstag on March 5] the neighbors and passers-by heard the screams and moans of people inside." When the police finally broke in, they found 70 Communists—several dead, the others badly beaten. In the Charlottenburg prison, storm troopers shoved sticks into prisoners' anuses or lifted them with ropes a few feet above the floor as they pounded on their bare feet with rubber truncheons: every blow, said one prisoner, felt like it slammed into his "bare brain." A doctor showed up occasionally, not to reprimand the Nazis but to determine whether the torture could continue. Usually it could. At least two Communists were beaten to death at the Charlottenburg prison; a third died after his hands were chopped off.

In the cold, dank basement of the Pape-strasse prison, the facility where Hanussen was taken, about two hundred prisoners were kept in 13 cells. Each cell was about 535 square feet; each held 20 to 30 prisoners. The lucky few got out in a week or two; most were locked up for months. They had no heat, no blankets, and little food. Female prisoners were tied to a vaulting horse and raped by one storm trooper after another as other women were forced to watch. In another room, prisoners faced a wall as storm troopers used them as targets for shooting practice. In a cell used exclusively for interrogations, sulfuric acid was injected into the penis of at least one prisoner. A layer of sand covering the floor soaked up the blood as prisoners were beaten to a pulp. When a neighbor complained about the racket from the prison, he was dragged inside and tortured for a few hours himself. One cell was reserved for disloyal party members. They could rehabilitate themselves by beating other prisoners—lining up along the

90-foot corridor as prisoners ran up and down the passageway and hitting them with clubs until they dropped.[20]

Most prisoners at the Pape-strasse prison were given numbers. Number 235—Erich Simenauer—was a psychoanalyst and a Rilke scholar. Severely beaten, he somehow survived. Prisoner 45—Leo Krell, a journalist for a socialist newspaper—wasn't so lucky. Dumped in the prison on March 16, he died from his beatings on March 21—three days before Hanussen was taken there.[21]

No number has been found for Hanussen. Nor is it certain exactly what happened to him after he was escorted through the prison's green wooden doors. He may have been thrown into a cell in the basement with other prisoners. Probably not, as he returned home a few hours later—shaken but unharmed. And one storm trooper later said that Hanussen's good-bye from the prison was "an absolutely friendly one"—so friendly that Hanussen walked back into the building and asked for a drink of water. If he wasn't taken to the basement where the tortures and the rapes and the beatings occurred, perhaps he climbed the seven steps to the prison's first floor to be interrogated in a slightly more cordial atmosphere than he would have found in the basement. What is certain is that he arrived during the prison's wildest phase: Seven people were murdered there within a week of his arrival. The storm troopers were flexing their muscles: Nothing is more anarchic than a totalitarian state that is just getting its bearings, calibrating how much terror it can get away with. And surely, the storm troopers had been emboldened by what the Reichstag had done the day before Hanussen's arrest.[22]

On March 23, the Reichstag had approved the Enabling Act (or, to use its full title, the Law for Removing the Distress of People and Reich). Its five paragraphs repealed the Reichstag's power to legislate, approve treaties with other countries, control the budget, and initiate amendments to the constitution. All these powers now resided with the Reich cabinet, whose laws—drafted by Chancellor Hitler himself— "might," the Enabling Act warned, in one of the great understatements of the twentieth century, "deviate from the constitution." The act passed overwhelmingly, 441 to 94, thanks partly to Hermann Goering, who, as president of the Reichstag, had lowered the number of deputies required for a quorum by not counting the Communists. After the vote, the Nazis marched around the hall, singing their anthem, the Horst Wessel song:

> *Raise high the flags! Stand rank on rank together,*
> *Storm Troopers march with steady, quiet tread ...*

By a purely legal procedure, the Nazis had hijacked the government. Hitler now had license to do whatever he wished. That was the law.[23]

This dissolution of Germany's binding legal strictures could be how Hanussen ended up at the Pape-strasse prison. Before passage of the Enabling Act, most people whom the Nazis had tortured or killed had been political foes. There were certain ideological reasons to dispatch them. Hanussen was different. He was a celebrity. His fame extended beyond politics, although he had certainly served a political function—turning his newspaper into a propaganda sheet for Hitler, lending Helldorf (and other Nazis) tens of thousands of marks, and providing boots, cars, and money for the storm troopers. He had served the Nazis well. Nine days before the elections earlier in March, Hanussen had demanded in his newspaper, "Away with the Reichstag! An end to the parliament! Carte blanche to the defenders of the Fatherland!" Speaking as the all-seeing, all-knowing clairvoyant who had dazzled audiences throughout Europe, Hanussen had predicted that Germans would "voluntarily and faithfully" place their country's future in the hands of the Nazis, the only people who could save the nation from becoming "a slave to bolshevism." "The time of debates is over," Hanussen declared. "The time of the parliamentarian is over. Germany's fate lies in the hands of men and not in the whims of parliamentary trends."[24]

Hanussen knew the party line, and he was good at it. But the Nazis didn't need his help now, not with Hitler installed as chancellor and the Reichstag passing the Enabling Act and the SA taking over the streets. With Hanussen's Jewish identity becoming widely known, his inability to remain silent about the Reichstag fire, and his attempt to make a profit from the Mosse publishing company deal by using Helldorf's IOUs against the Nazis, he had transformed almost overnight from an asset to a liability.

As the Nazis were reaching their fatal conclusions about Hanussen, Count Helldorf was less available to him than ever. The conservatives who were not Nazis had frustrated Goering's plans to name Helldorf Berlin's police chief: putting the city's safety in the hands of the man who had led the anti-Semitic riot on the Kurfürstendamm two years before was too risky. Instead, Goering appointed Helldorf police chief of Potsdam, a suburb of Berlin where his past would be less ironic. With Helldorf in Potsdam—and control of the storm troopers in Berlin passing to Karl Ernst, a former bouncer at a gay nightclub—there was one less buffer between Hanussen and the growing number of Nazis who were gunning for him. The séance at Hanussen's palace the night before the Reichstag fire was probably the last time Helldorf saw Hanussen. The séance, in particular, had sealed the psychic's fate.[25]

# CHAPTER 14

# Three Bullets in the Woods

After Hanussen disappeared, rumors were flying all over Berlin. He was sick. He had fled to Prague. He had settled in Zurich. He had been seen in Berlin with his head wrapped in bandages. Someone had seen him being driven, blindfolded, through the capital. Where he was being taken, no one knew. One especially melodramatic rumor was that Hanussen's troubles dated to the housewarming for his Palace of the Occult: After midnight, the party had degenerated into an orgy. Three days later, Hitler had received photos showing Helldorf and other Nazis in compromising positions. The pictures "spoiled . . . [Hitler's] appetite for the day and his good humor for the week," one reporter wrote, especially since they were accompanied by a ransom note: The negatives would cost Hitler 100,000 marks. After paying the blackmailer, who just happened to be Hanussen, Hitler gave Helldorf an ultimatum: either get out of town or end your friendship with Hanussen. Helldorf preferred the latter. In a showdown with Hanussen, went this rumor, Helldorf told him that his Jewish arrogance had gotten both of them in trouble. A few days later, storm troopers whisked Hanussen from his apartment. Not long after that, he checked into a clinic with a broken nose and bruises all over his body, telling doctors he was moving to Paris as soon as he was able to travel. Helldorf learned where Hanussen had holed up, and, that night, storm troopers pulled up to the clinic and threw him into their car. He was never seen again.[1]

The real story was nothing like these fictions. While Hanussen was at the Pape-strasse prison on March 24, several storm troopers had demanded that he give them all the IOUs he had been collecting. Hanussen refused, knowing they were his best weapons against the Nazis—perhaps his only one. At one point, the SA men left the room where they had been grilling Hanussen. Frustrated, they stood in the doorway, yelling threats at him. Sensing that he was losing his leverage, Hanussen offered to exchange the IOUs for the money that was owed him. The Nazis rejected his offer. Hanussen and the Nazis had reached a stalemate.[2]

The clairvoyant was released around midnight. Returning home, he found his apartment a mess. Furniture and clothing were strewn all over. While he had been at the prison, several storm troopers had ransacked the place, searching for the IOUs. Hanussen called his ex-wife, Fritzi. They had been divorced for about a year, but he still relied on her, especially in a crisis. Despite his infidelities, they remained friends. As they were discussing calling a lawyer, three storm troopers walked into the room and the phone went dead. It was a little after 1 a.m.[3]

The storm troopers were led by Wilhelm Ohst, the SA major who had engineered the Mosse publishing company takeover. Ohst knew Hanussen well. The other storm troopers were Rudolf Steinle and Kurt Egger, who had never seen Hanussen before. When Ohst knocked on the door to Hanussen's apartment, Hanussen's secretary told him, "Just go up. The boss is up there." Even after the SA's ransacking of the apartment earlier that night, and after Hanussen's return from one of the storm troopers' notorious prisons, the secretary still greeted Ohst casually, almost offhandedly, perhaps because he knew that Ohst and Hanussen were acquaintances and he assumed that the SA major wasn't necessarily there on official business. Maybe Ohst had come to assist Hanussen in some way? Hanussen had helped the SA for so long that it's conceivable his secretary thought Ohst was there to return the favor.

Ohst knew exactly where to go in the apartment; he had been there many times. When he found Hanussen and told him he was under arrest again, the clairvoyant was incredulous. "My dear Ohst," Hanussen said, thinking about this night of revolving-door arrests, and his assumption that he had nothing to worry about after his release from the Papestrasse prison just a few hours earlier, "that cannot be true. Don't make jokes like that when I have helped you so many times." Cutting him off, Ohst demanded, "Where are the papers?" Realizing this wasn't the time to argue, Hanussen told one of his aides to get the IOUs. The large pile included two signed by Helldorf for fifteen hundred marks (more than $6,300 in 1933) and one signed by another SA officer, Achim von Amim, for four hundred marks (then about $2,000).

Once Ohst had the IOUs, he told Steinle and Egger that he was sorry he had to treat Hanussen this way. Ohst and Hanussen had known each other for quite a while. But Karl Ernst, the new commander of the SA in Berlin, had ordered Ohst to show no sympathy toward the psychic. That afternoon, Ohst and Ernst had sat down to figure out what to do about Hanussen. He had already attempted to use those IOUs to profit from the Mosse sale. That hadn't worked, but it also hadn't stopped Hanussen from loudly bragging in restaurants that he had bribed some of the most powerful SA members in the city, and then naming them: Helldorf, Ernst, and Ohst. For half an hour, Ohst tried to persuade Ernst to show some mercy toward Hanussen. The psychic was sneaky, manipulative, and always scheming, but he did not necessarily deserve the fate Ernst had in mind. Ernst glowered. "Are you going soft on me?" he asked Ohst.[4]

The storm troopers threw Hanussen into their car outside his apartment building. One later said his "demeanor was that of a creditor toward a debtor. Even while we were driving, he was still asking Ohst why he had come to arrest him when he had only done him good at all times."[5]

They took Hanussen back to the Pape-strasse prison. On his earlier visit—roughly 8 p.m. to midnight—he had witnessed the kinder face of the prison. This time, the storm troopers shoved him down the stairs, to the level of the cells and the torture chambers, where they pumped three bullets into him: one to his neck, one to his abdomen, and one to the back of his head. Then they dragged his body up the stairs, threw it back into their car, and drove south. After almost an hour, they pulled over in a forest not far from the town of Zosse, dumped his body in the woods, and drove back to Berlin. Once there, Ohst called Ernst to say he had accomplished his mission. Now there would be no one to squeal about the Nazis' secret plans at late-night séances or to blackmail them about borrowing money from a Jew. Ohst assured Ernst that he had all the IOUs. Hanussen had thought the IOUs were his lifeline; rather, they had ensured his demise. He was 43 years old.[6]

The next morning, one of Hanussen's secretaries—not the one who had been there the previous night—walked into the ransacked palace. She couldn't call the police; the telephone wires had been cut. She and Hanussen's business manager walked to a police station and reported Hanussen missing.[7]

★   ★   ★

Two days after Hanussen was killed, Ohst showed up at his new job at the publishing company. He hadn't been seen since Hanussen disappeared.

Casually handing the trousers from his uniform to one of the office boys, Ohst asked him to take them to the nearest branch of the Landrock Laundry. The boy did as he was told. Later, he told the few people he trusted at the firm that the pants had been stained with blood.[8]

Ernst, the storm trooper who had ordered Ohst to kill Hanussen, had also borrowed money from the psychic. Like the other Nazis who had taken money from the clairvoyant, Ernst kept it quiet. But he had another secret: He was gay. In fact, a few years before, people were calling him "Frau Rohrbein" because he was having a fling with Paul Rohrbein, the first SA commander in Berlin. Ernst was so leery of being outed that, in September 1933, he went to the trouble of getting married. The marriage was brief. On June 30, 1934, as Ernst and his wife left their hotel in Bremerhaven for a belated honeymoon, they were surrounded by several SS men. Ernst was hustled onto a waiting plane and flown to Berlin, where he was executed. Ernst's honeymoon was a fake. The Gestapo had learned that he was fleeing Germany. Ernst had recognized that the SA was losing a power struggle within the fledgling Nazi regime and planned to tell the major foreign powers about Hitler's real intentions and urge them to sever relations with Germany. To prove Hitler was a criminal, Ernst was reportedly carrying documents that implicated the Nazis in the Reichstag fire.[9]

Although Ernst had risen quickly within the SA—a year or two before, he had been working at a gay club in Berlin—he didn't have the power to order Hanussen's murder on his own. For that, we have to turn to Ernst Roehm, the SA commander for the entire country. Roehm had a unique place in the Nazi hierarchy. He was the only member of Hitler's inner circle allowed to call the fuehrer by the familiar German form *du,* or "you," rather than the more formal *Sie.* They had been comrades since 1919 when Roehm helped install Hitler as head of the Nazi Party. After organizing the SA in 1921, Roehm

stole weapons for them from army depots. If anyone was indispensable to Hitler's early rise, it was Roehm. And if anyone was faithful
to Hitler, it was Roehm. But in 1928, he left Germany to train the
Bolivian army after arguing with Hitler about the best route to power.
Roehm, the military man, favored another putsch. Hitler, the evolving
politician, favored elections—a slower, more plodding route but one
that had the patina of legitimacy. Two years later, Roehm returned
to Germany at Hitler's request. The storm troopers were too violent,
too undisciplined, and Hitler was sure Roehm was the only man who
could control them. Reaching out to Roehm was a risk, Hitler knew.
Independent and stubborn, Roehm was never averse to letting Hitler
know about their differences, perhaps because they had been friends
for so long. But Hitler understood that Roehm was loyal to him and to
the goals of the Nazi Party. Hitler was already tired of the quarreling
rivals who were surrounding him; honesty and allegiance meant a lot
to the fuehrer.[10]

But then there was Roehm's sexuality. Like Karl Ernst, he was gay.
This disgusted Heinrich Himmler, who ran the SS and the Gestapo.
To Himmler, gays were a plague, afflicted with an infection that could
destroy the country. At the very moment that Germany needed a larger
population, homosexuals were doing nothing to increase the birthrate.
Their disease had to be eradicated, not to make them better people—
they were beyond hope—but so Germany could soar with a pure and
virile master race. Oddly, while Himmler was ranting against homosexuals, Hitler was essentially apathetic toward them. This was obvious
from his blueprint for saving Germany, *Mein Kampf*. He devoted 176
pages to Jews, but didn't refer to homosexuals once. Eventually, the
Nazis turned on homosexuals because Himmler won the argument
that their sexual deviancy threatened "the battle for the birth rate."
But unlike the Jews, who were a fairly easy target—they stated their

religion on census forms, birth certificates, and official documents—homosexuals were a relatively elusive, almost invisible target. A full-scale "homosexual Holocaust" would have been difficult to implement: The Nazis never agreed on how to define *homosexual*. They didn't know exactly where to locate them. And the vast numbers—on the eve of World War II, there were at least two million homosexuals in Germany versus 250,000 Jews—would have made exterminating homosexuals a staggering project even for the Nazis, who otherwise proved they could elevate mass murder to a cruel science. That homosexuals were spared the same numerical suffering as Jews is not to minimize their pain: about fifteen thousand were taken to concentration camps, thousands more were castrated, and about 100,000 were imprisoned, where they were often brutally beaten and sometimes died.[11]

Hitler knew that Ernst Roehm was not ashamed of his sex life. So long as Roehm and his storm troopers (many of whom were also gay) did their jobs, the fuehrer was willing to overlook their peccadilloes. "I won't spoil any of my men's fun," Hitler told one politician. "If I demand the utmost from them, I must also leave them free to let off steam as *they* want, not as churchy old women think fit.... I take no interest in their private lives, just as I won't stand for people prying into my own." But soon homosexuality was so extensive in the SA that one of the storm troopers warned Hitler that male prostitutes all over Berlin were tittering about a "homosexual chain" that ran through the entire Nazi apparatus. Worse, Hitler was told, "rumors are being spread that you yourself, my most esteemed Fuehrer, are also homosexual." Hitler was not pleased. He was even less pleased with Roehm's demands in late 1933 and the first half of 1934 for a "second revolution" that would more aggressively pursue social equality for workers, strengthen the unions, and stop the new government's suppression of civil liberties. Roehm's sin was that he had fallen for the "socialism" half of national socialism. His other sin was that he was convinced that his long friendship with Hitler—and the veritable army of storm troopers that Roehm commanded—would insulate him from any dire consequences. He called Hitler a "rotten...weakling" who was "badly in need of a vacation." "Stupid, dangerous creatures"—reactionaries— were manipulating the fuehrer, who was

> betraying all of us.... His old comrades aren't good enough for him.... Adolf is and always will be a civilian, an "artist," a dreamer. Just leave me be, he thinks. Right now, all he wants to do is sit in the mountains and play God. And guys like us have to cool our heels, when we're burning for action.... The chance to do something new and great—it's a chance in a lifetime. But Hitler keeps putting me off. He wants to let things drift. Keeps counting on a miracle. That's Adolf for you.[12]

Like Karl Ernst, Ernst Roehm was killed on June 30, 1934—the Night of the Long Knives, when the Nazis killed about a thousand Germans: storm troopers, journalists, rivals of Hitler, the minister of transport, even a former Reich chancellor. One victim was a Catholic priest who had helped Hitler write *Mein Kampf.* Some—such as a music critic and the head of the Hitler Youth in Saxony—were killed by mistake. Their widows received their ashes in the mail, along with a note of apology.[13]

Roehm and Ernst weren't killed because they were gay; rather, their crime was political—the climax of a power struggle with the army, Goebbels, Goering, and Hitler on one side and Roehm and his restless storm troopers on the other. Roehm's murder, in particular, warned every Nazi not to deviate from their fuehrer's thinking. It also showed how callous Hitler could be: Roehm was one of his oldest friends. This was a fuehrer not to be trifled with.[14]

Hanussen's murder in 1933, and Roehm's and Ernst's and all the other murders a year later were stepping-stones in the Nazis' reign of terror: the beginning of the fear that would make a nation forget what it had been. The season of killings was the warm-up act for all those that would follow. Roehm gave the order for Karl Ernst to kill Hanussen. Proud of his storm troopers, Roehm couldn't stomach a mind reader bragging all over Berlin that he had Roehm's army in his vest pocket. Proud of his friendship with Hitler, there was no way he could anticipate that, 15 months later, he would be dead too.[15]

★  ★  ★

On April 7, two lumberjacks found a body in the woods south of Berlin. It had been badly disfigured by wild animals. The jacket of the suit the man had been wearing had two labels. One had the name of the tailor: Hoffman. The other had the name of the man for whom the jacket was made: Hanussen. Several of Hanussen's employees went to the morgue to identify the body. Police ruled out robbery—the only item missing from the body was his watch. Thirty marks were in his jacket pocket, a not-so-subtle suggestion that Hanussen was a Judas to Germany's new rulers.[16]

Except for a brief item in Goebbels's newspaper, *Der Angriff*, the murder was almost ignored in Germany: "The body of a Jew was found in an evergreen grove on the road from Bayreuth to Neuhof. He had been shot to death. His face was unrecognizable. At the morgue, he was identified as Hermann Steinschneider, who, under the name of Hanussen, had a certain vogue in Berlin as a clairvoyant." "A certain vogue" would have infuriated Hanussen. With three words, his entire career was reduced to ephemera.[17]

Outside Germany, the murder was reported extensively. In Vienna, a left-wing newspaper, the *Arbeiterzeitung*, blamed it on the Nazis. Under the headline "Another Lynch Killing by the Nazis?" the paper traced Hanussen's friendships with high Nazis, the very people who "decided to rid themselves of the unpleasant and inconvenient Jew in their midst," a task "easily accomplished by the Nazis whose motto is 'As soon as you've served your purpose, you can go.' No sooner does a Nazi think this than a dead body is found in the forest." And beyond Europe, almost every paper reported on the killing. "Noted Clairvoyant Found Murdered," the *Canberra Times* announced. "Seer Who Told Hitler's Rise Found Slain; Hanussen Was Adviser to European Royalty," proclaimed the *New York Times*. In upstate New York, the *Syracuse Herald* ran a 40-inch story: "Bullets End Amazing Career of Hanussen, Germany's Rasputin." Even the *Daily Call* in little Piqua, Ohio—population sixteen thousand—put the murder on Page One: "Remains of Erik Hanussen Located."[18]

Hanussen's death told the future more accurately than anything he had ever divined. It was a future of gas and fire, ovens and bullets, graves and tears. No one saw this future, not even "Europe's best known fortuneteller." Yet his murder was a sign that the beast had arrived, that the future—always Hanussen's bread and butter—would be an implacable and merciless plague. Hanussen would not see its full ferocity. This he was spared, and for that he should have been grateful. No one should have witnessed what was to come, though, surely, Hanussen would have been proud that, in his death, he had performed the greatest act of clairvoyance of his entire life.

Glimpses into the true state of Hanussen's mind had surfaced three years earlier in his autobiography, *Meine Lebenslinie*. After more than 270 pages of boasting about his feats or complaining about the hardships he had overcome, in the book's last five pages, the curtain rises on the man behind the myth. What we see is someone at odds with himself. On one side—the Hanussen side—he is timorous and ambivalent. On the other side—the side of Herman Steinschneider, the "real" side, not an invention for the stage—he is driven and ambitious. Just past his forty-first birthday when he wrote the book, Hanussen/Steinschneider was not at ease with himself: quarreling about his purpose, his goals, his very reason for being.

In these final pages, Steinschneider meets privately with Hanussen. Until now, he was "too much of a coward" to turn his powers upon himself, the same powers he had used to fill theaters all over Europe. It was finally time for him to benefit from himself.[19]

The hotel room where Hanussen was conducting private consultations was a mess. Letters and newspapers were strewn all over the place. "You don't look comfortable," Steinschneider told Hanussen. "In fact, you don't seem to be enjoying your life very much."

Hanussen had been stuck in this gloomy dungeon most of the day. Thirty, maybe 40, people had sought his wisdom and his insights. "People think I know everything," he complained to Steinschneider. "And horribly enough, I do know most of it. I long for not seeing clear to the bottom of everyone's soul. I want to close my eyes before the visions that come to me. I struggle with myself."[20]

Yet Hanussen rallied as this new customer—the other half of himself—stood before him. "You are here to gain some clarity about yourself," he said. "You want to know what you represent in this world, what is going on with you, why you exist."

Steinschneider smiled. "You guessed wrong, Mr. Clairvoyant," he said. "I know who I am. I am someone who wants to eat well, drink well, and sleep well. I want to make as much money as possible and I want to work as little for it as possible."

"That isn't true," Hanussen countered. "With your talents, it would not be difficult for you to make money in another line of work. Now you earn your money with great difficulty, then you spend it quickly. Really, why do you love money?"

"Money is nice when you get older, Mr. Hanussen," Steinschneider answered lamely, adding, "You can buy friends with money."

"You can buy parasites," Hanussen countered. "Those aren't friends. You won't ever have a real friend, sir. Do you know that tale about Rübezahl, Mr. Steinschneider?"

"Rübezahl? Wasn't that the mythical character who turned turnips into human beings?"

"Exactly," said Hanussen. "He raised his wand and suddenly the turnips in his field turned into friends and women, horses and wagons, flowers and elegant dresses for beautiful women."

"Nice," said Steinschneider. "I want to be able to do that."

"You *are* capable of doing that," said Hanussen. "You've been doing that your whole life. You raise your wand and turn turnips into human beings. But turnips don't last forever. They get old and wrinkly, dry and ugly. With you, it's always been just turnips, not human beings. It's turnips that your wand sets alive."[21]

The room grew silent as the darkness closed in on them. Steinschneider was getting chilly. The hollowness of his life was being held up before him. "You scare me," he told Hanussen. "You make my flesh creep. I don't want to be near you. You're really quite horrible."

With that, Steinschneider left the room, glad to put some distance between himself and Hanussen, who, as it turned out, was more sensible than the man who had invented him. Hanussen knew it was time for a respite from a constant pursuit of fame and wealth. But Steinschneider was in no mood to be kind. Joined at the hip, he and Hanussen would go forward together, getting as ugly as a dried-up turnip against which no wand could do its magic.

★ ★ ★

Seven people attended Hanussen's funeral—barely enough to fill a single pew. The Nazis had advised Hanussen's friends and business associates to stay away. Most did. Other than the small turnout, Hanussen would have enjoyed his funeral. There was some pomp and some ceremony, and he was never averse to that. The chapel was a jewel box of a building, with a highly varnished dark brown wood exterior and carvings near the entrance so detailed and graceful that they could have been exhibited at a crafts museum. And the seven middle-aged men—employees of the Southwest Cemetery—who wheeled Hanussen's casket out of the chapel provided the liveried escort that had eluded him in life, although with their baggy uniforms, polished black shoes, and caps with shiny visors, they resembled streetcar conductors more than somber functionaries at a cemetery.[22]

Hanussen would have been pleased that, for once, he was being treated with the dignity and respect he was due. This was no ordinary cemetery. In the early 1900s, when it was apparent that Berlin was running out of room for the dead, the Protestant church had bought five hundred acres in Stahnsdorf, a small town south of the capital. The church built a state-of-the-art cemetery there, with fountains, reflecting pools, glades, 100,000 trees, and paths of various lengths and widths that crisscrossed and intersected with each other. All this established a calm and peace that many of the dead had never enjoyed in life. Soon it was among the most prestigious cemeteries in Berlin, drawing the wealthy and the famous, for whom immense mausoleums and ambitious monuments were erected. But not for Hanussen. His resting place is marked by a tall brown stone, three feet wide at its bottom and almost four feet tall. About halfway up, a gradual tapering culminates in a rounded point at its peak. All that is written on the stone is "Erik Jan Hanussen." No dates of birth or death. No bromides about whether Hanussen would rest in peace or if God or the angels would protect him through all eternity. No descriptions of his accomplishments. Just "Erik Jan Hanussen," although, almost perversely, this might have satisfied him: a true celebrity should be recognized by name alone.

Hanussen's grave is well maintained. The day I was there, a small pot of fresh lavender flowers rested in front of the tombstone. But it is hard to find. Getting to the cemetery required a long ride on a subway from Berlin, then a lengthy bus ride, then a long walk down a cobblestone road with small country houses on the right and tall pine trees on the left. Then it took me two hours of wandering around the cemetery to find the gravesite. The cemetery has deteriorated since Hanussen was buried there, its grand design now overgrown with weeds and underbrush. Some paths have entirely disappeared; others have narrowed so much they are more like vague suggestions than well-defined trails. The place is a maze: paths meet other paths that take you nowhere or disappear after several hundred feet or join trails where you've already been or take you past graves you've already seen or mausoleums and memorials you don't want to see—and all the while you don't run into anyone because the cemetery is as empty of life as it is neglected. Truly, this is a place of the dead. After being lost for so long, I was so elated when I found Hanussen's grave that, after muttering inches from his tombstone, "Where the hell have you been, Hanussen?," I called a friend in Berlin on my cell phone to brag of my success.

During the hour and a half I spent near Hanussen's grave, two people came by: a man in his mid-twenties who wanted to show his elderly mother where Erik Jan Hanussen lay. She had heard about him from her parents, who had seen him perform. And her son had heard how, during World War I, Hanussen had read the minds of soldiers by bribing a friend in the platoon's mailroom to withhold their mail until he read it. To mother and son, Hanussen was damaged goods.

In death, Hanussen is as elusive as in life. After paying my respects to him, I had dinner at a café opposite the cemetery entrance. A wedding reception that was being held there seemed friendly enough, so after enjoying my meal, I congratulated the bride and groom and asked several guests about Hanussen. No one had ever heard of him. What I told them about the man was ancient history—someone their grandparents might have known about. Not them. History is like that: It can hide right in front of you: in this case, across the street in the largest cemetery in Germany. Unless someone brings it up, it lies buried and inert. And, anyway, the wedding guests were eager to get on with their celebration, an urge that Hanussen surely would have appreciated: the man so fond of parties might have injected some life into this one, which was quiet and dull. For, if anything, Hanussen was about life: He quarreled with it, enjoyed it, resented it, and tried, passionately and tirelessly, to shape it to his liking. Unwilling to settle for the smallness of the lives of others, he was full of tricks, even up to the last minute. He was among the first Jews killed in the Holocaust, but by the night of his murder, he was officially a Protestant. He had converted a few weeks before—a last-ditch effort to save his life. The conversion was Hanussen's final illusion.

Four years after Hanussen was killed, the Nazis were still obsessed with him. In the fall of 1937, the weekly newspaper of the SS, *Das Schwarze Korps*, attacked Hanussen as a Jew who used "demonic affectations, colossal impudence and brazen tricks" to accumulate fame, wealth, and a string of decadent possessions (fancy cars, a luxurious yacht, a sprawling apartment). Hanussen personified Jewish trickery and capitalism at its worst. With his smooth patter and slick tricks, he had blinded people to reality, encouraging them to return to a past ruled by wonder and superstition and an unwavering adherence to the power of the irrational.[23]

The attack on Hanussen was part of a series in the paper against the occult. Called "Dangerzone Superstition," the articles argued that charlatans like Hanussen were part of an international conspiracy engineered by Jews and Catholics to manipulate Germans. Priests, psychics, and spiritualists were dispensing the same deceptions. Astrologists, too, for how could an Aryan and a black child born on the same day share a horoscope and thus the same fate? This was an assault on reason, on destiny. It was also a violation of the law: in June 1937, the Nazis had outlawed all occult activities.[24]

One reason the Nazis banned the occult was so there would be one less influence on public opinion: totalitarian regimes prefer to control their own narratives. Yet the Nazis exploited the occult when it suited them. In 1943, for instance, when the Germans wanted to rescue Mussolini after the Italian was deposed in a bloodless coup, Himmler—an unwavering believer in clairvoyance—set up a team of psychic wizards in a villa on Lake Wannsee near Berlin. There they enjoyed good food, good wine, and good cigars while swinging pendulums over maps of Italy, trying to determine where Il Duce was being held. Two years later, as the Allies closed in on Berlin and Germany was in ruins, Joseph Goebbels, Hitler's faithful propaganda chief, turned to horoscopes for predictions that contradicted the dire military conditions. And when Goebbels learned that Franklin Roosevelt had died the day before, the Reich's minister of propaganda called Hitler in his bunker, almost shouting into the phone, "My Fuehrer, I congratulate you. It is written in the stars that the second half of April will be the turning point for us. Today is Friday, April 13. It is the turning point."[25]

Nothing turned. The stars did not favor Hitler. They had not favored Erik Jan Hanussen either.

★   ★   ★

A year after the Nazis banned all occult activity came Kristallnacht—November 10, 1938. In one night, the Nazis destroyed almost fourteen hundred synagogues. It was apparent that Jewish life in Germany had no future. This catastrophe helped make sense of a note that Hanussen had smuggled out of Germany not long before his murder. In the note, Hanussen admitted his mistakes to Ernest Juhn, who had been his manager for two years. "I have no time for long explanations," he told Juhn.

> Let's be friends again at the end. I wasn't as shrewd as I thought, nor as stupid as you believed. But stupid enough. . . . I always thought that business about the Jews was just an election trick [of the Nazis]. It wasn't. Read carefully what [the prophet] Daniel has to say on the subject in chapters 11 and 12. Count the days, but only after they have destroyed a hundred temples in a single day—that's the time to start counting. The first date you get will mark the fall of the man who wants to become the ruler of the world by brute force. And the second date will mark the day on which will occur the triumphal entry of the victors. This is my farewell to you.[26]

And what a farewell it was. The Book of Daniel is full of visions about the end of days and the coming of the messiah and reassuring stories about faithful Jews exiled in Babylon who walked unscathed out of lions' dens and fiery furnaces, protected by God. The Book of Daniel was consolation for a people who were doubting their much-promised redemption and deliverance. Daniel's core message was that empires may rise and fall, but everything, even the fate of the powerful and the mighty, is determined by God, whose divine plan would ultimately be fulfilled, though in the timely measure of the Lord, not the impatient timetable of his people here on Earth. The final chapters of Daniel—the chapters to which Hanussen alluded in his note—attempt to work out the date of the end of the world, the cataclysmic days when immense, terrifying battles will rage between "the king of the north" and "the king of the south," nations will be wrenched by lies and betrayals, and women will commit heinous and blasphemous abominations. Daniel looked beyond all this. He promised hope—the hope of salvation. The faithful, the weak, and the frail would be saved. Everyone else would be damned. This was the end of life as we know it, and the beginning of eternity as we've heard of it.

Juhn wasn't a scholar or particularly religious, but to decipher Hanussen's cryptic message, he focused on the eleventh and twelfth verses of chapter 12 in the Book of Daniel: "And from the time that the daily sacrifice shall be taken away, and the abomination that maketh desolate set up, there shall be a thousand two hundred and ninety days. Blessed is he that waiteth, and cometh to the thousand three hundred and five and thirty days."[27]

In his note, Hanussen instructed Juhn to start counting "only after they have destroyed a hundred temples in a single day." The Nazis were destroying or desecrating synagogues regularly but never in the numbers Hanussen stipulated. Then came Kristallnacht, when the Nazis destroyed 13 times as many synagogues as Hanussen had specified. That didn't matter: Destroying one hundred temples was as outrageous as destroying almost fourteen hundred. Either number represented a despicable plunge into human depravity.

So Juhn began counting. According to Hanussen's formula, 1,290 days after Kristallnacht—May 23, 1942—Hitler would fall. And 1,335 days after Kristallnacht—July 7, 1942—the Allies would triumphantly enter Berlin. As it turned out, the Soviets entered Berlin in late April 1945; Hitler committed suicide on April 30; and Germany surrendered on May 7. Hanussen's prediction would have shortened the war by three years, saving tens of millions of lives and halting the worst of the Holocaust.

Thoroughly believing the prophecy, *Redbook* magazine announced in early 1942 that "in May and July of this year"—when the greatest clairvoyant of his time had predicted the war would end— "Hanussen...will find his definite place in the annals of our age." Surely, anyone who accurately forecast the end of the worst war in history was worthy of honors. But *Redbook*, Juhn, and anyone else who fell for Hanussen's prediction might have been smarter to place their faith in Daniel himself, not in a latter-day prophet who sullied himself with scams, tricks, and Nazis. Even Nebuchadnezzar in ancient Babylon knew that Daniel's wisdom was "ten times better than all the magicians and astrologers" in his entire realm. But faith has to be placed somewhere and, in time of war, when the human spirit clings to whatever hope it can find, a discredited clairvoyant may seem as good a place as any.[28]

PART THREE

# The Daughter

There is no remedy for love but to love more.
—*Henry David Thoreau*

# CHAPTER 15

# The View from Italy

Erika Steinschneider-Fuchs lives in a nursing home in Merano, the town in northern Italy that Hanussen visited in the fall of 1932, hoping to convince his daughter and ex-wife to run away to America with him. Her room is a shrine to her father, with black-and-white photos of him on almost every wall and colored photos of the elaborate staterooms on his yacht next to a snapshot of a white-flanneled Hanussen strolling in a square with the boat's burly captain. On a table, a frame displays an eight-by-ten photo of Hanussen a few inches from a small painting of the Virgin Mary looking demurely toward her right, almost as if she is blessing Hanussen. In the photo, Hanussen is wearing a three-piece suit, a white shirt, and a dark tie. A white handkerchief is tucked into his jacket pocket. The photo is dated "5★XII★32"—December 5, 1932. It is inscribed, "To my dearest photo companion, from your father, Erik."

Erika is the child Hanussen saw for eight days in 1932. He had not seen her for almost a decade. He would never see her again.

For a 90-year-old, Erika is tireless—full of charm and vigor and innocent flirtations and a peppy garrulousness. Often, most of this conversation is about her father, whom she really only knew for a week and a day 79 years ago: eight days that remain the cardinal moments in her long life.

Erika's devotion to Hanussen is disproportionate to his devotion to her. From 1924, when he divorced Therese, to 1932, he ignored his daughter. Then, suddenly, he showed up, thinking perhaps that by wooing little Erika, he might persuade Therese to join him in the United States. Knowing Hanussen's character, it was not beyond him to use the child to gain her mother. Even Erika, sitting in an overstuffed armchair under all those photos of her father, is open to this possibility. "He realized they were both getting older," she acknowledges, "and that she was the mother of his only child and he would probably never have another one. He had always wanted a child, and she had given him one. That is why he wanted her back."[1]

Other than being Hanussen's daughter, Erika has another reason to be so concerned about him. As a Catholic, she cares deeply about his soul. When she was a little girl, she studied with a rabbi for a few years, then converted to Catholicism when she was eight to please her mother and her new stepfather, who came from a wealthy and powerful family in Merano. By the time Hanussen visited Erika there, she had been confirmed and was attending mass every Sunday. Although largely dismissive toward religion, Hanussen admired this. "He asked me, 'Do you still adore Jesus?'" Erika recalls. "When I said yes, he looked at me with a certain wonder." Perhaps Hanussen was witnessing an unfamiliar sight—one that he had been trying to evoke from his audiences for decades: the faith of a child—deep and impenetrable.

Given a chance, Hanussen would have always remained in Berlin. "He wanted to live only there," Erika says. "Berlin was the only place where he felt at home." He knew he was a marked man in Germany, yet there was no place else for him to turn. Therese would not reconcile

with him and move to New York, and he could not remain in Merano.
He would have been uncomfortable there, says Erika, with Therese's
husband "controlling everything. His family was enormously influential, especially in politics. My father would not have wanted to stay
here. He wanted to be the king of everything. Here he would have
been a nonentity. A no one. My stepfather would have made sure he
stayed that way."

On the day Hanussen arrived in 1932, Erika was waiting for him
inside her house on Maiastrasse, peeping through the curtains. Her
mother had taken her out of school for a few days so she could enjoy
the time with her father. When Erika spotted Hanussen in the garden,
she ran outside and flew into his arms. He cried as he held her. Was
it a father's joy at being reunited with his daughter? Or a clairvoyant's
hunch that the reunion was also their farewell? Hanussen may not have
come to Merano to induce his daughter and ex-wife to join him. He
may have come to say good-bye.

During their few days together, Hanussen showed Erika pictures
of his boat and said he would change its name from *Ursel IV* to *Erika*.
He promised to take her on a long trip on the boat in the spring. They
went for walks and took photos together. He bought her a bike—her
first—and taught her how to ride, running behind to help balance it.
And he took her mother aside and warned that her second marriage
would not last long and she would have a sad Christmas. He was right.
Not long after Hanussen left, Therese learned that her husband was
having an affair. They soon divorced.

Erika is not sure if Hanussen told Therese that her marriage would
crumble out of sheer petulance after she refused to come to America
with him. She is sure that his powers were real. Otherwise, she said,
"I could not have inherited them," alluding to healing a woman who
had arthritis. The woman had gone as far as Innsbruck to consult with

a doctor, who could not help her. When the woman returned to the nursing home, Erika laid her hands on her. The woman's pain disappeared. Erika's mother was also sure that Hanussen's powers were real. "She told me about my father solving a bank robbery and seeing him hypnotize a woman during one of his shows into believing she was a cat and trying to crawl up the curtain on the stage. She knew Hanussen was authentic. She was not a clairvoyant, but she was very intuitive. She worried that he might destroy himself in the end."

And he did. Hanussen, says Erika, "knew too much. His fame meant power and the Nazis didn't want to have that used against them. Any Jew who wielded as much influence as Hanussen was a problem. Hitler asked him to visit one day so he could learn about his future. My father told the truth: 'If you don't leave the Jews in peace, you will have no luck.' He also said he saw darkness at the end of Hitler's life. Which means he had to disappoint Hitler. With that, things got out of hand for my father. Perhaps, though, he understood this was inevitable. He told me nobody can escape their own fate."

Hanussen respected fate. And he respected death. In the 1950s, Erika remembers, Elizabeth Heine, one of Hanussen's employees (and one of the seven people who attended his funeral), told her about a woman who consulted with Hanussen. "As soon as she entered his private office, he told her to go away because he couldn't help her. She was quite upset and left. When she crossed the street outside my father's office, she was hit by a car and died. My father said that he had seen death behind her and he had no power to help her."

Perhaps when Hanussen visited Erika in Merano, he knew death was behind him. And that he had no power to help himself.

To some degree, Erika has conflated Hanussen and Jesus. These two men—the prophet and the savior—have sustained her since an afternoon in 1933 when she went to a friend's house to play and was barely in the door before her friend waved a newspaper in her face. "Look," she said, "they killed your father." Erika ran home crying. Her mother already knew about Hanussen's murder—a lawyer had called her with the news—but she had not told Erika: How do you tell a child that her father has been killed? That should never be a mother's duty, and hearing it should never be a child's fate. Therese, says Erika, "was scared. My father's apartment had been ransacked. There was nothing left, though he wanted to give everything to me. My mother didn't want any money. She wanted to be left alone. She wanted to be left in peace."

For Erika, Hanussen was not unlike Jesus: Both accepted their fate. Both men were dedicated to their mission and their purpose. "With my father," notes Erika, "it is like what Jesus said: 'You are either with me or against me'"—a categorical distinction that culminated with a crucifixion in one case and a gangland-type slaughter in the other. In both cases, death.

★ ★ ★

Erika yearns for that most peaceful of places—heaven—and she does what she can to ensure that this will be her final destination. The other residents in her nursing home might sit on a patio outside, doing arts and crafts or singing "Der Froeliche Wanderer" ("I love to go a-wandering, Along the mountain track, And as I go, I love to sing, My knapsack on my back"). Erika lives her own life there, an independent one, and she admits to the paradox that she knew her father "so little in life, and now that he is somewhere else, I know him so well. He is always present. His soul is tightly bound to mine." She attends mass every day in the chapel of the nursing home "and every time I pray, I tell the Virgin Mary to take care of my father.

'Please look after my father,'" Erika prays. "'I don't know how he behaves up there. I am only a human whose father was taken away much too early.'"

In Erika's room, two crucifixes hang next to a photo of Pope John Paul II. Underneath them on a table are two foot-tall statues—one of Jesus, one of the Virgin Mary. Freshly cut roses are arranged in front of them. Faithful and devout, Erika is confident that in heaven she will be with Jesus—and with Hanussen. Almost everyone else familiar with Hanussen deems this improbable. They envision a less pleasant destination for him. Erika counters their intense dislike of her father with a love and absolution he never found on Earth, but which, she is sure, he has found for eternity with his Maker.[2]

Erika is so devoted to Hanussen that it is tempting to suspect that the 90-year-old suffers from a form of arrested development. Her life has been centered for so long on those eight days with her father that everything before and after those 192 hours pales by comparison. Those few days define her, perhaps because she sees her father's visit not as an act of desperation—a panicked dodge from the Nazis—but as his final gift to her. "He was a clairvoyant," she says. "He knew he was going to die. He wanted to see his daughter before his death. He wanted to get to know me." Hanussen was telling her: Even during my long absence, I did not forget you. You are my daughter and I will love you forever, in heaven as I have not done very well on Earth.

Erika is certain she convinced Hanussen to convert to Christianity. "At my Catholic boarding school, I found my big love—Jesus. I told my father that he should learn to love Jesus too." Joining the church, she told him, meant joining her in paradise. With his soul allied with Christ, cleansed by baptism, and purified through Communion, "after death," says Erika, "Jesus would not come between us." And why should he? She was just getting to know her father—her real father.

And surely Jesus was familiar with the complexities of the father-child relationship.

* * *

During her nine decades, Erika has survived the Depression and the hardships of a war and then what came after the war. She survived the divorce of her parents and being married to someone 20 years her senior while having an affair with a man she calls "the real love of my life. My mother always said I didn't deserve my husband. He was such a gentleman." As if these sorrows were not enough, Erika knows that almost everyone familiar with her father considers him a swindler, a crook, and a friend of evil and malificent men: "He had many enemies and only a few good friends." Yet she worships him. A girl—any girl—wants to think the best of her father, for this is the power of love. In Erika's case, it is also the power of longing for a life that she never had, a life that, to some extent, she expanded into a fantasy of familial togetherness. She had to. For most of her mother's marriage to Hanussen, her father wasn't home. He was tantamount to a rumor. Often her mother wasn't there either, once joining Hanussen for an extended trip to Asia and the Orient while Erika stayed in Vienna with her aunt. The trip was so lengthy that Erika didn't recognize Therese when she returned. "One day," she says, "I came home from school and there was this woman standing in the hallway. It was my mother. I couldn't identify her because they had been away for so long. I thought it was our dressmaker." As a family, there were no weekend trips, no Sunday outings, no drives in the country. "For anything like that," said Erika, "I only went with my mother or aunt. My father was never there. Family life like that only happened in Merano."

By then, Hanussen was long gone, and whatever semblance of normal family activities was truncated, anyway, with Erika attending a boarding school at a convent, with infrequent visits home and a stepfather who, while not a distant man, was, in some ways, cautious and controlling. So when Hanussen, her ghost of a father, showed up—glittering with fame and wealth and a raffish disregard for rules and convention—Erika begged, "I want to live with you. I don't want to stay here." "No," said Hanussen, "that is not a good idea. I'm always traveling. Stay here with your mother."

That was not the answer Erika wanted, though, at the time, it made sense. The real reason, she now says, is that "he didn't want to scare me." Soon after his visit, she remembers hearing, Hanussen told an audience in Stuttgart that he would die soon. You can tell strangers in Stuttgart a prediction about your own mortality. It is not something you tell your 12-year-old daughter who hasn't seen you for half her life.

Not long after Hanussen's murder, Erika began sensing that her father was with her, guiding her, advising her. She told few people about this and certainly not her priest: The church did not approve of communicating with the dead. That, plus the skepticism of our modern age, made it difficult for Erika to find the right person in whom to confide that she was in touch with her father. This troubled and frustrated her since she is ordinarily rather open and trusting. I was honored, then, that, on my second day of interviewing her, Erika said she had been in touch with her father and I had his blessing for writing this book. He was also watching over me and my translator, ensuring our safety, wherever we went. When the interview ended two hours later and I was driving down the narrow, winding streets of Merano in a tiny Fiat, past pastel-colored villas and young mothers pushing strollers, I turned to my translator. "We have Hanussen's blessing?" I laughed. "And he's protecting us? Yeah! Sure!" That was not a good moment for sarcasm: it was the only time during our fifteen-hundred-mile trip through Germany and Italy that the Fiat jumped the curb.

★ ★ ★

Merano may be in the Alps, but summers there can be scorchers. In July, when I visited, it was sizzling, with the deep valley where the town lies holding in the heat and the humidity. Everyone, especially the tourists, was wilting, cursing global warming and wondering why they weren't spending their time along some breezy, cool seashore. Erika seemed fine. She has spent most of her life there. She is accustomed to the summers and has more energy than a person half her age. She carries her 90 years lightly, with fading eyesight one of her few concessions to the rigors of age. But even with her sight waning, she has clear visions of the hills and peaks that surround the town, holding in the sizzling heat and holding her in, too, sheltering her from the pain of what happened to her father—"this great stranger in my life"—a long time ago, keeping it at a remove where she can absorb it, knitting it into a narrative that buoys and uplifts her, assuring her that there was a reason for the grieving and the sorrows and the tears.[3] These peaks are so high that, on certain days—lovely days—they get lost in the low, brilliantly white clouds, merging with the sky and everything beyond it to form one vast and endless vista: a spacious terrain of pristine whites and cerulean blues and a golden, celestial light. These mountains beckon Erika upward, toward the salvation she craves. Then at last, the little girl who begged to live in Berlin with a man she barely knew will reside with him in eternal and glorious splendor—at last, in peace. And at last, together.

# Acknowledgments

Every book begins with a small and, sometimes, idle thought, often in the middle of the night and often when nothing else is going on. Which is why the first person I'll thank is the guy who turned me on to Hanussen, Peter Lamont. If I hadn't been reading Peter's book, *The Rise of the Indian Rope Trick*, around three in the morning a few years ago, I'd never have heard of Erik Jan Hanussen. The entire book is riveting, but Peter's brief references to a Jew who was Hitler's "psychic consultant" in particular kept me awake the rest of the night. This is the sort of oxymoronic jostling that makes history fun. And disturbing. If I'd fallen asleep before I got to that section, I shudder to think how I might have spent the past two years.

From that simple discovery of a man named Hanussen, the net grew wider. Fast. Soon friends in other countries were helping with research—Sarah Glazer in London, Aurore Renaut in Paris—as well as some new friends I have yet to meet: Alexandra Nagel in Amsterdam and Yossi Chajes at the University of Haifa in Israel. Closer to home, thanks to other new friends—Duane Griffin, a geographer at Bucknell University; Geoffrey J. Giles, a historian at the University of Florida; the eminent Gerhard Weinberg, professor of history at the University of North Carolina at Chapel Hill; two savvy historians at the United

States Holocaust Memorial Museum in Washington, Steven Sage and Joseph White; and another historian generous with his time and knowledge, Bob Waite, who is lucky enough to divide his life between Berlin and upstate New York.

Since I'm tragically monolingual, *merci beaucoup* and *tak så meget* to a trio of translators: Jane Delury and Emily Blair for wrestling with French and Katherine Langballe Sorensen for deciphering Danish. Carol Vaeth and other librarians at the University of Baltimore found books, articles, and manuscripts around the globe. The university itself provided a sizable research and travel grant. Without that, I'd have been more tethered to home—not recommended when researching a book that requires extensive trips to Europe. Other Baltimoreans who were invaluable were Dai Andrews, who has keen insights about magic and mind reading; Justin Codd and Giordana Segneri, each of whom transcribed key interviews I conducted; and Tara Bostock, whose sharp ideas about strategic sections of the manuscript and warnings about goofs of logic, holes in research, and troublesome potholes of grammar were of vast assistance. A classy publisher in New York should snap her up.

From the Washington metropolitan area, Phillip Steinschneider, a distant relative of Hanussen's, offered his extensive research into the family's genealogy.

Dedication is an understatement when it comes to my agent, Kathy Anderson. Kathy works hard. She knows how publishing works and where publishing is heading and instantly knows the merits of an idea when she hears it. She negotiates a contract like a hound, ferreting out clauses that don't belong or cajoling clauses into a contract that were mysteriously missing. Kathy elevates the definition of "agent". I am proud I know her. I am delighted she represents me.

At Palgrave Macmillan, Alessandra Bastagli immediately understood what this book was about; Luba Ostashevsky edited with diligence and wisdom, especially regarding structure and tone; her assistant, Laura Lancaster, addressed all the wonkiness—to use her word—that annoys writers but is unavoidable when bringing a book into the world; and publicist Siobhan Paganelli and marketing director Christine Catarino imaginatively thought of every angle, contact, television show, radio host, website, lecture series—hither and, often, yon—that would ensure *The Nazi Séance* was not a closely guarded secret, the death knell for any book. Kudos to production manager, Donna Cherry, for gracefully shepherding the book over the many hurdles that distinguish a pile of paper known as a manuscript from a bound volume known as a book. A tip of the hat to copy editor Debra Manette, whose keen eyesight would make an eagle jealous. And a cornucopia of appreciation to Polly Kummel, "Polly Proofreader," as she should be known in the trade, is tireless and discerning, with a good sense of humor and a deep love of horses (which has absolutely nothing to do with this book).

If you've seen the magicians Penn & Teller, you know that one is boisterous, the other silent. Offstage, Teller, the quiet guy, is a formidably articulate observer of our human predicament. He graciously took time out from his busy schedule to discuss the history and dynamics of his craft—what kind of people are drawn to it and what audiences seek and how performers satisfy that yearning. There is more to magic than meets the eye, precisely because it doesn't meet our eyes. It is the art of the invisible. Teller is a master not only of that art but also of expressing the ineffable.

In Germany, where I had never been, I met or spoke with the sweetest, most thoughtful people. To Daniela Gauding, Uwe Schellinger, Matthias Heisig, Martin Schaaff, Tillman Hellwig, Rolf Scholz: *Vielen herzlichen Dank*. The same goes for Satori, whose business card says he is "The Man Who Knows Almost Everything!" True, but he is overly modest. Satori brings to mentalism a staggering originality and to relationships an enriching kindness. And, anyway, somehow he could read my mind. How, I'll never know. In fact, I don't want to know: it's more fun *not* knowing.

In the small Italian town of Merano, Delia Muller was an exquisite hostess. She showed me all the nooks and crannies of Merano, including the best pizza joint. She also introduced me to friends who insisted I go hang gliding with them in the Alps—an offer I could not refuse.

Finally, the three people who were most indispensable for *The Nazi Séance:* Erika Steinschneider-Fuchs—Hanussen's only child—allowed me to interview her for many hours over three days about her father, her mother, her life. Erika was patient and comprehensive. The one thing I foolishly didn't ask was the secret of her longevity: she was 90 years old when we spoke.

Gary Bart, the great-nephew of Sigmund Breitbart, is a man of character and perspective. The wonder that Breitbart kindled in him when he was a kid has yet to be extinguished. It's the kind of wonder that is a rare commodity in today's rushed, mercantile world, and that he should treasure. Gary and I had many conversations about Breitbart and the era in which he performed. Gary's collection of rare, contemporary articles about Breitbart, Hanussen, and Marta contributed significantly to the fullness of the first part of this book.

Erika Otto is in a category by herself. Smart as whip and kind as a saint, Erika was involved with *The Nazi Séance* from a few weeks after I got my book contract to the last translations that I needed the very day I finished the manuscript. Her skills as a translator and researcher are impeccable. Her enthusiasm for this project—and the historic, philosophical, and psychological insights she brought to it—is staggering. Erika wrote her own job description as we went along: What she expected from herself I would not have expected from anyone. Her high standards raised the standards for the book. Exceeding these were her generosity, hospitality, and patience, admirable traits in anyone, surely, and second nature for Erika. If you are thinking about writing a book that involves anything Germanic, sorry, I will not give you Erika's address or phone number. I've already reserved her for my next project.

So a late-night reading of a book that I accidentally picked up in a bookstore culminated in a journey on which I encountered wonderful people and odd and peculiar ideas. I also encountered historical figures who forced me to ponder our potentially fatal vanities. I hope reading this book has done the same for you.

# Notes

PREAMBLE   "HE CANNOT DOUBT THE GENUINENESS
OF HIS MISSION"

1. Bruno Frei, *Hanussen: A Report* (Strasbourg, France: Sebastian Brant, 1934), 142–143.
2. Ted Harrison, "Count Helldorf and the German Resistance to Hitler," Working Papers in Contemporary History and Politics, no. 8, European Studies Research Institute, University of Salford, Salford, UK, January 1996, 17, 19, 21, 26, 30.
3. Frei, *Hanussen: A Report,* 144–145; "Nazidom's Rasputin," *True Mystic Science,* November 1938, 74; Martin Schaaff, interview by author, February 10, 2010.
4. Dusty Sklar, *The Nazis and the Occult* (New York: Dorset, 1977), 122.
5. Frei, *Hanussen: A Report,* 142, 145–146.
6. Frederick Marion, *In My Mind's Eye* (New York: E. P. Dutton, 1950), 94; Arthur Koestler, *Arrow in the Blue* (New York: Macmillan, 1952), 298.
7. *Neues Weiner Journal* (Vienna), February 22, 1922, Albert Hellwig Archives, Institut fur Grenzgebiete der Psychologie und Psychohygiene, Freiburg, Germany.
8. Ibid.
9. *Erik Jan Hanussen's Berliner Wochenschau,* July 24, August 8 and 24, October 8 and 24, November 10 and 24, 1932, Hellwig Archives.
10. Alexandra Richie, *Faust's Metropolis* (New York: Carroll & Graf, 1999), 387, 398.
11. Thomas D. Grant, *Stormtroopers and Crisis in the Nazi Movement* (New York: Routledge, 2004), 35; William L. Shirer, *The Rise and Fall of the Third Reich* (New York: Touchstone, 1990), 42–43.
12. Grant, *Stormtroopers and Crisis in the Nazi Movement,* 6, 54–55; Jacques Delarue, *The Gestapo* (New York: Skyhorse, 2008), 6–7; Conan Fischer, *The German Communists and the Rise of Nazism* (New York: St. Martin's, 1991),

82–83, 144–145; Richard Bessel, *Political Violence and the Rise of Nazism* (New Haven, CT: Yale University Press, 1984), 51.

13. Delarue, *Gestapo,* 7; Bessel, *Political Violence and the Rise of Nazism,* 47.

14. Pierre van Paassen, "The Date of Hitler's Fall," *Redbook,* May 1942, 85–86; Bella Fromm, *Blood & Banquets* (New York: Birch Lane, 1990), 78.

15. Franz Polgar, *The Story of a Hypnotist* (New York: Hermitage House, 1951), 72.

## CHAPTER 1   ONE OF THE FINEST LIARS IN EUROPE

1. In an apparent effort to connect Hanussen with Jewish mystics, researchers into his early life have speculated that his family name—Steinschneider, or "stone carver"—is related to Ba'al Shem Tov, the founder of the sect of Jewish mysticism known as Chasidism. These efforts are misguided and strained. Ba'al Shem Tov is Hebrew for "master of the good name," not for "amulet carver," as revisionists claim. At best, a "cultural translation" can be applied to Ba'al Shem Tov so it roughly corresponds to Steinschneider, since the Ba'al Shem Tov dispensed cures through amulets containing the name of God. But such a holy, sacred skill is quite distant from carving stone.

2. By most standards, Berlin's conversion rate was substantial: three thousand of its Jews had converted in recent decades. In Vienna, three times as many Jews converted during the same period. Half of all Viennese Jews who left Judaism became Catholics, and one-quarter became Protestants. The rest stated that they had no religion. While Baron Hirsch was bitter about other Jews' ambitions, he wasn't stingy—he donated more than $100 million to Jewish causes. Most of that money, though, went toward resettling Jews from Europe, mostly to Argentina, an aspiration that makes us ponder Hirsch's true goal: Did he seek to improve Jews' conditions or to send them far away so he would not have to deal with them? Jewish plutocrats weren't the only self-haters. The Socialist Party's newspaper, largely staffed by Jews, campaigned against "Jewish interests," attacked the mainstream press as a pro-Jewish conspiracy, and sympathized with the slogan of an anti-Semitic party: "Down with the domination by the Jews" (George L. Berkley, *Vienna and Its Jews* [Lanham, MD: Madison Books, 1998], 54–55).

3. Erik Jan Hanussen, *Meine Lebenslinie* (Berlin: Universitas, 1930), 19–20.

4. Ibid., 37.

5. Ibid., 46.

6. Ibid., 41–46. Martin Schaaff, interview by author, February 9, 2010.

7. Hanussen, *Meine Lebenslinie,* 46–47.

8. Ibid.

9. Ibid., 49–50.

10. Ibid., 54.

11. Ibid., 55.

12. Ibid.
13. Ibid., 55–56.
14. Ibid., 56.
15. Ibid.
16. Ibid., 57.
17. Ibid., 58.
18. Ibid., 59. Over the years, there has been speculation that the circus Hanussen joined was the famous Carl Hagenbeck Circus. That's preposterous. The only clue that supports this is Hanussen calling the circus "Circus H" in his autobiography. But the "H" doesn't necessarily stand for Hagenbeck, nor would Carl Hagenbeck have tolerated whipping a lion across the face. To this day, Hagenbeck is considered one of the greatest animal trainers of all time. He was the first to establish the principle of training animals through trust, friendship, and kindness, not through fear or intimidation. The only weapon he allowed trainers was an ordinary kitchen chair that they held with the legs in front of them to bear the weight of a sudden attack. Hagenbeck would have banned the sort of whip Hanussen said he used to beat Sultan, and Hagenbeck surely would not have allowed a kid with zero experience with lions to step into their cage. Not only was Hermann far too young for such dangerous work, but he would have lacked the trust from the lions that could have come only from months of practice. (Background on Hagenbeck from Joan Selby-Lowndes, *How the Circus Works* [London: Routledge & Kegan-Paul, 1962], 68–71.)
19. Hanussen, *Meine Lebenslinie*, 59.
20. Teller, email to author, October 15, 2010.

## CHAPTER 2   THE PSYCHIC GRAVEDIGGER

1. Erik Jan Hanussen, *Meine Lebenslinie* (Berlin: Universitas, 1930), 56, 59.
2. Ibid., 59–63.
3. Ibid., 64.
4. Ibid., 64–65.
5. Ibid., 69–70.
6. Ibid., 70.
7. Ibid., 107.
8. Ibid., 110.
9. Ibid., 111.
10. Ibid., 112.
11. Ibid., 114–116.
12. Ibid.
13. Ibid., 117–118.
14. Ibid., 120–121.
15. Ibid., 122.

16. Ibid., 82–103.
17. Wilfried Kugel, *Hanussen* (Dusseldorf: Grupello, 1998), 26–27.
18. Ibid., 123–126.
19. Franz Hollering, "I Was an Editor in Germany, Part II: Fire in the Reichstag!" *Nation*, February 12, 1936, 183.
20. Ibid., 130; Dr. Allan Gold email to author, March 14, 2010; Robert Foley, *German Strategy and the Path to Verdun* (New York: Cambridge University Press, 2004), 138–145.
21. Hanussen, *Meine Lebenslinie*, 131, 134; Adam Borosz, "Jewish War Cemeteries in Western Galicia," n.d., website of Muzeum Okregowe w Tarnowie, www.muzeum.tarnow.pl.
22. Hanussen, *Meine Lebenslinie*, 136–137.
23. Ibid., 156.
24. Ibid., 158, 160–161.
25. Ibid., 161.
26. Ibid., 162.
27. Ibid., 164.
28. Ibid., 166–168, 170. Translation of program from Hanussen's November 11, 1918, performance, in the Bart Collection, a private archive in Los Angeles owned by Gary Bart, great-nephew of Siegmund Breitbart, the "Jewish strongman" with whom Hanussen had a rivalry in the early 1920s.
29. *Neues Weiner Journal* (Vienna), February 22, 1922, Albert Hellwig Archives, Institut fur Grenzgebiete der Psychologie und Psychohygiene, Freiburg, Germany.
30. Ibid.

## CHAPTER 3 "A CONJUROR IS AN ACTOR PLAYING THE PART OF A MAGICIAN"

1. Erik Jan Hanussen, *Mind Reading and Telepathy*, trans. and ed. Bill Palmer (Vienna: Jimmy Bix Versand, 2008), 44–45, 48–49.
2. Ibid., 52–54.
3. Ibid., 58–59.
4. Ibid.
5. Ibid., 48, 64–65.
6. Ibid., 65–66.
7. Ray Hyman, "Ouija, Dowsing and Other Seductions of Ideomotor Action," in Sergio Della Shea, ed., *Tall Tales about the Mind and Brain: Separating Fact from Fiction* (New York: Oxford University Press, 2007), 412–414, 418–420.
8. Ricky Jay, *Learned Pigs & Fireproof Women* (New York: Farrar, Straus and Giroux, 1998), 194. G. M. Stratton's study of Rubini, "The Control of Another Person by Obscure Signs"—*Psychological Review* 28, no. 4 (July

1921): 301–314—is a bit naive; even its title is off, since Rubini never claimed to control anyone. But it does provide an interesting peek at an early study of purported psychic ability.

9. Stratton, "Control of Another Person by Obscure Signs," 301–314.
10. Teller, interview by author, May 22, 2009.
11. "Legerdemain," *Encyclopedia Britannica* (New York: H. G. Allen, 1888), 14: 415.
12. Satori, email to author, January 15, 2010, and interview by author, December 21, 2009, Berlin.
13. Franz Polgar, *The Story of a Hypnotist* (New York: Hermitage House, 1951), 68–69.
14. Delia Muller, *The Bitter Heritage* (Bozen, Italy: Athesia Spectrum, 2006), 21.

CHAPTER 4  THE IRON QUEEN AND THE JEWISH SAMSON

1. Delia Muller, *The Bitter Heritage* (Bozen, Italy: Athesia Spectrum, 2006), 37.
2. Ibid.
3. Ibid.
4. Erika Steinschneider-Fuchs, interview by author, July 20, 1011.
5. Muller, *Bitter Heritage,* 38. Hanussen's solution for the Indian rope trick from *Berliner Illustrierte Zeitung*, October 31, 1930, translation in Harry Price Collection, Senate House Library, University of London, www.shl.lon .ac.uk/specialcollections/hpl.shtml.
6. *Berliner Illustrierte Zeitung*, October 31, 1930.
7. Ibid.
8. Erik Jan Hanussen, *Meine Lebenslinie* (Berlin: Universitas, 1930), 178–181; Muller, *Bitter Heritage,* 45.
9. Gary Bart, "Zisha Breitbart (1893–1925): The Strongest Man in the World & Jewish Defender," manuscript, 2001, 8, in the personal files of Gary Bart.
10. Ibid., 2, 3, 5; Gary Bart, email to author, December 23, 2010; Daniela Gauding, *Siegmund Sische Breitbart* (Berlin: Hentrich & Hentrich, 2006), 51; Sharon Gillerman, "Samson in Vienna: The Theatrics of Jewish Masculinity," *Jewish Social Studies* 9 (Winter 2003): 86–88.
11. Gillerman, "Samson in Vienna," 86.
12. Ibid.; Edwin A. Goewey, "How 'Feats of Strength' Are Faked," *Muscle Builder*, December 1925, 43. Ironically, adjacent to Goewey's column debunking feats of strength was an ad from the body-building company that Breitbart owned: "I can bite thru heavy chains! Lift 4,000 lbs on my chest! Drive nails thru 5 in. boards! Bend a ¾ in. horseshoe with my bare hands! You too can know the thrill of strength and be the Man you've always wished to be!...My secret method is now YOURS! Nothing like it has

ever been known! It has revolutionized all conceptions of physical culture methods! It's newer-better-different-better-SURE." Readers were asked to fill out a coupon, mail it with a dime (for shipping and postage) to Siegmund Breitbart, Dept. H-5, 1819 Broadway, New York, NY and receive—"FREE, without any obligation"—a "new 64-page book, MUSCULAR POWER, and one of our MUSCLE METERS." It's impossible to know how many readers asked for the book and a "muscle meter." It is possible to say that there wasn't a subsequent epidemic of American he-men bending horseshoes and biting through chains.

13. "Marta Farra: Queen over Her Kingdom of Willpower," *Der Tag* (Vienna), January 31, 1923; Florence E. McIntyre, "She Broke Heavy Crowbars, Tossed Elephants and Lifted Horses, But When She Had a Tiff with Eric…!," 1924; "The Iron King at Court," *Kleine Volks-Zeitung*, February 24, 1923; ads for Marta in two Viennese newspapers, *Weiner Sonn-und Montags-Zeitung*, January 29, 1923, and *Der Tag*, January 30, 1923, all in the Bart Collection, a private archive in Los Angeles owned by Gary Bart, great-nephew of Siegmund Breitbart.
14. *Illustrierte Kronen-Zeitung*, February 3 and 4, 1923; "The Exposed Telepathist," *Der Tag*, February 3, 1923, both in Bart Collection.
15. "Exposed Telepathist."
16. *Illustriertes Wiener Extrablatt* and *Neue Frie Presse*, February 3, 1923, Bart Collection.
17. Ibid.
18. Bart, email to author; "The Truth about Breitbart and Farra," *Weiner Sonn-und Montags-Zeitung*, February 5, 1923, and *Illustrierte Kronen-Zeitung*, February 3, 1923, both in Bart Collection.
19. Leo Singer, letter to the editor, *Programm*, September 3, 1929, Bart Collection.
20. Film and theater ads, *New York Times*, April 21, 1924, 20.
21. Marta Farra, "I Am the Strongest Woman Alive," *Muscle Builder,* July 1924, 10; Norman Clarke, *The Mighty Hippodrome* (South Brunswick, NJ: A. S. Barnes, 1968), 23, 34–36, 114–131; John E. DiMeglio, *Vaudeville U.S.A.* (Bowling Green, OH: Bowling Green University Popular Press, 1973), 129.
22. Quotes from reviewers of Hippodrome shows from unknown New York newspapers, April 1924; McIntyre, "She Broke Heavy Crowbars"; Rosetta Hoffman, "The World's Strongest Woman," *Health & Strength,* July 1937, 31, all in Bart Collection.
23. McIntyre, "She Broke Heavy Crowbars."
24. "Marta Farra Admits 'Copying' Breitbart," May 1924, Bart Collection.
25. "Bring on Tigers! Cries This She-Samson Who Tamed a Man," *New York Star,* n.d., Bart Collection.
26. Hanussen, *Meine Lebenslinie*, 250.
27. Ibid., 251, 254.

## CHAPTER 5   THE KING OF EVERYTHING

1. Peter Lamont, *The Rise of the Indian Rope Trick* (New York: Abacus, 2004), 178; Franz Polgar, *The Story of a Hypnotist* (New York: Hermitage House, 1951), 65–67.
2. Martin Schaaff, interview by author, February 10, 2010, Berlin. Unless otherwise indicated, details come from this interview.
3. Polgar, *Story of a Hypnotist,* 13–15.
4. Ibid., 37.
5. Ibid., 65.
6. Ibid., 67.
7. Ibid., 66–67.
8. Ibid., 67.
9. Ibid., 67–68.
10. Ibid., 68.
11. Ibid., 19.

## CHAPTER 6   HITLER: "THERE'S ROOM FOR A LITTLE SUBTLETY

1. Erik Jan Hanussen, *Meine Lebenslinie* (Berlin: Universitas, 1930),257–260; "Hanussen—Failure in Investigation Cases," *Ekstra Bladet* (Copenhagen), September 1, 1932, Albert Hellwig Archives, Institut fur Grenzgebiete der Psychologie und Psychohygiene, Freiburg, Germany.
2. Adolf Hitler, *Mein Kampf* (New York: Mariner, 1999), 57, 65, 138–139, 140, 290, 296, 619, 640, 672, 674, 688.
3. Joseph W. Bendersky, *A History of Nazi Germany: 1919–1945* (Chicago: Burnham, 2000), 165; William L. Shirer, *Rise and Fall of the Third Reich* (New York: Touchstone, 1990), 234, 240.
4. Guenter Lewy, *The Catholic Church and Nazi Germany* (New York: McGraw-Hill, 1964), 4, 26; Guenter Lewy, *The Holy Reich* (Cambridge: Cambridge University Press, 2003), 46; Susannah Heschel, *The Aryan Jesus* (Princeton, NJ: Princeton University Press, 2008), 5, 190–191; Uriel Tal, *"Political Faith" of Nazism Prior to the Holocaust* (Tel Aviv: Tel Aviv University, Chaim Rosenberg School of Jewish Studies, Diaspora Research Institute, 1978), 30–31. Despite his contempt for Christianity, Hitler remained a member of the Catholic Church until his death. The church returned the favor, neither excommunicating him nor banning his writings, although it had ample opportunity to add *Mein Kampf* to its Index of Prohibited Books.
5. Adolf Hitler, *Hitler's Table Talk, 1941–1944: His Private Conversations,* trans. Norman Cameron and R. H. Stevens (New York: Enigma, 2000), 143; Speer, *Inside the Third Reich,* 143.
6. Alexandra Richie, *Faust's Metropolis* (New York: Basic Books, 1999), 372–373; John Toland, *Adolf Hitler* (New York: Anchor Books, 1992), 222. Banning Jews from the Stahlhelm was not the only insult to Jews

who served in the Germany military. The army suppressed the number of Jews killed in World War I: ten thousand (Richie, *Faust's Metropolis*, 373).

7. Paramahansa Yogananda, *Autobiography of a Yogi* (Los Angeles: Self-Realization Fellowship, 1975), 419–420. Therese's reputation for eating only Communion wafers was bolstered when she didn't apply for ration cards during World War II. Rather, she received extra cards for soap, which she needed on Fridays, the day when, according to a devotee, "her hair is matted with blood from the crown-of-thorn wounds." Cleaning her, he said, was "a wearying as well as painful task." In 1932, the Vatican discouraged pilgrimages to Therese. Stirring Rome's skepticism about her was the lack of a consensus about her bleedings. In 1927, a medical laboratory in Munich had determined that the blood covering her face and wrists on Fridays was, indeed, human, but the low number of corpuscles in it correlated with menstrual flow, not with the level found in non-menstrual blood. Several doctors who examined Therese found no stigmata, one or two doctors were sure she had cut holes into her hands and feet from which the blood flowed, and a few speculated that an ulcer behind Therese's eyes made blood pour from them. Not helping her credibility was her insistence that no one stay in her room when she began bleeding. And over time, her "nail wounds"—wounds allegedly from the same nails that had been pounded into Jesus—shifted from round to rectangular, "presumably," said one skeptic, "as... [Therese] learned the true shape of Roman nails."

While it's easy to doubt her stigmata, her influence in another sphere may be more important—and more saintly. She spoke out repeatedly against the Nazis, often encouraging opposition to them. She was closely observed by the Gestapo, although they never bothered her. Whether her stigmata were genuine or not, her courage in the face of the Nazis cannot be disputed. She especially encouraged Fritz Gerlich, a liberal editor whose newspaper, *Der Gerade Weg*, opposed communism, Nazism, and anti-Semitism. Gerlich was taken to Dachau in March 1933. He was killed 15 months later. As a journalist, he had intended to expose Therese as a fake in 1927. Instead, under her influence, he converted to Catholicism in 1931. His resistance to national socialism subsequently was inspired by the social teachings of the Catholic Church (Albert Paul Schimberg, *The Story of Therese Neumann* [Milwaukee, WI: Bruce Publishing, 1947], 15; "Fritz Gerlich," Wikipedia, http://en.wikipedia.org/wiki/Fritz_Gerlich).

8. Yogananda, *Autobiography of a Yogi,* 420–422.
9. "Hanussen's 4th Lecture: From Konnersreuth to Telepathy," *Kassler Tageblatt* (Kassel, Germany), August 4, 1929, Hellwig Archives.
10. Frank Polgar, *The Story of a Hypnotist* (New York: Hermitage House, 1951), 72–73.

11. David Waxman, *Hartland's Medical and Dental Hypnosis* (London: Bailliere Tindall, 1989), 156–162.
12. Wilfried Kugel, *Hanussen* (Dusseldorf: Grupello, 1998), 17.
13. Heschel, *Aryan Jesus,* 201; Michael Burleigh, *The Third Reich* (New York: Macmillan, 2001), 100; Claudia Koonz, *The Nazi Conscience* (Cambridge, MA: Belknap, 2003), 143.


CHAPTER 7   "THIS MAN MUST BE IN LEAGUE WITH THE DEVIL"

1. Erik Jan Hanussen, *Meine Lebenslinie* (Berlin: Universitas, 1930), 261.
2. Ibid., 263–294.
3. Ibid., 261.
4. "The Trial against Hanussen," *Prager Tagblatt* (Prague), December 17, 1929, translation in the Bart Collection, a private archive in Los Angeles owned by Gary Bart, great-nephew of Siegmund Breitbart.
5. Erik Jan Hanussen, *Mind Reading and Telepathy*, trans. and ed. Bill Palmer (Vienna, Austria: Jimmy Bix Versand, 2008), 17. I found the Ostermann testimony in the Albert Hellwig Archives at the Institut fur Grenzgebiete der Psychologie und Psychohygiene in Freiburg, Germany. I spent several days with the large, uncataloged collection in July 2009 and, much to my chagrin, later realized that I had failed to note in which specific documents I came across Ostermann's testimony.
6. "Trial against Hanussen."
7. Ibid.
8. Ibid.
9. Ibid.
10. "Experiments at Court?" *Prager Tagblatt* (Prague), December 18, 1929, translation in Bart Collection.
11. "100 New Witnesses," *Prager Tagblatt* (Prague), December 19, 1930, translation in Bart Collection. Admittedly, the odds that Hanussen's vision bore any resemblance to reality were slim. However, he didn't describe the man in his vision or specify how he was related to the doctor. Also, the doctor overlooked the possibility that *he* was psychic too. Otherwise, why would he have been crying at the moment his brother had a fatal heart attack? Unlike Hanussen, perhaps the doctor was too modest to make such a claim.
12. "Hanussen Trial Postponed," *Prager Tagblatt* (Prague), December 20, 1929, translation in Bart Collection.
13. Ibid.
14. Ibid.
15. "The New Hanussen Trial," *Prager Tagblatt* (Prague), May 23, 1930, translation in Bart Collection.
16. Ibid.; "Clairvoyant Does Tricks for Court," *Rock Valley (IA) Bee*, August 15, 1930, 11.

17. "New Hanussen Trial."
18. "Hanussen Experiments," *Prager Tagblatt* (Prague), May 27, 1930, translation in Bart Collection.
19. Ibid.; "Clairvoyant Proves Power in Czech Court," *New York Times*, May 29, 1930, 8.
20. Hanussen, *Meine Lebenslinie,* 268.
21. "Hanussen Experiments." European legal experts and experts in the history of magic confirmed for me that Hanussen's courtroom demonstration of his powers was the first—and only—time a psychic has been allowed to perform in a Czech court.
22. "Hanussen Experiments."
23. Ibid.
24. Ibid.; "Clairvoyant Proves Power in Czech Court."
25. "Hanussen Experiments."
26. Ibid.; Franz Polgar, *The Story of a Hypnotist* (New York: Hermitage House, 1951), 75.
27. "Hanussen Experiments."
28. Some of these stories began appearing in European newspapers and magazines in the mid- and late 1930s; a number began showing up in certain American magazines—*Redbook, True Detective, Mystic*—during World War II. Most likely, these were part of an effort to expand the mythology about Hanussen by illustrating his phenomenal powers—and then to denigrate his character by pondering why someone with Hanussen's almost otherworldly skills would eventually aid Nazis and anti-Semites. The fictive quality of these stories is apparent after an exhaustive reading of contemporary newspaper accounts of Hanussen's trial. None of these reports the more far-fetched feats attributed to Hanussen that would gradually appear in newspapers and magazines. Certainly, if Hanussen had told a sergeant in the courtroom how many teeth were missing from his comb or advised police to dash to the train station to apprehend a bank robber, newspapers of the day would have trumpeted these with 72-point headlines the next day. Instead, the papers reported about Hanussen's more sedate, but surely impressive, performance before Judge Schalek.
29. P. Voigt, "Clairvoyant Hanussen Acquitted in Leitmeritz," translation in Bart Collection; "Clairvoyant Proves Power in Czech Court."
30. Ibid.; Hanussen, *Meine Lebenslinie,* 268–269.
31. "Clairvoyant Proves Power in Czech Court."

### CHAPTER 8    TRIUMPH IN BERLIN

1. Mark Twain, *A Tramp Abroad* (New York: Dover, 2003), 56; Karl Baedeker, *Berlin and Its Environs* (New York: Charles Scribner's Sons, 1910), 54.
2. Otto Friedrich, *Before the Deluge* (New York: Harper & Row, 1972), 12–13.

3. John Toland, *Adolf Hitler* (New York: Anchor Books, 1992), 148–149. Interestingly, the suicide rate in Berlin was highest among Jews: 68 per 100,000 versus 45 per 100,000 for Protestants and 32 per 100,000 for Catholics. In 1925, Jews committed 12 percent of all suicides in Berlin, although they comprised only 4 percent of the city's population. In addition to the poverty that afflicted all Berliners was Jews' significant loss of self-esteem as they were trying desperately fit into the broader society (Donald L. Niewyk, *The Jews in Weimar Germany* [Baton Rouge: Louisiana State University Press, 1980], 20).

4. Corinna Treitel, *A Science for the Soul* (Baltimore: Johns Hopkins University Press, 2000), 57.

5. Ibid., 15–16, 59, 64, 70, 175.

6. Dusty Sklar, *The Nazis and the Occult* (New York: Dorset, 1989), 118–119.

7. Arthur Koestler, *Arrow in the Blue* (New York: Macmillan, 1952), 298–300.

8. Ibid.

9. Ibid.

10. Ibid., 298–300.

11. Stephen Spender, *The Temple* (New York: Grove, 1988), 156–162.

12. PEM, *Homesick for the Kurfurstendamm* (Berlin: Lothar Blanvalet Verlag), 65–66.

13. Ibid., 66.

14. Ibid., 66–67.

15. Ibid., 67.

16. Adolf Hitler, *Hitler's Table Talk* (New York: Enigma Books, 2000), 583–584, 694–695.

17. Timothy W. Ryback, *Hitler's Private Library* (New York: Alfred A. Knopf, 2008), 238–239; Treitel, *A Science for the Soul*, 213.

18. Balthasar Gracian, *The Art of Worldly Wisdom,* trans. Joseph Jacobs (Mineola, NY: Dover, 2005), 1, 54, 59, 64, 87.

19. Toland, *Adolf Hitler,* 23–24.

20. Raymond L. Sickinger, "Hitler and The Occult: The Magical Thinking of Adolf Hitler," *Journal of Popular Culture* 34, no. 2 (Fall 2000): 108, 115; H. R. Trevor-Roper, *The Last Days of Hitler* (New York: Macmillan, 1947), 70–71; Walter C. Langer, *The Mind of Adolf Hitler: The Secret Wartime Report* (New York: Basic Books, 1972), 56–57.

21. Heather Pringle, *The Master Plan* (Toronto: Viking Canada, 2006), 179–180; Paul Roland, *The Nazis and the Occult* (Edison, NJ: Chartell Books, 2008), 148–149, 153–154; Duane Griffin, "What Curiosity in the Structure: The Hollow Earth in Science," manuscript, 25–26, 29–30, in the personal files of Duane Griffin. Goering wasn't the only one who believed the hollow earth theory. In 1933, the city council of Magdeburg funded a test to prove Bender's theory. The idea was that a rocket launched vertically from Magdeburg would soar through the hollow earth and land south of New Zealand. The rocket caught on the launch tower and was flung horizontally,

flew about 330 yards parallel to the ground, then slid along in the dirt for another ten yards. The only thing hollow was the brains of the people who designed it ("Magdeburg," *Encyclopedia Astronautica,* www.astronautix.com /lvs/mageburg.htm).

22. Dr. Alfred Gradenwitz, "The Clairvoyant Transcends Time and Space," *Reclams Universum* (Leipzig), no. 47 (August 21, 1930); Dr. Leo Jacobsohn, "Medical Encounter," *Die Medizinische*, no. 35, n.d., both in Bart Collection, a private archive in Los Angeles owned by Gary Bart, great-nephew of Siegmund Breitbart.

## CHAPTER 9   AN ALLIANCE OF SCOUNDRELS

1. "Hanussen Sues Berliner Herold," *Berliner Herold*, April 1, 1930, Albert Hellwig Archives, Institut fur Grenzgebiete der Psychologie und Psychohygiene, Freiburg, Germany.
2. Albert Hellwig to Ernst Juhn, 1930, Hellwig Archives.
3. Tillman Hellwig, interview by author, October 29, 2010; Gerhard Hellwig to Tillman Hellwig, June 13, 2002, in the personal files of Tillman Hellwig.
4. Corinna Treitel, *A Science for the Soul* (Baltimore: Johns Hopkins University Press, 2000), 145.
5. Hellwig manuscript and test results from Akademic MAP Psychological Institute, Hellwig Archives.
6. Nikolaus Wachsmann, *Hitler's Prisons* (New Haven, CT: Yale University Press, 2004), 19; Heather Wolfram, "Crime, Clairvoyance and the Weimar Police," *Journal of Contemporary History* 44, no. 4 (2009): 512, 584–585, 589. The desperate conditions that led normally law-abiding Germans to break the law were apparent when they reported to prison. Of one hundred men who were sent to the Poltzensee prison in Berlin, 50 showed up without a shirt, 60 without shoes, and 80 without socks.
7. Wolfram, "Crime, Clairvoyance and the Weimar Police," 581–583; Albert Hellwig, "Criminal Telepathy in the Kurten Case," *Nove Freie Presse* (Vienna), April 26, 1931, Hellwig Archives.
8. Margaret Seaton Wagner, *The Monster of Dusseldorf* (London: Faber & Faber, 1932), 111, 145–152, 234; Dr. C. V. Looz-Corswarem, email to author, July 16, 2010.
9. Wagner, *Monster of Dusseldorf*, 69–72; George Godwin, *Peter Kurten: A Study in Sadism* (London: Acorn, 1938), 17–18; Todd Herzog, *Crime Stories* (New York: Berghahn Books, 2009), 112.
10. Hellwig, "Criminal Telepathy in the Kurten Case"; Dusseldorf police chief to Hellwig, September 15, 1930, April 26, 1930, and November 29, 1930, Hellwig Archives; newspaper articles in Hellwig Archives.
11. Hellwig manuscript, n.d., Hellwig Archives.

12. Dr. Basten to Hellwig, October 31, 1931, and Hellwig to mayor of Godesberg, February 2, 13, and 19, 1932, all in Hellwig Archives; "A Tour through German Spas & Watering Places," German Tourist Information Office, Berlin, 1931, 1–4.

13. Dr. Basten to Hellwig, February 16, 1932; Hellwig to Godesberg mayor, January 21, 1933; and German Society Against Medical Fraud to Hellwig, n.d., all in Hellwig Archives; Treitel, *A Science for the Soul,* 156–157.

14. Erik Jan Hanussen, "Forecast for the Year 1932," *Der Querschnitt* (Berlin), December 1931, 829–832.

15. Ibid., 832. Hanussen also predicted that communism would collapse in Russia "not by military force, but by a massive lack of money"; Gandhi would become ill; England's head of state would "be in mortal danger"; and there would be riots in South America and famine in India. Overall, his predictions for Germany in 1932 were hopeful but vague. Artur Schumacher, an astrologer whose column ran next to Hanussen's in that issue of *Der Querschnitt,* was much bolder. Schumacher named names, one in particular. "It is astonishing," he wrote, "that the astrological constellations for Hitler, who people have been saying will have great success in 1932, are as bad as [President] Hindenburg and [Chancellor] Bruning." Schumacher might have been predicting "big conflicts and setbacks" for Hitler because Schumacher had less to lose than Hanussen, who by now had hitched his wagon to the Nazis. Their future was his. Schumacher, however, was a relative nonentity (Hanussen, "Forecast for the Year 1932," 830; Artur Schumacher, "Forecast for the Year 1932," *Der Querschnitt* 11, no. 2 [December 1931]: 832).

16. John Toland, *Adolf Hitler* (New York: Anchor Books, 1992), 260; Joachim C. Fest, *Hitler* (New York: Harcourt Brace, 1974), 316–317; Alexandra Richie, *Faust's Berlin* (New York: Carroll & Graf, 1998), 391.

17. Fest, *Hitler,* 319.

18. Ted Harrison, "Count Helldorf and the German Resistance to Hitler," Working Papers in Contemporary History and Politics, no. 8, European Studies Research Institute, University of Salford, Salford, UK, January 1996, 1, 2, 67; Konrad Heiden, *The Fuehrer* (London: Robinson, 1999), 294.

19. Harrison, "Count Helldorf and the German Resistance to Hitler," 3.

20. Ibid., 4–5.

21. Ibid., 5–10.

22. Ibid., 10–12.

23. Ibid., 12–14; "Anti-Semitic Leaders Are Fined in Berlin," *New York Times,* February 10, 1932, 8. Originally, the prosecutor asked for three years' imprisonment for Helldorf. Helldorf claimed that when he learned what was happening on the Kurfürstendamm, he went there "to prevent possible 'thoughtless acts'" by the storm troopers. Rather than incite violence, he explained, his presence "had a steadying influence." In November 1931, Helldorf was sentenced to six months in jail. An appeal reduced this to a fine of 100 marks

and no jail time ("Anti-Semitic Leaders Are Fined in Berlin"; "Nazi Storm Troopers Sentenced for Riots," *New York Times,* November 8, 1931, 14).

24. "Nazi Storm Troopers Sentenced for Riots," 15–16; Toland, *Adolf Hitler,* 186.

25. Harrison, "Count Helldorf and the German Resistance to Hitler," 18, 29–30.

26. Ibid., 17, 19, 21, 26, 30; Thomas D. Grant, *Stormtroopers and Crisis in the Nazi Movement* (New York: Routledge, 2004), 100–102; William L. Shirer, *The Rise and Fall of the Third Reich* (New York: Touchstone, 1990), 166, 171–172; Richard Bessel, *Political Violence and the Rise of Nazism* (New Haven, CT: Yale University Press, 1984), 56.

27. Wilfried Kugel, *Hanussen* (Dusseldorf: Grupello, 1998), 196; Hans Hein, "Die Magier von Berlin," *Die Welt am Abend* (Berlin), November 13, 17, and 20 and December 6 and 8, 1930; Bruno Frei, *Hanussen: A Report* (Strasbourg, France: Sebastian Brant, 1934),160–161.

28. Frei, *Hanussen: A Report,* 161; Kugel, *Hanussen,* 200–201.

29. Frei, *Hanussen: A Report,* 161.

30. Ibid., 144–145; "Nazidom's Rasputin," *True Mystic Science,* November 1938, 74.

31. Ad for golomboy in *Hanussen-Almanac 1933* (Berlin: Erik Jan Hanussen Publishing, 1933).

32. *Erik Jan Hanussen's Berliner Wochenschau,* July 24, August 8 and 24, October 8 and 24, November 10 and 24, 1932, Hellwig Archives.

33. Frei, *Hanussen: A Report,* 165; Treitel, *A Science for the Soul,* 232–233.

34. Frei, *Hanussen: A Report,* 164–165.

35. Ibid.; Alfred Neubauer, *Speed Was My Life* (New York: Clarkson N. Potter, 1960), 37–38. At the Grand Prix, just before the first turn, the prince's Bugatti left the track, hurtled across the grass between the two long straightaways, shot 60 feet into the air, smashed into three trees, and landed on the electric railway line. The driver's skull was shattered. It was Prince Lobkowicz. After a few more laps, the race turned into a duel between two drivers, Rudi Caracciola in a red Alfa and Manfred von Brauchitsch in his Mercedes. In the ninth lap, Brauchitsch took the lead. In the twelfth, Caracciola was ahead again. In the final lap, Brauchitsch began edging up until he and Caracciola were side by side at 140 miles an hour. Pressing down on the accelerator, Brauchitsch shot past Caracciola. He won the race by 3.6 seconds (Neubauer, *Speed Was My Life,* 37–38).

36. Kugel, *Hanussen,* 199–200.

37. Wouter Melissen, "Bugatti Type 54 Grand Prix," October 23, 2006, Ultimatecarpage.com, www.ultimatecarpage.com/car/2927/Bugatti-Type-54-Grand-Prix.html; "Type 54," www.bugatti.com/en/tradition/bugatti-models/t54.html.

38. Frei, *Hanussen: A Report,* 163; Kugel, *Hanussen,* 199–200.

39. Kugel, *Hanussen,* 199–200.

CHAPTER 10   THE NOOSE TIGHTENS

1. George Borup, *Copenhagen and Environs* (Copenhagen: Borup's Rejseforer, 1925), 46.
2. "Hanussen—A Failure in Investigation Cases," *Ekstra Bladet* (Copenhagen), September 1, 1932, 1; "The Police Initiate Investigation of Erik Jan Hanussen," *Dagens Nyheder* (Copenhagen), September 2, 1932, 5; "Imprisonment and Deportation Face Mr. Hanussen," *Exstra Bladet* (Copenhagen), September 2, 1932, 5; German embassy in Copenhagen to German Medical Society, September 28, 1932; Copenhagen Police Investigator Stamm to Judge Albert Hellwig, September 9, 1932, all in Albert Hellwig Archives, Institut fur Grenzgebiete der Psychologie und Psychohygiene, Freiburg, Germany; "Weird Finale of the 'Miracle Man' Who X-Rayed Park Avenue Women's Souls," *Salt Lake City (UT) Tribune*, May 21, 1933, 38.
3. "Hanussen—A Failure in Investigation Cases," 1.
4. "Police Initiate Investigation."
5. Ibid.; Stamm to Hellwig.
6. "Police Initiate Investigation."
7. Police President of Berlin to German Medical Society, December 24, 1932, Hellwig Archives. The letter was sent in late December, but the police chief was referring to Hanussen's September 2, 1932, attempt to enter Norway.
8. Michael Burleigh, *The Third Reich* (New York: Hill and Wang, 2000), 117; Joachim C. Fest, *Hitler* (New York: Harcourt Brace, 1974), 339, 341; Alexandra Richie, *Faust's Metropolis* (New York: Carroll & Graf, 1999), 386–387; Conan Fischer, *The German Communists and the Rise of Nazism* (New York: St. Martin's, 1991), 148, 151.
9. Burleigh, *Third Reich,* 117, 131; Eve Rosenhaft, *Beating the Fascists?* (New York: Cambridge University Press, 1983), 141; Pierre Aycoberry, *The Social History of the Third Reich, 1933–1945* (New York: New Press, 1999), 18.
10. *Le Journal de la Prestidigitation* (Paris), no. 67 (January–February 1933); Keith Clark, *Silks Supreme* (Cincinnati, OH: Silk King Studios, 1942), 1–18; review of *Celebrated Cigarettes,* an ebook on magic at Trickshop.com, www.trickshop.com/celebrated_cigarettes.com; "Speaking of Pictures...A Crack Magician Explains Some Tricks," *Life Magazine*, April 7, 1941, 8–10.
11. Francois Lassagne, "Le Prophete Assassine," *Vu Magazine*, July 12, 1933, 1064; "Séances Yield Nothing," *New York Times*, July 7, 1922; *Le Journal de la Prestidigitation*. To lend Hanussen some credibility before a French audience, Paul Heuze introduced him every night. Heuze had written several books about psychic phenomena, participated in experiments about the long-term effects of hypnosis, and organized séances at the Sorbonne. In the end, the scientists who monitored the séances concluded that they proved nothing about the existence of life in other dimensions. (A Madame Bisson, who had helped arrange the sessions, said the medium "had not been in possession

of all her faculties." Her disclaimer could be interpreted in several ways.) (Lassagne, "Le Prophete Assassine"; "Séances Yield Nothing.")

12. Lassagne, "Le Prophete Assassine," 1064; Claire Lemercier, "The Club of Faubourg: Open Forum of Paris, 1918–1939," paper presented to the Institute of Political Studies of Paris, November 30, 1995, 1, 10–11, 17.

13. Erika Steinschneider-Fuchs, interview by author, July 21, 2009.

14. Hanussen, postcard to Erika Steinschneider-Fuchs, December 1932, courtesy of Erika Steinschneider-Fuchs.

15. Fest, *Hitler*, 338–389; Wilfried Kugel, *Hanussen* (Dusseldorf: Grupello, 1996), 192.

16. "Weird Finale of the 'Miracle Man,'" 38.

17. Christoph Schroeder, "Hanussen and Metaphysics," n.d.; J. R., "In Berlin, They Talk About...," *Die Wahrheit* (Berlin), March 4, 1933, both in Hellwig Archives.

18. J. R., "In Berlin, They Talk About."

19. Ibid.


## CHAPTER 11   THE FUEHRER'S COURT JEW

1. *Erik Jan Hanussen's Berliner Wochenschau*, January 8 and 24, February 16, 1933, Albert Hellwig Archives, Institut fur Grenzgebiete der Psychologie und Psychohygiene, Freiburg, Germany.

2. John Toland, *Adolf Hitler* (New York: Anchor Books, 1992), 290–291; Alexandra Richie, *Faust's Metropolis* (New York: Carroll & Graf, 1999), 405, 408.

3. Brian Ladd, *The Ghosts of Berlin* (Chicago: University of Chicago Press, 1997), 134–137; "Germany: Jewish Population in 1933," *Holocaust Encyclopedia*, U.S. Holocaust Memorial Museum, Washington, D.C., http://webcache .googleusercontent.com/search?q=cache:rhaGvRfgqKEJ:www.ushmm.org /wlc/en/article.php%3FModuleId%3D10005276+jewish+population+ger many+1933&cd=1&hl=en&ct=clnk&gl=us&source=www.google.com.

4. Francois Lassagne, "The Murdered Prophet," *Vu*, July 12, 1933, 1064.

5. Ibid. If these stories are true, why were these photos not published after Hanussen's murder?

6. Name changes could be subtle. One of Hanussen's friends, for instance, the actor Siegfried Aron, had studied in an Orthodox yeshiva in Hamburg. His name had originally been Siegfried Aaron—a more "Jewish spelling" than his stage name.

7. Robert Gessner, *Some of My Best Friends Are Jews* (New York: Farrar & Rinehart, 1936), 79–80; Claudia Koonz, *The Nazi Conscience* (Cambridge, MA: Belknap, 2003), 40.

8. Gessner, *Some of My Best Friends Are Jews*, 81; Michael Brenner, *The Renaissance of Jewish Culture in Weimar Germany* (New Haven, CT: Yale University Press,

1996), 51; Donald L. Niewyk, *The Jews in Weimar Germany* (Baton Rouge: Louisiana State University Press, 1980), 165, 166, 169, 170, 175. In an aside in his book that unwittingly evokes Hanussen, Niewyk says that, despite the efforts of some Jews to ingratiate themselves with the Nazis, "nothing short of *clairvoyance* could have spared...[them] from a fate that could be determined in the first place by the larger society...and ultimately by one man—Adolf Hitler" (199, emphasis added).

9. Pierre van Paassen, "Hitler's Private Seer, 'On Top of World,' Predicts Marxist Doom in 6 Years," *Syracuse (NY) Herald,* March 2, 1933, 1; Erik Jan Hanussen, "Payoff," *Hanussen-Zeitung,* March 8, 1933, 2, Hellwig Archives.

10. Erik Jan Hanussen, "An Open Letter from Hanussen to Hitler," *Hanussen-Zeitung,* February 8, 1933, 1, Hellwig Archives.

11. Ibid.

12. Ibid.

13. Adolf Hitler, *Mein Kampf,* trans. Ralph Manheim (New York: Mariner, 1999), 355; William L. Shirer, *The Rise and Fall of the Third Reich* (New York: Touchstone, 1990), 30; Toland, *Adolf Hitler,* 9–12, 61; David Redles, *Hitler's Millennial Reich* (New York: New York University Press, 2005), 95, 149–151.

14. Toland, *Adolf Hitler,* 139; Adolf Hitler, *Hitler's Table Talk, 1941–1944,* trans. Norman Cameron and R. H. Stevens (New York: Enigma Books, 2000), 414.

15. Toland, *Adolf Hitler,* 218, 222. A similar story about Hanussen being Hitler's speech coach and helping him stage his mass rallies appears in *The Mind of Adolf Hitler* (New York: Basic Books, 1972), a secret wartime study of Hitler commissioned by William Donovan, who ran the World War II spy agency, the Office of Strategic Services. For this, the author of the study, Walter Langer, a psychoanalyst, relied on accounts from Otto Strasser, a Nazi dissident who had fled Hitler and was living in Canada.

16. Lassagne, "The Murdered Prophet," 1926.

17. Heinrich Hoffman, *Hitler Was My Friend* (London: Burke, 1945), 46.

18. Ibid., 41, 49, 105, 160.

19. "Nazidom's Rasputin," *Mystic Magazine,* November 1938, 74; Pierre van Paassen, "Prelude to a Tyrant," *Redbook,* July 1940, 58.

20. Bella Fromm, *Blood & Banquets* (New York: Birch Lane, 1990), 98.

21. Toland, *Adolf Hitler,* 282.

22. Ibid., 283.

23. Van Paassen, "Prelude to a Tyrant," 59–60.

24. *Screen Files: Hanussen,* French television show, January 1971.


CHAPTER 12   THE FIRE THAT KILLED A COUNTRY

1. Hanussen to Therese Fuchs, February 4, 1933, in Delia Muller, *The Bitter Heritage* (Bozen, Italy: Athesia Spectrum, 2006), 57.

2. Ibid.

3. Frederick Marion, *In My Mind's Eye* (New York: E. P. Dutton, 1960), 96.

4. Ibid., 97.

5. Ibid., 95.

6. Ibid.

7. "Private Séance at Erik Hanussen's House," *12 Uhr Blatt* (Berlin), February 27, 1933, Albert Hellwig Archives, Institut fur Grenzgebiete der Psychologie und Psychohygiene, Freiburg, Germany; Franz Polgar, *The Story of a Hypnotist* (New York: Hermitage House, 1951), 76.

8. "Private Séance at Erik Hanussen's House"; World Committee for the Victims of German Fascism, *The Brown Book of the Hitler Terror and the Burning of the Reichstag* (New York: Alfred A. Knopf, 1933), 171. The fascist credentials of Hans Ewers, the failed novelist who attended the opening of the Palace of the Occult, were, at best, dubious. In 1922, he had expressed sympathy for the Jews in a foreword to *The Voice of Jerusalem,* a pro-Zionist polemic by the British Jewish author Israel Zangwell. And once the Nazis attained power, they added two of Ewers's pornographic novels to their list of "filthy and disgusting literature." But writers—even poor ones—are adept at cutting their conscience to suit the latest fashions. Ewers was a hack, but a good enough tailor of his own scruples for Goebbels, Hitler's propaganda guru, to appoint him head of the Association of German Authors toward the end of 1933.

9. Maria Paudler, *Laughing Also Has to Be Learned* (Berlin: Universitas, 1978), 121–122; "Nazidom's Rasputin," *Mystic Magazine,* November 1938, 74; Pierre van Paassen, "Prelude to a Tyrant," *Redbook,* July 1940, 92–93; Bella Fromm, "Under the Nazi Terror," *True Detective,* May 1942, 82.

10. Paudler, *Laughing Also Has to Be Learned,* 122.

11. Ibid., 123.

12. Ibid.

13. Ibid.; "Nazidom's Rasputin," 74; Van Paassen, "Prelude to a Tyrant," 92–93; Fromm, "Under the Nazi Terror."

14. Fromm, "Under the Nazi Terror"; Bella Fromm, *Blood & Banquets* (New York: Birch Lane, 1990), 78; John Weitz, letter to the editor, *New York Times,* February 1, 1994, A16.

15. Franz Hollering, "I Was an Editor in Germany," *Nation,* February 12, 1932, 183.

16. Ibid.; Fritz Tobias, *The Reichstag Fire* (New York: G. P. Putnam's Sons, 1964), 23–24, 29; World Committee for the Victims of German Fascism, *Brown Book,* 111.

17. Hollering, "I Was an Editor in Germany," 183.

18. William L. Shirer, *The Rise and Fall of the Third Reich* (New York: Touchstone, 1990), 191; Heinrich Hoffman, *Hitler Was My Friend* (London: Burke, 1955), 302.

19. Alexandra Richie, *Faust's Metropolis* (New York: Carroll & Graf, 1999), 409–410; Shirer, *Rise and Fall of the Third Reich*, 191; Sefton Delmar, *Trail Sinister* (London: Martin Secker & Warburg, 1961), 186.
20. Shirer, *Rise and Fall of the Third Reich*, 191–192; Hoffman, *Hitler Was My Friend*, 72.
21. Delmar, *Trail Sinister*, 188.
22. Ibid., 189.
23. Shirer, *Rise and Fall of the Third Reich,* 194.
24. Anson Rabinbach, "Staging Fascism: The Brown Book of the Reichstag Fire and Hitler Terror," *New German Critique* 35, no. 1 (Spring 2008): 100–101; World Committee for the Victims of German Fascism, *Brown Book*, 52.
25. Tobias, *Reichstag Fire*, 117–118.
26. Delmer, *Trail Sinister*, 194; Tobias, *Reichstag Fire*, 14. For almost three decades, most historians swallowed *The Brown Book*'s scenario about the Nazis' manipulating a loony, gay ex-Communist who had morphed into a dedicated Nazi. Then in 1960, a West German journalist, Franz Tobias, also concluded that *The Brown Book* was hooey and laid the fire at the door of the Communists. That view dominates today, although it must be remembered that, when Tobias was writing, scholarship in West Germany was often not divorced from politics. Blaming the fire on Communists—or on just one Communist—discredited the regime to the East. At the time, both German governments were vying for legitimacy. Manipulating history was simply one tool in the struggle.
27. Ted Harrison, "Count Helldorf and the German Resistance to Hitler," Working Papers in Contemporary History and Politics, no. 8, European Studies Research Institute, University of Salford, Salford, UK, January 1996, 22; "Surprising Evidence at the Reichstag Trial," *Manchester (UK) Guardian*, October 31, 1933, 18.
28. Van Paassen, "Prelude to a Tyrant," 92.
29. Van der Lubbe quote from "Nazi Case Shaken in Reich Fire Trial," *New York Times*, September 29, 1933, 10. While the fire has never been traced directly to Hitler, there is no doubt the fuehrer was obsessed with flames. Writing from Spandau Prison in 1947, Albert Speer, Hitler's uber architect, "unhesitatingly" said that "fire was Hitler's proper element.... [Fire] always stirred a profound excitement in him." In his Chancellery during the war, Hitler ordered newsreels shown of exploding convoys and London burning and a "sea of flames over Warsaw." He watched with "rapture" and "a kind of delirium," ecstatically describing his plans for destroying New York "in a hurricane of fire"—"skyscrapers turning into gigantic burning torches, collapsing upon one another, the glow of the exploding city illuminating the dark sky." This fixation with fire may have been contagious, with Goering, Goebbels, Helldorf, and others using fire as a tool to please their boss. And

as historian Steven Sage has pointed out, Hitler had already seized on one fire. In 1931, soon after the Glass Palace in Munich burned to the ground, Hitler commissioned an architect to design a new structure, explaining that his first building project when taking power would be a gallery for German art. The Glass Palace's modern art collection had appalled Hitler, who was living only a few minutes' walk from the palace before it burned and had to put up with its aesthetic abominations almost every day (Steven F. Sage, *Ibsen and Hitler* [New York: Carroll & Graf, 2006], 230–233).

30. "Nazidom's Rasputin," 74; Van Paassen, "Prelude to a Tyrant," 92–93; Fromm, "Under the Nazi Terror," 82.
31. Van Paassen, "Prelude to a Tyrant," 92–93.
32. Ibid.
33. In some postwar versions of what happened at the séance at the Palace of the Occult, it was Maria Paudler, as Hanussen's transmitter, who talked about the imminent fire at the Reichstag. When Paudler first read this version of that famous night in *Munich Illustrated* in 1951, she was furious. The author had written the article without relying on a single witness who was there that night. Paudler particularly disliked being called a prophet for the Third Reich. Suing for libel, she got a retraction (Paudler, *Laughing Also Has to Be Learned*, 123–124).

## CHAPTER 13   A RIDE TO A WILD PRISON

1. Joe Labero, *Men of Wonder, I Reveal Your Secrets!* (Leipzig, Germany: Wahrheit Ferdinand Spohr, 1933), 51.
2. Teller, interview by author, May 22, 2009.
3. Labero, *Men of Wonder*, 51.
4. PEM, *Homesick for the Kurfurstendamm* (Berlin: Lothar Blanvalet, 1952), 66.
5. George L. Mosse, *Confronting History* (Madison: University of Wisconsin Press, 2000), 8–9, 11, 13–17, 23, 27.
6. Ibid., 23, 25, 33–36, 42.
7. Ibid., 43.
8. Ibid., 71–72.
9. Francois Lassagne, "The Murdered Prophet," *Vu,* July 12, 1933, 1064.
10. Ibid.
11. Mosse, *Confronting History*, 44–46, 72; Anthony Read, *The Devil's Disciples* (New York: W. W. Norton, 2004), 333. According to Read, by the time the Nazis finished their buying spree, they owned more than 83 percent of the German press (334).
12. Mosse, *Confronting History,* 73; "Milestone," *Time Magazine,* May 1, 1944, www.time.com/time/magazine/article/0,9171,774912,00.html; Bella Fromm, *Blood & Banquets* (New York: Birch Lane, 1990), 78.

13. Ibid., 70–72; Pierre van Paassen, "Bullets End Amazing Career of Hanussen, Germany's Rasputin," *Syracuse (NY) Herald,* May 14, 1933, 27.

14. PEM, *Homesick for the Kurfurstendamm*, 73.

15. Ibid., 74.

16. Alexandra Richie, *Faust's Metropolis* (New York: Carroll & Graf, 1999), 416.

17. Read, *Devil's Disciples*, 302.

18. Ibid., 302–303; Herman Beck, *The Fateful Alliance* (New York: Berghahn Books, 2008), 115.

19. Geoffrey Megargee, ed., *United States Holocaust Museum Encyclopedia of Camps and Ghettoes, 1933–1945* (Bloomington: United States Holocaust Memorial Museum and Indiana University Press, 2009), 1:29, 31–32, 34; Matthias Heisig, interview by author, July 3, 2009; Joe White, interview by author, September 20, 2010.

20. Megargee, *United States Holocaust Museum Encyclopedia* 1:29, 31–32, 34; Heisig, interview; Claudia Koonz, *The Nazi Conscience* (Cambridge, MA: Belknap, 2003), 37.

21. Megargee, *United States Holocaust Museum,* 29; Heisig, interview.

22. William L. Shirer, *The Rise and Fall of the Third Reich* (New York: Touchstone, 1990), 196–200.

23. Ibid.; SA field police to IV-c-Administration, n.d., signature partly illegible but may have been that of Wilhelm Ohst, Bundesarchiv, Berlin; Eleanor Hancock, *Ernst Rohm* (New York: Palgrave Macmillan, 2008), 124.

24. Wilfried Kugel, *Hanussen* (Dusseldorf: Grupello, 1998), 223.

25. Ted Harrison, "Count Helldorf and the German Resistance to Hitler," Working Papers in Contemporary History and Politics, no. 8, European Studies Research Institute, University of Salford, Salford, UK, January 1996, 19, 21; Kugel, *Hanussen,* 223.

## CHAPTER 14   THREE BULLETS IN THE WOODS

1. Pierre van Paassen, "Bullets End Amazing Career of Hanussen, Germany's Rasputin," *Syracuse (NY) Herald*, 32; "The Third Reich's Prophet," *Arbeiterzeitung* (Vienna), April 11, 1933.

2. Wilfried Kugel, *Hanussen* (Dusseldorf: Grupello, 1998), 348.

3. PEM, *Homesick for the Kurfurstendamm* (Berlin: Lothar Blanvalet, 1952), 75; Bruno Frei, *Hanussen: A Report* (Strasbourg, France: Sebastian Brant, 1934), 140.

4. Rudolf Steinle, interview by SA, September 18, 1934, and Karl Ernst to Police Station "K," Berlin, March 29, 1933, both in Bundesarchiv, Berlin; Kugel, *Hanussen*, 252–253.

5. Steinle, interview.

6. Senior Prosecutor County Court II, Berlin, to Minister of Prussian Department of Justice, "Investigation into the Murder of Steinschneider-Hanussen," April 10, 1933, Bundesarchiv, Berlin.

7. Kugel, *Hanussen*, 253.

8. PEM, *Homesick for the Kurfurstendamm,* 74.

9. Lothar Machtan, *The Hidden Hitler* (New York: Basic Books, 2001), 185; Eleanor Hancock, *Ernst Rohm* (New York: Palgrave Macmillan, 2011), 148.

10. William L. Shirer, *The Rise and Fall of the Third Reich* (New York: Touchstone, 1990), 39, 143; Joachim C. Fest, *Hitler* (New York: Harcourt Brace, 1974), 231; Jacques Delarue, *The Gestapo* (New York: Skyhorse, 2008), 27.

11. Adolf Hitler, *Mein Kampf* (New York: Mariner, 1999), 58, 253, 304; Geoffrey J. Giles, "The Denial of Sexuality: Same-Sex Incidents in Himmler's SS and Police," in Dagmar Herzog, ed., *Sexuality and German Fascism* (New York: Berghahn Books, 2005), 202–203, 289; Nikolaus Wachsmann, *Hitler's Prisons* (New Haven, CT: Yale University Press, 2004), 144; Geoffrey J. Giles, "Why Bother about Homosexuals?" J. B. and Maurice Shapiro Memorial Annual Lecture, May 30, 2001, United States Holocaust Memorial Museum, Washington, DC, 1, 2, 4.

12. Shirer, *Rise and Fall of the Third Reich*, 221–222; John Toland, *Adolf Hitler* (New York: Anchor Books, 1992), 250, 263; Machtan, *Hidden Hitler,* 185–191, 194, 207: Heinz Hohne, *The Order of the Death's Head* (New York: Penguin Books, 1971), 71; Fest, *Hitler*, 451–453, 455. Not only was Roehm frank about his sexuality, he was almost neutral about Jews. Asked in 1934 whether he had anything against Jews, Roehm said, "The question is idiotic. I have neither something against the Jews nor something for the Jews. They are a matter of complete indifference to me." While Roehm said he could imagine the Nazi revolution without anti-Semitism, he advised his friend who had posed the question that Hitler was adamant on this issue (Hancock, *Ernst Rohm*, 91).

13. Delarue, *Gestapo,* 119–121; Edouard Calic, *Reinhard Heydrich* (New York: William Morrow, 1982), 114–115.

14. Calic, *Reinhard Heydrich*; Wachsmann, *Hitler's Prisons*, 145.

15. Kugel, *Hanussen*, 230.

16. PEM, *Homesick for the Kurfurstendamm,* 75; Senior Prosecutor County Court II, Berlin, "Investigation into the Murder of Steinschneider-Hanussen"; "Hanussen Murdered," *Prager Tagblatt* (Vienna), April 9, 1933, 1, Bart Collection, a private archive in Los Angeles owned by Gary Bart, great-nephew of Siegmund Breitbart.

17. "Hanussen Murdered."

18. Ibid.; "Clairvoyant Hanussen Found Murdered: Another Lynch Killing by the Nazis?" *Arbeiterzeitung* (Vienna), April 9, 1933, in Bart Collection; Senior Prosecutor County Court II, Berlin, "Investigation into the Murder

of Steinschneider-Hanussen"; Pierre van Paassen, "Prelude to a Tyrant," *Redbook*, August 1940, 94; "Noted Clairvoyant Found Murdered," *Canberra Times*, April 11, 1933, 1; "Seer Who Foretold Hitler's Rise Found Slain; Hanussen Was Adviser to European Royalty," *New York Times,* April 9, 1933, 12; "Bullets End Amazing Career of Hanussen, Germany's Rasputin," *Syracuse (NY) Herald*, May 14, 1933, 27; "Remains of Erik Hanussen Located," *Piqua (OH) Daily Call,* April 8, 1933, 1. In *Time Magazine*, the "bullet-riddled body of one of Europe's best known fortunetellers" helped illustrate how the Nazis were quickly transforming Germany. Hanussen's murder was part of a pattern of terror and repression: already, only 35 of Berlin's two thousand Jewish lawyers were allowed to practice; a Protestant pastor praised the storm-troopers for doing God's work more than the church, which was "not jubilantly join[ing]" in celebrating the Third Reich, and the government was "strongly hinting" that any official should divorce his Jewish spouse if he wanted to keep his job ("Germany: Co-ordination," *Time Magazine,* April 17, 1932, www.time.com/time/magazine/article/0,9171,847291,00.html).

19. Erik Jan Hanussen, *Meine Lebenslinie* (Berlin: Universitas, 1930), 269.
20. Ibid., 270–271.
21. Ibid., 271–272.
22. Delia Muller, *The Bitter Heritage* (Bozen, Italy: Athesia Spectrum, 2006), 144.
23. "Dangerzone Superstition," *Das Schwarze Korps*, October 7, 1937, 12, library, United States Holocaust Memorial Museum.
24. Ibid.
25. Fest, *Hitler*, 734.
26. Pierre van Paassen, "The Date of Hitler's Fall," *Redbook*, May 1942, 85, 86.
27. Daniel 12:11–12, *The Holy Bible* (Standard King James translation) (Nashville, TN: Royal, 1971), 977.
28. Daniel 1:20; Van Paassen, "Date of Hitler's Fall," 86. Since Hanussen's note to Juhn was not published until May 1942, it has to be treated with a healthy skepticism. Quite possibly, Hanussen never wrote it, and it was a clever piece of wartime propaganda, written by the author of the *Redbook* article, by a propagandist in the U.S. government, or by Juhn himself.


CHAPTER 15   THE VIEW FROM ITALY

1. Unless otherwise attributed, all details come from Erika Steinschneider-Fuchs, interview by author, July 20–22, 2009.
2. Delia Muller, *The Bitter Heritage* (Bozen, Italy: Athesia Spectrum, 2006), 142.
3. Ibid.

# Index